Alan Sutton Publishing Limited
17a Brunswick Road
Gloucester GL1 1HG

First published 1822
This edition published 1980
in collaboration with
SOMERSET RECORD SOCIETY

British Library Cataloguing in Publication Data

Greenwood, C
   Somersetshire delineated.
   1. Somerset, Eng. – Description and travel
   I. Title   II. Greenwood, J
   914.23'08'0474   DA670.S5

   ISBN 0-904387-53-4

Printed in Great Britain by
Redwood Burn Limited,
Trowbridge & Esher

SOMERSETSHIRE

Delineated:

BEING

A TOPOGRAPHICAL DESCRIPTION

OF EACH

TOWN, PARISH, CHAPELRY, &c.

In the County,

WITH THEIR RESPECTIVE DISTANCES AND BEARINGS·

TO WHICH ARE ADDED, THE

NAMES OF THE INCUMBENTS,

AND THE

DATE OF INDUCTION TO EACH LIVING.

LIKEWISE THE

Population Returns for the Years 1801, 1811, & 1821.

A WORK OF VERY GENERAL UTILITY,

AND USEFUL AS

AN INDEX

TO

A SURVEY MADE IN THE YEAR 1821.

BY C. AND J. GREENWOOD,

SURVEYORS OF THE SEVERAL COUNTIES OF ENGLAND AND WALES.

London:

PRINTED BY T. BENSLEY,
Crane Court, Fleet Street.

PUBLISHED BY C. AND J. GREENWOOD, 174, PICCADILLY;
AND SOLD BY ALL BOOKSELLERS.

INTRODUCTION

Christopher Greenwood was born in 1786 in the parish of Gisburn in Yorkshire, the son of a small farmer. In 1817 he began a project which was to make an obscure country surveyor into something of a national figure. He conceived of an atlas of all the counties of England, to be produced individually at a uniform scale of one inch to one mile, a project which would be the culmination of cartographical improvements made in the previous half century, and which would at the same time illustrate every corner of the countryside at a particularly rapid period of change. It was also a period when the Ordnance Survey was at work, and there is little doubt that Greenwood owed at least something to that great undertaking, though exactly how much only a detailed comparison of each can finally settle.

Greenwood and his partners in the scheme, 'proprietors' as he refers to them in the *Prospectus*, were undertaking a commercial enterprise, one which had to be brought to a premature end in 1834 before the whole scheme was quite finished. The *Prospectus* itself refers to financial difficulties as early as 1822, and left to himself Greenwood the surveyor might well have floundered as a business man. After only a year on the project Greenwood had moved his office from an address in Wakefield to London. In 1820 George Pringle and his son and namesake joined him in partnership. George the elder was a solicitor, having professional contacts with civil engineering schemes in North London; George the son acted as publisher of the maps. By 1822 Greenwood himself had an office at 174 Piccadilly, and Pringle was to be found at 70 Queen Street, Cheapside, in the heart of the City of London, at the 'Repository for the sale of Greenwood's County Maps'. One more name was by now also officially linked with the enterprise. John Greenwood, much younger than his brother Christopher, seems to have been a junior in the Greenwood business ever since about 1812. Perhaps in consequence of the firm's expansion in the early 1820s, John's name came to be linked with Christopher's as surveyor, for clearly other staff were being taken on. The *Prospectus* refers to a 'considerable' increase in the number of surveyors and artists, for it was becoming important to produce the maps as quickly as possible. Financial success depended on the satisfaction of 'numerous' subscribers and the public at large.

There was, of course, no doubt about public interest. Upwards of ten thousand names had been collected by 1822, and a selection of them was duly appended to the new *Prospectus* for that year, beginning with the King and his royal brothers, and continuing with a fine collection of the aristocracy. Rather few bishops were interested in the details of their dioceses, and curiously absent were the Archbishop of Canterbury and the Duke of Wellington. But there in the list were to found the famous names of nineteenth-century England like Earl Grey, Lord Melbourne or Sir Robert Peel; and there were the gentry of county significance, on whom the practical success of the enterprise so much depended. Somerset landowners were there in plenty, from the Duke of Somerset and the Marquis of Bath, the Earl of Darlington, Lord Arundell, Lord Glastonbury and Lord Huntingfield, to Sir Charles Bampfylde, Sir John Trevelyan, Sir Abraham Elton, Sir Richard Colt Hoare, Sir W.E. Medlycott and Sir Alexander Hood. Somerset, at any rate, supported the Greenwoods well.

It may or may not have been a coincidence that when the Greenwoods began a new but related enterprise in 1822 Somerset with Worcestershire should have been the first counties to benefit. Maps of both appeared in that year and, accompanying each of them, a gazetteer of which the present volume is a reprint. This new venture was no doubt designed to strengthen the firm's financial position, by providing, in addition to their maps, a volume containing details of the towns and villages whose relationship to each other they had drawn so carefully. It was, of course, something that the Ordnance was not doing; and it was later to be copied on a commercial basis by the Post Office and the firm of Kelly among others in the second half of the nineteenth century. The Greenwoods were, perhaps, premature. *Worcestershire Delineated* and *Somerset Delineated* were followed only by a volume for Surrey in 1823, and then the scheme was abandoned.

The information contained in *Somerset Delineated* pretends to no great detail and originality, only to general usefulness. Of that there was no doubt then, nor is now. Greenwood himself wrote that the material was gathered 'if not perhaps from any very recondite sources, yet carefully and from approved authorities'. Clearly the sources included the Census Reports of 1821, for the volume is arranged, like the Reports, by parish and township rather than by village and hamlet; it gives the number of inhabited houses, the number of families occupying them, and the general type of employment. The population figures for 1801 and for 1811 are also included. Today, such information is still not always easily discovered, and is a serious contribution to the local history of every place. Thus Bath had 5157 inhabited houses in 1821 into which 8546 families, some of them doubtless visitors, were somehow squeezed. Wookey, on quite a different scale, had a similar problem, 190 houses for 223 families. The rather bald division between agriculture and trade is perhaps less helpful, though local information from South Somerset reveals how Lopen, itself a rare example of a country parish where agriculture was not supreme, comprised 46 farming families and 50 involved principally in the making of dowlas.

Other information to be found in the gazetteer came from different sources. Clergy lists probably provided the details about clergymen and their benefices; books of fairs or Travellers' Companions gave dates of markets and fairs and of their special commodities. But also included are notes of schools and charities and roads, of the structure of the parish church, perhaps brief descriptions of public buildings or neighbouring seats. Many of these pieces of information were clearly derived from local sources of a less formal kind, and are thus all the more valuable. So Radstock had about 100 families involved in coal mining. In contrast the entry for Bath is much less factual: 'as a considerable proportion of the Bath visitants come more for the purpose of enjoying than acquiring a sound constitution there is no deficiency of placed of public amusement', though it was noted that the Lower Assembly Rooms had lately been destroyed by fire. Such a comment is, perhaps, not exactly to be expected from a sober and factual gazetteer. Perhaps Bath did not appeal to the tastes of the practical Yorkshireman in Greenwood. More to his liking may have been the small towns and villages of the countryside, each of which figure in *Somersetshire Delineated* with more objective information. The project was, after all, as Greenwood himself claimed, 'a work of very general utility, and useful as an index' to his survey.

That utility is undoubtedly greater today than in Greenwood's own time, and the appearance of a reprint, coinciding with the publication of a reproduction of his and an earlier map of Somerset by the Somerset Record Society, is a major contribution to the available sources for local study in the county. An appraisal of Greenwood as a surveyor and cartographer by Dr J.B. Harley which accompanies the map is a continuation of Dr Harley's work on Greenwood which appeared in 1962 (J.B. Harley, *Christopher Greenwood, county map-maker, and his Worcestershire Map of 1822*, Worcestershire Historical Society) to which this introduction is heavily indebted.

Robert Dunning.
Taunton, 1980.

A

TOPOGRAPHICAL DESCRIPTION

OF

SOMERSETSHIRE.

———————

ABBOTS-LEIGH—a parish in the hundred of Portbury, 4½ miles
W.N.W. from Bristol; containing 54 inhabited houses, occu-
pied by 62 families, whereof 38 are employed in agriculture.
It formerly belonged to the Abbots of St. Augustine, in Bristol,
from which circumstance it received its designation. The place
is remarkable for having proved an asylum to King Charles the
Second, who was concealed in the house of Sir George Norton,
till means could be provided for his escape into France. *Abbots-
Leigh-Park* is now the residence of *P. J. Miles, Esq.* member for
Bristol, who has lately purchased the estate. The church consists of a nave, chancel, and south aisle, with an embattled
tower at the west end. The living is united with Bedminster;
Rev. R. M. Whish, incumbent; instituted 1806. Population,
1801, 292—1811, 341—1821, 317.

ABDICK and BULSTONE—the name of a hundred, con-
taining the following parishes, viz. ASHILL, BEER-CROCOMBE,
BICKENHALL, BRADON (NORTH and SOUTH,) BROADWAY, BUCK-
LAND-ST. MARY, CRICKET-MALHERBE, CURLAND, CURRY-MALLET,
CURRY-RIVEL, DONYATT, DOWLISH-WEST, DRAYTON, EARNS-
HILL, FIVEHEAD, HATCH-BEAUCHAMP, ILMINSTER, ILTON, ISLE-
ABBOTS, ISLE-BREWERS, LACKINGTON-WHITE, PUCKINGTON,
STAPLE-FITZPAINE, STOCKLINCH-MAGDALEN, STOCKLINCH-OTTER-
SAY and SWELL; containing 1584 inhabited houses, 1912 families;
4822 males, and 4823 females. Total population, 9645.

ALFORD—a parish in the hundred of Catash, 2½ miles W. from Castle-Cary; containing 17 inhabited houses, and 29 families, whereof 23 are employed in agriculture. At a farm-house called Alford Well, in this parish, is a mineral spring, which was formerly held in great repute for its medicinal virtues, but it is now quite neglected. The church consists of a nave and chancel, with a low tower containing three bells. Alford is a rectory, in the deanery of Castle-Cary; Rev. J. G. D. Thring, incumbent; instituted 1808. Population, 1801, 99—1811, 96—1821, 136.

ALLER—a parish in the hundred of Somerton, 2 miles N.N.W. from Langport, near the banks of the river Parret, which river divides it from East-Lyng and the Isle of Athelney; containing 80 inhabited houses, and 85 families, whereof 72 are employed in agriculture. At Aller Moor, in this parish, a remarkable battle took place between the royalists and the parliament army. The church consists of a nave only, with a tower at the west end, and appears of Saxon architecture. It is a rectory, and a peculiar, in the deanery of Ilchester; Rev. Joseph Mends, incumbent; instituted 1809. Population, 1801, 389—1811, 409—1821, 454.

ALLERTON-CHAPEL—a parish in the hundred of Bempstone, 4½ miles S.S.W. from Axbridge; containing 46 inhabited houses, and 58 families, whereof 47 are employed in agriculture. This village was called Chapel-Allerton, to distinguish it from a place called Stone-Allerton, about a mile distant, the former having a place of religious worship. The living is a rectory, in the deanery of Axbridge; Rev. P. L. Parfit, incumbent; patron, the Dean of Wells. Population, 1801, 226—1811, 225—1821, 335.

ALMSFORD—a parish in the hundred of Catash, half a mile N.N.W. from Castle-Cary; containing 48 inhabited houses, and 54 families, whereof 25 are employed in agriculture. The church consists of a nave only, with a tower and three bells, and is

dedicated to St. Andrew. The living is a rectory, in the deanery
of Cary; Rev. F. Woodward, incumbent; instituted 1793. Population, 1801, 237—1811, 244—1821, 300.

ANDERSFIELD—the name of a hundred in the centre of
the county, between Taunton and Bridgewater; it took its name
from a small hamlet in the parish of Goathurst, where the
hundred courts were formerly held; it consists of six parishes,
viz. BROOMFIELD, CREECH ST. MICHAEL, DURLEIGH, ENMORE,
GOATHURST, and LYNG; containing 432 inhabited houses, 464
families; 1208 males, and 1184 females. Total population, 2392.

ANGERSLEIGH—a parish in the hundred of Taunton and Taunton-Dean, 4 miles S.S.W. from Taunton; containing only 9
inhabited houses, and 11 families, whereof 9 are employed in
agriculture. The church is small, consisting of a nave, and a
tower at the west end. The living is rectorial, in the deanery of
Taunton; Rev. J. Gale is both patron and incumbent. Population, 1801, 62—1811, 54—1821, 64.

ASHBRITTLE—a small parish in the hundred of Milverton,
4½ miles W. from Wellington, on the borders of Devonshire;
containing 111 inhabited houses, and as many families, whereof
72 are employed in agriculture. The church is a small structure,
consisting of a nave only, and is dedicated to St. John. The
living is a rectory, in the deanery of Taunton; Rev. Andrew
Quicke, incumbent; instituted 1811. Population, 1801, 595—
1811, 508—1821, 579.

ASHCOTT—a parish in the hundred of Whitley, 5 miles W.S.W.
from Glastonbury; containing 99 inhabited houses, and 129
families, whereof 97 are employed in agriculture. The church,
which stands upon rising ground, is dedicated to All Saints, and
consists of a nave, and tower at the west end. The living is a
vicarage, united with Shapcot, in the deanery of Glastonbury;

Rev. G. H. Templer, incumbent in his own right. Population, 1801, 358—1811, 462—1821, 712.

Ashill—a parish of considerable extent in the hundred of Abdick and Bulstone; containing 69 inhabited houses, and 70 families, whereof 41 are employed in agriculture. Jordans, the residence of William Speke, Esq. is situated to the S. E. of this parish, which place received its name from the small river Jordan, which divides this place from Ilminster. In a field to the north is a medicinal spring, called Skipperham Well, the water of which has a very peculiar property; it ebbs and flows every day, and is very cold, but never freezes; it is used as an antidote in scorbutic eruptions, and is classed among the light chalybeats, which require to be used upon the spot. The church, which is dedicated to St. Mary, is a neat Gothic structure, consisting of a nave and chancel, with a quadrangular embattled tower upwards of fifty feet in height. The living is vicarial, and a peculiar belonging to the prebendary; Rev. S. Smith, incumbent; instituted 1805. Population, 1801, 316—1811, 399—1821, 378.

Ashington—a parish in the hundred of Stone, 3 miles E. S. E. from Ilchester, divided on the north and east from Chilton-Canteloe by the river Yeo; containing 9 inhabited houses, and 18 families, the whole of whom are employed in agriculture. The church is a small structure, consisting of a nave only, with a turret at the west end. It is a rectory, in the deanery of Marston; Rev. John Williams, incumbent; instituted 1785. Population, 1801, 62—1811, 71—1821, 81.

Asholt—a parish in the hundred of Cannington, 3 miles S. from Nether Stowey; containing 33 inhabited houses, and 40 families, whereof 33 are employed in agriculture. The church (which is dedicated to All Saints) consists of a nave, chancel, and south aisle, with a tower containing three bells at the west end. The living is a rectory, in the deanery of Bridgewater ; and the Rev. John Brice is both patron and incumbent. Population, 1801, 136—1811, 159—1821, 178.

ASHTON-LONG—a parish in the hundred of Hartcliffe with Bedminster, 3 miles W. S. W. from Bristol ; containing 202 inhabited houses, and 227 families, of whom 126 are employed in agriculture. The parish contains upwards of 4000 acres of land, principally pasture and meadow, and the Bristol market has a large supply of milk and butter from the dairies ; likewise all kinds of vegetables, in the cultivation of which a considerable part of the population is employed. At Rownham is a ferry over the Avon, which river divides this parish from Bristol and Gloucestershire. The dowager *Lady Smith* resides at *Rownham-Lodge*, between which and the village of Long-Ashton, is *Ashton-Court*, the residence of *Sir J. H. Smith, Bart.* who is lord of the manor and patron of the living, to whose family it came by purchase in the year 1603. The church is a noble structure, dedicated to All Saints, and consists of a nave, north and south aisles, a chancel, with a chapel on each side, and a tower at the west end containing six bells. The benefice is vicarial, in the deanery of Redcliff and Bedminster ; Rev. Israel Lewis, incumbent ; instituted 1794. Population, 1801, 895—1811, 1073—1821, 1168.

ASHWICK—a parish in the hundred of Kelmersdon, 3½ miles N. from Shepton Mallet, containing 193 inhabited houses, and 219 families, whereof 80 are employed in agriculture. An extensive brewery and some coal-works have been established here, which has increased the population considerably. The Roman fosse runs through this parish, on the west side of which is a Roman camp, called Masberry Castle, consisting of a double rampire and ditch, about three furlongs in circuit, having two opposite entrances, guarded by oblique turns of the vallum, which is upwards of fifteen feet deep. Ashwick is a chapel to

Kilmersdon; Rev. Charles Neve, incumbent. Population, 1801, no return—1811, 710—1821, 829.

AXBRIDGE—an ancient borough and market town, in the hundred of Winterstoke, 10 miles from Wells, 18 from Bristol, and 18 from Bridgewater; containing 172 inhabited houses, and 210 families, whereof 61 are employed in agriculture, 107 in trade and manufacture, and 42 not comprised in either class. It takes its name from the river Axe, on which it is situated. The town principally consists of one street, three-quarters of a mile in length from east to west, and was anciently a borough by prescription. At the conquest it had 32 burgesses, and from the 23d of Edward I. till the 17th of Edward III, it sent members to Parliament, after which it was excused upon the petition of its inhabitants. Axbridge was formerly governed by a portreeve and assistant, but afterwards it was incorporated under the title of a mayor, aldermen, and burgesses, which charter was confirmed by Henry the Eighth, Queen Elizabeth, and James the First. The corporation at present consists of a mayor, recorder, town clerk, ten aldermen, and twenty-two burgesses, from whom are chosen a sheriff, serjeant at mace, and constables. The only manufacture in Axbridge is that of knit hose. It has a market on Saturday, and two fairs annually, viz. the day before Candlemas and Lady-day.

The church, which stands upon an eminence, at a short distance from the present market place, is a large handsome structure, in the Gothic style, built in the form of a cross, and consists of a nave, north and south transept, north and south isles, and two chapels, one on each side of the chancel, with a lofty tower, rising at the west end, adorned with two statues, in niches, one of them a king bearing a sceptre, and the other that of a prelate, in his pontifical robes. The living is a rectory, in the deanery of Axbridge; Rev. R. J. R. Jenkins, incumbent; instituted 1796; patron, Bishop of Bath and Wells. Population, 1801, 819—1811, 835—1821, 988.

BABCARY—a parish in the hundred of Catash, 6 miles N.N.E. from Ilchester, and 5½ E. from Somerton, containing 86 inhabited houses, and 93 families, 79 of whom are employed in agriculture. The river Cary, which rises at Castle-Cary, runs through and gives its appellation to this parish. The church consists of a nave only, with a strong embattled tower, containing five bells, and is dedicated to the Holy Cross. The living is a rectory, in the deanery of Cary; Rev. John Wicher, incumbent; instituted 1787. Population, 1801, 337—1811, 330—1821, 422.

BABINGTON—a parish in the hundred of Kilmersdon, 6 miles W.N.W. from Frome, containing 37 inhabited houses, and as many families, 8 of whom are employed in agriculture. *Babington-House*, the residence of Colonel Knatchbull, is pleasantly situated near the church; and about half a mile to the south-west is *Newberry-House*, the residence of John Paget, Esq. The church is a neat edifice, dedicated to St. Margaret, and was built in 1750. The living is a rectory, in the deanery of Frome, Rev. Thos. R. Jolliffe, incumbent; instituted 1810. Population, 1801, 215—1811, 176—1821, 156.

BACKWELL—a parish in the hundred of Hartcliffe with Bedminster, 7 miles S.W. from Bristol, containing 131 inhabited houses, and 156 families, 86 of whom are employed in agriculture: a market was formerly held here, on Mondays, by a grant from Edward the Second, and confirmed by Henry the Seventh; and a fair, by royal charter, also, is still held here, on Sept. 21, for cattle and pedlery ware. The church is a handsome stone structure, consisting of a nave, chancel, two side isles, a chapel and vestry-room, with an elegant embattled tower at the west end, with open turreted pinnacles. The rectory was granted by Ralph de Salopia, Bishop of Bath and Wells, in 1306, to the brethren of St. John the Baptist, at Redcliffe-Pit, Bristol; who, in 1343, admitted a vicar to the said church. The rectory is now a sinecure, belonging to H. E. Bridgeman; and the Rev. W. R. Wake, is incumbent to the vicarage. Population, 1801, no return—1811, 593—1821, 863.

The great increase of population is attributed to the establishment of coal works in the above parish.

BADGWORTH—a parish in the hundred of Winterstoke, 3½ miles S. W. from Axbridge; containing 51 inhabited houses, and 68 families, 44 of whom are employed in agriculture. Near the church is a spring of mineral water, which issues out of a cavity, and forms a rivulet which runs into the Axe. The church consists of a nave only, with a tower at the west end containing five bells. The living is a rectory, in the deanery of Axbridge; Rev. Charles Mordaunt, incumbent; instituted 1800. Population, 1801, 260—1811, 305—1821, 319.

BAGBOROUGH-WEST—a parish in the hundred of Taunton and Taunton Dean, 8 miles N.N.W. from Taunton; containing 80 inhabited houses, and 82 families, 68 of whom are employed in agriculture. This village is pleasantly situated under the western ridge of the Quantock hills, and commands an extensive view over the vale of Taunton. *Bagborough-House,* the residence of Francis Popham, Esq. is situated near the church, which is dedicated to the Holy Trinity, and consists of a nave and chancel, with an embattled tower at the west end. The living is a rectory, in the gift of the Archdeacon of Bristol; Rev. Joseph Guerin, incumbent; instituted 1798. Population, 1801, 352—1811, 376—1821, 421.

BALTONSBOROUGH—a parish in the hundred of Glaston-Twelve-Hides, 5 miles S.E. from Glastonbury; containing 107 inhabited houses, and 130 families, 108 of whom are employed in agriculture, and 22 in trade. The church is dedicated to St. Dunstan, and consists of a nave, chancel and porch, with an embattled tower containing five bells. The living is a chapel to Butleigh, though privileged with burials. Population, 1801, no separate return—1811, 644—1821, 671.

BANWELL—an extensive parish in the hundred of Winterstoke, 4½ miles N. N. W. from Axbridge, on the north side of Winthill ; containing 252 inhabited houses, and 290 families, 182 of whom are employed in agriculture. The church, which is dedicated to St. Andrew, is a large Gothic structure, consisting of a nave, side aisles, and chancel, with a tower at the west end 100 feet in height. The living is a vicarage and a peculiar, in the deanery of Axbridge ; Rev. F. Randolph, incumbent ; instituted 1817 ; patrons, the Dean and Chapter of Wells. Here are two fairs annually for cattle, viz. January 18 and July 18. Population, 1801, 1082—1811, 1162—1821, 1430.

BARRINGTON—a parish in the hundred of South Petherton, 3½ miles N. E. from Ilminster ; containing 71 inhabited houses, and 85 families, 63 of whom are employed in agriculture. The village consists of one street nearly half a mile in length. The lands in this parish are chiefly arable, and great quantities of hemp and flax are cultivated in the neighbourhood. The church, which is built in the form of a cross, has an octangular tower in the centre, containing a clock and five bells. The living is a curacy, in the deanery of Crewkern; Rev. Edward Combe, incumbent ; instituted 1821. Population, 1801, 374—1811, 402 —1821, 440.

BARROW-GOURNEY—a parish in the hundred of Hartcliffe with Bedminster, 6 miles S. W. from Bristol ; containing 47 inhabited houses, and as many families, 39 of whom are employed in agriculture. The manor house is situate near the church, and is now the residence of the Rev. Charles Gore, to whose family this estate came by purchase in the year 1659. The church consists of a nave, chancel, and south aisle, with a tower at the west end containing three bells. The living is a donative, in the deanery of Redcliffe and Bedminster; Rev. James Sparrow, incumbent. Population, 1801, 203—1811, 235—1821, 285.

BARROW-NORTH—a parish in the hundred of Catash, 4 miles S. W. from Castle Cary; containing 19 houses, and 27 families, 18 of whom are employed in agriculture. The church stands upon an eminence, and consists of a nave, chancel and porch, with a quadrangular tower at the west end upwards of 50 feet in height, containing four bells. The living is a rectory, in the deanery of Castle Cary; Rev. John Harbin, incumbent; instituted 1811. Population, 1801, 101—1811, 113—1821, 142.

BARROW-SOUTH—a parish adjoining the above, 4 miles S. S. W. from Castle Cary; containing 24 inhabited houses, and 27 families, the whole of whom are employed in agriculture. The church is a small structure, consisting of a nave only. The living is a rectory and a peculiar, in the deanery of Cary; Rev. Thomas Woodford, incumbent; instituted 1810; patrons, the Dean and Chapter of Wells. Population, 1801, 122—1811, 128 —1821, 155.

BARTON-ST. DAVID—so called from the dedication of its church, is a parish in the hundred of Catash, 4½ miles N. E. from Somerton; containing 48 inhabited houses, and 72 families, 42 of whom are employed in agriculture. The church, which is dedicated to St. David, consists of a nave, chancel, and side aisle, with an octangular tower at the west end. Over the north entrance is a fine Saxon arch of excellent workmanship. The living is a rectory, in the deanery of Cary, and in the patronage of the prebend of St. David; Rev. C. H. Pulsford, incumbent; instituted 1810. Population, 1801, 288—1811, 358—1821, 368.

BATCOMBE—a parish in the hundred of Whitestone, 3 miles N. from Bruton; containing 154 inhabited houses, and 175 families, 128 of whom are employed in agriculture. Batcombe is a considerable village, containing 4 hamlets, viz. WESTCOMBE, ASH-COMBE, ALLAM and SPARGROVE ; at the latter was formerly a church, dedicated to St. Lawrence, and united with Batcombe. The prospects from the hills to the north and south are very extensive, the sides of which are finely cultivated ; the chief part of the land in this parish is pasture. The church is dedicated to St. Mary, and consists of a nave, chancel, north and south aisles, and a tower at the west end containing six bells. The living is a rectory ; Rev. Thomas Coney, incumbent ; instituted 1790. Population, 1801, 677—1811, 719—1821, 792.

BATH FORUM—the name of a hundred, situate at the N. E. point of the County, being bounded on the north by Gloucestershire, on the east by Wilts, on the west by the hundred of Keynsham, and on the south and south-west by Wellow, and includes the following parishes, viz. BATH-EASTON, BATH-FORD, BATHWICK, ST. KATHERINE, FRESHFORD, KELWESTON, LANGRIDGE, LYNCOMBE and WIDCOMBE, MONKTON-COMBE, STOKE-NORTH, STOKE-SOUTH, SWANSWICK, WALCOT, WESTON and WOOLLEY ; containing (exclusive of the parish of Walcot, which is included in Bath return) 2727 inhabited houses, 3636 families, 7337 males, and 9278 females. Total population, 16,615.

BATH—a city in the hundred of Bath Forum, lying in latitude 51° 22′ 30″ N. and longitude 2° 21′ 30″ W. 12 miles E. S. E. from Bristol, and 105 from London ; comprising four parishes, viz. ST. JAMES, ST. MICHAEL, CHRIST-CHURCH, and ST. PETER and ST. PAUL, called the Abbey church ; containing 5157 inhabited houses, and 8546 families, of whom 191 are employed in agriculture, 4891 in trade, manufactures, or handicraft, and 3464 not comprised in either of the two preceding classes. Bath is considered one of the most celebrated cities in Europe, both as it regards the elegance of its buildings, and the beauty of the adjacent country, and is by far the most frequented and fashionable watering place in the kingdom ; it is nearly surrounded by an amphitheatre of hills of considerable height; this range of hills opens a course to the N.E. for the river Avon, which winds round the city to the east, south, and west, and proceeds nearly in a serpentine direction through Bristol to the Channel. This city owes its origin and importance to its medicinal springs, and appears to have been founded by the Romans about the middle of the first century, in the reign of the Emperor Claudius. The various remains of Roman grandeur which have been discovered from time to time tend to confirm this idea.

Most of the new buildings, and by far the largest and finest part of Bath, are without the walls, particularly the Circus, the houses of which are built on a uniform plan, with openings at equal distances leading into three several streets. The fronts of the houses are adorned with three rows of columns, in pairs, of the Doric, Ionic, and Corinthian orders, and the frieze embellished with sculpture. In the centre is a reservoir of water, filled with rising springs from the neighbouring hills. On the south side of the town are the north and south parades, paved with hewn stone, raised upon arches, having an elegant row of houses on one side, and a stone balustrade opposite. Of late years several new streets have been built, the advantages of building here being very great, as excellent free-stone, lime-stone, and slate, are readily found in the neighbourhood. Among these improvements are the Royal Crescent, St. James's Square, Lansdown Crescent, Catherine Place, &c. &c.; and indeed, even within the last twenty years, the number of houses in Bath, and the adjoining parishes, have increased one-third, the additional number being 3322.

The local jurisdiction of this city is governed by a mayor, recorder, aldermen (the number not to exceed ten, nor be less than four,) and twenty-four common council men. Two justices are chosen from among the aldermen, and a town clerk from the common council, except the senior, who is always chamberlain; these are assisted by constables and inferior officers, with two serjeants at mace   The charter which authorized the above body corporate, and declared Bath to be a city of itself, was granted by Queen Elizabeth, September 4, 1590; and in 1794 a new charter was granted by his late Majesty, with a trifling extension of ancient privileges.

The public baths are four in number : the King's bath and the Queen's bath, which are connected with each other ; the Hot bath and the Cross bath. There are likewise two private baths, one belonging to the corporation, in Stall-street, and the Duke of Kingston's, or Abbey bath, which is supplied from the same source as the great pump-room.

TheKing's bath is situated at the southern side of the pump-room, and is sixty-five feet ten inches in length, and forty feet ten inches in breadth, and when filled to its usual height contains upwards of three hundred and forty-six tons of water. In the central part, where the spring boils up, is a brass hand rail of an octangular form, and round the sides runs a Doric colonnade to shelter the bathers from the inclemency of the weather. The bath fills in nine hours, and in its hotest part raises the thermometer to 116, in its coolest to 100. Two commodious rooms open into this bath, fitted up with pumps and pipes, to direct the hot water to any particular part of the body. There are also fire-places and other conveniences for the use of the bathers. On the north side is the pump-room, where the nobility and gentry assemble every morning, between the hours of seven and ten, to drink the waters.

The Queen's bath is a square of twenty-five feet, behind the King's bath, and is furnished with similar conveniences ; the temperature is somewhat lower.

The Cross bath is situated at the extremity of Bath-street ; it is of a triangular form, and has a small neat pump-room attached to it. The appellation is derived from a cross which was erected in its centre by the Earl of Melfort, secretary to King James the Second, in commemoration of the benefit which the Queen derived from bathing in it. The cross is now removed.

The Hot bath stands about forty yards south-west from the

Cross bath, and is distinguished by the superior heat of its waters, their temperature being 117 degrees of Fahrenheit. The building includes a public bath, and several private ones, a vapour bath, dry pumps, and dressing rooms, and is provided with machines for assisting the infirm in bathing. A convenient pump room has been erected near this bath, which is peculiarly suited to invalids, on account of there being no steps to ascend.

The diseases in which the external and internal use of these waters render most service, are affections of the liver and stomach, induced by long residence in warm climates, excessive intemperance, jaundice, hypochondriasis and chlorosis. They are also particularly efficacious in that state of the gout termed atonic; in this disease the waters have a peculiar tendency to excite paroxysms, and to remove the debility consequent upon them. The external application of the water is highly beneficial in palsy, chronic rheumatism, and cutaneous diseases; also in local affections, of scrofula and rheumatism affecting the principal joints, as well as in lameness, contractions, and loss of power in different organs.

As a considerable proportion of the Bath visitants come more for the purpose of enjoying than acquiring a sound constitution, there is no deficiency of places of public amusement: among these may rank the upper and lower assembly rooms (the latter have lately been destroyed by fire, but will shortly be rebuilt); a public theatre, built in 1804, which, though small, is little inferior in point of elegance and attraction to those of the metropolis; the harmonic society, which was instituted under the patronage of the late Dr. Harrington, and another musical society called the York-house club. During the summer months, the residents in this city resort for amusement principally to Sydney Garden Vauxhall, at the extremity of Great Pultney-street; the amusements consist of public breakfasts, promenades, illuminations and music, and in the course of the season there are several gala nights. In fact, Bath is not wanting in any thing that tends to contribute to the gaiety and attraction of a place honoured by the visits of the very first personages in the empire.

The number of charitable institutions in Bath are considerable; that most worthy of remark is the general hospital established for the reception of all the sick poor in the United Kingdom (excepting those resident in the city of Bath) whose complaints are of a nature requiring relief from the waters. It is an elegant pile of building, 110 feet in breadth, and 90 in length ; the first stone was laid on the 8th July, 1738, by the Right Hon. William Pultney, afterwards Earl of Bath.

St. John's Hospital stands a little to the westward of the cross bath, and was built by Mr. Wood, the architect, on the site of an hospital erected in the reign of Queen Elizabeth. This hospital was founded by Reginald Fitz-Joceline in 1138; at present there are six infirm old men, and as many women, who receive 4s. 8d. per week each, with an allowance of coal.

Bellott's Hospital is situated in Belltree-lane, on land belonging to St. John's Hospital; it entertains twelve poor men and women, who have each an apartment, with the liberty of bathing, and an allowance of 1s. 10d. per week, the mayor for the time being nominating such persons as its physician shall recommend as proper objects for the charity. This hospital continues open only half the year, from Lady-day to Michaelmas.

To the south of the above is Bimberrie's, Black Alms, or Hospital of St. Katherine, founded in ancient times by two sisters of the name of Bimberrie. It was rebuilt in 1553 by the corporation, and contains fourteen tenements for as many poor persons of either sex, but inhabited only by ten, who are allowed 3s. 6d. per week each, and a black coat once in two years.

In 1747 an hospital was founded for the reception of diseased paupers belonging to the several parishes in the city of Bath, which continued to be called the Pauper Charity till 1792, when its appellation was changed to the Bath City Dispensary and Asylum, and is supported by annual subscriptions and collections at the different churches and chapels.

The Casualty Hospital was established in 1788, and affords an asylum to paupers injured by accident. It is situated in Mead-street, and is likewise supported by voluntary contributions.

Besides these institutions for the cure of bodily diseases, there is a public Grammar School, founded by Edward the Sixth, a subscription Charity School, a School of Industry, a Lancasterian School, and several Sunday Schools. Likewise a Female Penitentiary, on the same plan as the London Society established for that purpose.

The church of St. Peter and St. Paul, commonly called the Abbey church, is a noble structure, built in the form of a cross, with a magnificent tower rising in the centre, 162 feet in height, having an excellent peal of ten bells. It was founded by King Osric, together with the Abbey-house for nuns; but in the year 775 King Offa placed therein secular canons, who being expelled by King Edgar, he instituted Benedictine monks in their stead. It was frequently repaired and augmented, till Oliver King, about the year 1500, formed a design to rebuild it, but died previous to its completion. Upon the dissolution of religious houses, in the reign of Henry the Eighth, it came to the crown, after which it was entirely stripped of its lead, glass, timber, and other materials, in which state it remained till 1606, when it was restored to its present state by Dr. James Montague, then bishop of the diocese, and other benefactors. It contains many curious monuments, has a handsome altar-piece representing the Wise Men's Offering, given in the year 1725 by General Wade, then one of the representatives of the city; and an excellent organ, considered one of the best in Europe. The several parishes of St. Peter and St. Paul, St. James, and St. Michael, with Lyncombe and Wincombe, are consolidated into one rectory, in the deanery and arch-deanery of Bath; the Rev. Charles Crook, incumbent; instituted 1815; patrons, the Mayor and Corporation of Bath.

The parish church of St. James was rebuilt in 1768-9, under the direction of Mr. Palmer, architect, Bath. The ground plan is a parallelogram of sixty-one feet long by fifty-eight feet wide, and is a very neat freestone building. The tower has a peal of eight musical bells. In 1782 an excellent organ was erected in this church by Mr. Seed, Bristol. The living is a curacy, united with St. Peter and St. Paul.

The church, dedicated to St. Michael, was rebuilt in 1734, partly by a rate and partly by voluntary subscriptions, but was not entirely completed till 1742. It is of the Doric order, with a tower containing eight bells. The living is a rectory, united with St. Peter and St. Paul.

The parish of Walcot includes all those parts of the city that lie on the north, north-east, and north-west sides of the parish of St. Michael; likewise the Circus, the Crescent, and all other buildings on the declivities of Lansdown and Beacon-hills. The church, which is dedicated to St. Swithin, was rebuilt in 1780, after a design from St. James's church, and is a modern edifice, with a small tower, containing a clock and three bells, surmounted by a neat spire. The living is a rectory; Rev. C. A. Moysey, incumbent; instituted 1821.

The population of the parish of Walcot having increased so rapidly, other places of worship were necessary; hence four chapels and one church have been erected. The first of these, in point of date, is

Queen-square Chapel, which stands at the south-west corner of Queen-square. It was built by Mr. Wood, from a design formed after an ancient temple at Athens. The external parts are of the Doric order, and it is open towards the square by a handsome portico. It is a chapelry to St. Peter and St. Paul; the Rev. E. Ravenshaw is the officiating minister.

Margaret Chapel is a spacious building, and was erected in 1773. It received its name from Mrs. Margaret Garrard, at that time lady of the manor, and patroness of the living of Walcot.

All Saints Chapel, situated immediately under Lansdown-hill, is an elegant structure, in the Gothic style, and was completed in 1794.

Kensington Chapel is situated on the eastern side of the London-road, and was built by subscription, in 1795.

Christ Church was built for the express purpose of providing a place of worship for the poor, on a piece of land in Montpelier-row, presented by Lord Rivers to the trustees appointed to manage the fund subscribed for its establishment. The whole of the area is appropriated to the use of persons who cannot afford to pay for seats, and the galleries only are reserved for letting. From the rent they produce the expenses of the institution are defrayed.

On the east side of Milsom-street is a neat chapel, called the Octagon Chapel, completed in 1767; and in Henrietta-street is Laura Chapel, built on a tontine scheme, 1796.

In addition to the places of worship in the church establishment, there are several appropriated to the use of various classes of Dissenters, particularly an Independant Calvinist Chapel in Argyle-street, a meeting for the Society of Friends, a chapel in connection with the late Countess of Huntingdon, a Baptist Chapel, a Wesleyan Methodist Chapel, and some others.

Bath returns two members to parliament, and conjointly with Wells forms a Bishopric, called the Bishopric of Bath and Wells, which comprehends the whole of the county of Somerset, except a few churches in the city of Bristol. The principal markets are held on Wednesdays and Saturdays, and here are two fairs annually, viz. February 14 and June 30. Population, 1801, 27,686—1811, 31,496—1821, 36,811.

BATHEALTON, or BADIALTON—in the hundred of Milverton, 3 miles S.W. from Milverton; containing 22 inhabited houses, and as many families, 19 of whom are employed in agriculture. The church is dedicated to St. Bartholomew; it is a small structure, but neatly ornamented within, having an elegant altar-piece. The living is a rectory, in the deanery of Taunton, and in the patronage of the bishop of the diocese; Rev. E. Webber, incumbent; instituted 1788. Population, 1801, 123—1811, 138 —1821, 105.

BATHEASTON—a parish in the hundred of Bath-Forum, 2 miles

N. E. from Bath; containing 253 inhabited houses, and 275 families, 164 of whom are employed in agriculture. On the south-east this parish is bounded and divided from Bath-Hampton by the river Avon, and on the west Salisbury-hill rises with a steep ascent to the height of nearly 600 feet from the river; on its summit is an entrenchment, generally supposed to be Saxon, and to have been thrown up by that people at the time they laid siege to Bath, A.D. 577. To the south of the village is *Bailbrook-House*, the residence of Colonel Tufnell. The church, which is dedicated to St. John, is a Gothic structure, and consists of a nave, chancel, and porch, with a quadrangular tower, at the west end, of excellent workmanship, 100 feet in height, containing six bells. The living is a vicarage, in the deanery of Bath, and in the gift of Christ Church College, Oxford; Rev. J. J. Coneybeare, incumbent; instituted 1812. Population, 1801, 1072—1811, 1208—1821, 1330.

BATHFORD—a parish in the hundred of Bath-Forum, 3 miles N. E. from Bath, so designated from its having a ford over the river Avon, and from its vicinity to Bath. It contains 133 inhabited houses, and 149 families, 164 of whom are employed in agriculture. The village is situate to the east of the river Avon, on an eminence, at the declivity of the point of a bold hill, called Farley Down, which rises to the height of nearly 700 feet; and on the opposite side Hampton Cliffs rise with great magnificence. The road from Bath to London runs through the parish. At Warley, the residence of Mr. Skrine, was found a Roman pillar of very curious workmanship, of which an etching was made by Sir H. C. Englefield; and on the down, above the village, is a Roman tumulus, and the vestiges of an encampment. About 2½ miles north from the village of Bathford is *Shockerwick-House*, the residence of John Wiltshire, Esq. The church consists of a nave, chancel, and porch, with a square tower containing two bells, and is dedicated to St. Swithin. The living is a vicarage, consolidated with that of Bath-Hampton; Rev. R.

Bedford, incumbent; instituted 1816. Population, 1801, 565—1811, 660—1821, 688.

BATH-HAMPTON—a parish in the liberty of Hampton and Claverton, and locally in the hundred of Bath-Forum, 2 miles N. E. from Bath, and bounded on the north and east by the river Avon; containing 37 inhabited houses, and 47 families, 39 of whom are employed in agriculture. The village is situate in the centre of a valley, which extends from Bath to Bathford. The houses are chiefly built of rough stone, and form one irregular street from the north-east to the south-west. The lands are in general rich pasture and meadow, and considerable quantities of vegetables are grown here for the supply of the Bath market. The church is a Gothic structure, dedicated to St. Nicholas, and consists of a nave, south aisle, and chancel, with a handsome embattled tower at the west end. In 1754 this church was repaired and beautified, and the south aisle rebuilt by Ralph Allen, Esq. in which a monument of white and Sienna marble is erected to his memory.

After the dissolution of monasteries, 34th of Henry the Eighth, the rectory and advowson of this church were granted to the Dean and Chapter of Bristol, who are the present patrons. The living has been augmented with Queen Ann's bounty, and is now consolidated with the vicarage of Bathford. Population, 1801, 157—1811, 227—1821, 243.

BATHWICK—a parish in the hundred of Bath-Forum, pleasantly situated on the banks of the river Avon, which divides it from Bath; containing 559 inhabited houses, and 844 families, 141 of whom are employed in agriculture, 264 in trade, manufactures, or handicraft, and 439 not comprised in either of the two preceding classes. The lands in this parish are frequently under water, from the overflowing of the river Avon, which renders the situation not very desirable in the winter season ; but it is much frequented in the summer, having several agreeable walks, and a number of private gardens with small summer houses, to which the tradesmen of Bath retire after the bustle of the day, to enjoy the delightful scenery with which this place is surrounded. The church is a modern Gothic building, dedicated to St. Mary; the first stone was laid by the Right Hon. the Earl of Darlington, lord of the manor, on the first day of September, 1814, and was consecrated on the 11th of February, 1820, by the Bishop of Gloucester. The living is a rectory, consolidated with Woolley; Rev. P. Gunning, incumbent; instituted 1805. Population, 1801, 2720—1811, 3172—1821, 4009.

BAWDRIP—a parish in the hundred of North Petherton, situate near the river Parrot, 3½ miles N. E. from Bridgewater ; containing 72 inhabited houses, and 79 families, 67 of whom are employed in agriculture. The church is dedicated to St. Michael, and is built in the form of a cross, with a plain tower in the centre. It is a rectory, in the deanery of Pawlet ; Rev. W. S. Knott, incumbent ; instituted 1806. Population, 1801, 244—1811, 315—1821, 372.

BECKINGTON—a parish in the hundred of Frome, situated on the turnpike road between Bath and Frome, being 10 miles S. S. E. from the former, and 3 miles N. N. E. from the latter ; containing 246 inhabited houses, and 254 families, 78 of whom are employed in agriculture, and 131 in trade and manufacture. It was formerly a town of considerable importance, and carried on a large manufacture of woollen cloths, some of which are still made. It is bounded on the west by the river Frome, and extends westward to the borders of Wiltshire. The church is an ancient structure, dedicated to St. Gregory, and consists of a nave, chancel, two side aisles, a vestry room, and two porches, with an embattled tower at the west end, containing a clock and six bells. The living is rectorial, united with Standerwick, in the deanery of Frome; Rev. H. Sainsbury, incumbent; instituted 1792. Population, 1801, 1469—1811, 1551—1821, 1645.

BEDMINSTER—a parish in the hundred to which it gives name,
1 mile S. from Bristol, on the great Western road from that
city; it contains 1412 inhabited houses, and 1673 families, 61
of whom are employed in agriculture, 595 in trade, manufacture,
or handicraft, and 1017 are returned as not being comprised in
either of the two preceding classes. The population of this
parish was formerly very inconsiderable, but it is now become so
crowded with buildings as to form an extensive suburb to the city
of Bristol. The church is dedicated to St. John, and consists of
a nave, chancel, and north aisle, with a large square tower at
the west end, with open ballustrades at top. The steeple was
thrown down in 1563. The living is a vicarage, with the
chapels of Abbots-Leigh and St. Mary Redcliff annexed, and is
a prebend in the cathedral church of Salisbury; Rev. R. Martin
Whish, incumbent; instituted 1806. Population, 1801, 2278
—1811, 4577—1821, 7979.

BEER-CROCOMBE—a small parish in the hundred of Abdick
and Bulstone, 8 miles S.E. from Taunton; containing 29 inhabited
houses, and 36 families, 32 of whom are employed in agriculture.
The situation is flat, and the soil a wet clay; the lands are almost
in equal proportions of arable and pasture. The church consists
of a nave, chancel, and porch, with a tower at the west end. The
living is a rectory, in the deanery of Crewkern; Rev. James
Upton, incumbent; instituted 1803. Population, 1801, 137—
1811, 172—1821, 186.

BEMPSTONE—a hundred which takes its name from a large
stone in the parish of Allerton, at which the courts were formerly
held. It is situated in the north-west part of the county, on the
eastern side of Bridgewater Bay. It is divided from Winterstoke
hundred by the river Axe, and from that of Whitley by the river
Brew. It comprises the following parishes, viz. CHAPEL-ALLER-
TON, BIDDESHAM, BREANE, BURNHAM, MARK, OVER-WEARE and
WEDMORE; and contains 1136 inhabited houses, 1286 families,
3214 males, and 3292 females. Total population, 6506.

BERKLEY—a parish in the hundred of Frome, 2½ miles N. E. from Frome, containing 94 inhabited houses, and 109 families, 60 of whom are employed in agriculture. This parish is situated on the borders of Wiltshire, and extends to the river Frome westward. The lands are mostly pasture, and the soil various. The Rev. J. M. Rogers resides at *Berkley-house;* and about a mile and a half north is *Standerwick-court,* the residence of H. F. E. Edgell, Esq. The church is a neat modern building, dedicated to St. Mary, built in 1751. Its dimensions are forty-one feet square; over the centre is an octagonal dome, supported by four Ionic columns, and terminated by a skylight; and at the westward is a neat tower, with ballustrade railing. The living is a rectory, in the deanery of Frome; the Rev. J. M. Rogers is both patron and incumbent. Population, 1801, 598—1811, 577—1821, 550, exclusive of Standerwick.

In the census of 1811, Berkley and Standerwick made a joint return, but they have lately been separated, in consequence of a new county-rate arrangement; therefore, in addition to the above return, in 1821, Standerwick contains 14 houses, 15 families, and 86 inhabitants, making the total population of Berkley, 636.

BERROW—a parish in the hundred of Brent with Wrington, situated upon the Severn sea, 10 miles from Axbridge, containing 68 inhabited houses, and 83 inhabitants, 44 of whom are employed in agriculture. The beach is a fine smooth sand, nearly half a mile broad at low water. From this place you have a view of the coast from Uphill to Minehead, and the Welch coast for sixty miles in length. The church, which is dedicated to St. Mary, stands near the sea, and consists of a nave, chancel, south aisle, and porch, with a plain square tower, containing five bells. The living is a vicarage, in the deanery of Axbridge; Rev. Charles Johnson, incumbent; instituted 1792; patron, the Archdeacon of Wells. Population, 1801, 371—1811, 480—1821, 449.

The decrease of population in 1821, is attributed to the distressed state of agriculture.

BERWICK—a parish which formerly gave name to a hundred of itself, but now in the hundreds of Houndsborough, Berwick and Coker, 2 miles S. from Yeovil; containing 70 inhabited houses, and 85 families, 39 of whom are employed in agriculture, 42 in trade, manufactures, or handicraft, and 4 not included in either class. *Stoford*, a hamlet about a mile eastward, was formerly a very considerable town belonging to the Lords of Berwick, by whom it was erected into a borough, but its privileges have long since been lost. A short distance to the north-east of the chureh is *Berwick-House*, the residence of John Newman, Esq. The church is a neat edifice, dedicated to St. Mary, and consists of a nave, chancel, and side aisles, with a tower on the north side containing five bells. The living is a rectory, in the deanery of Marston, in the gift of the lord of the manor, J. Newman, Esq.; Rev. T. Warry, incumbent; instituted 1781. Population, 1801, 339—1811, 352—1821, 400.

BICKENHALL—a parish in the hundred of Abdick and Bulstone, formerly a hamlet to Staple-Fitzpaine, but now a reputed parish, situate 6 miles N. W. from Ilminster, and contains 34 inhabited houses, and 36 families, 23 of whom are employed in agriculture. The church is a small building, consisting of a nave and chancel, with a tower at the west-end. The living is annexed to Staple-Fitzpaine; Rev. Thomas Parfit, incumbent. Population, 1801, 155—1811, 179—1821, 215.

BICKNOLLER—a parish in the hundred of Willerton and Freemanners, 4 miles S. E. from Watchett; containing 37 inhabited houses, and 50 families, 29 of whom are employed in agriculture: it is situated under the south-west slope of the Quantock-hills, and is considered to be a place of great antiquity, from the circumstance of Roman coins having been found here in great abundance. The church consists of a nave, chancel, and aisle, with a tower at the west-end. The living is united with Stogumber; Rev. William Phelps, incumbent. Population, 1801, 246—1811, 204—1811, 251.

BIDESHAM—a parish in the hundred of Bempston, 3½ miles W. S. W. from Axbridge, on the right of the turnpike-road to Bridgewater, and bounded on the north by the river Ax. It contains 18 inhabited houses, and 29 families, 26 of whom are employed in agriculture. The church is small, and has a tower at the west-end; the living is a vicarage, and a peculiar, in the deanery of Axbridge, belonging to the Dean and Chapter of Wells; Rev. B. Newton, incumbent. Population, 1801, 88— 1811, 88—1821, 136.

BINEGAR—a parish in the hundred of Wells-Forum, 3½ miles N. from Shepton Mallet, on the road to Bath; containing 77 inhabited houses, and 86 families, 50 of whom are employed in agriculture. There is a large fair held here the whole of the Whit-sun-week, for cattle, woollen cloth, and toys; it was anciently held at Wells, but was removed from thence on account of the plague, which prevailed in that city in the seventeenth century, and has continued at Binegar ever since. The church consists of a nave, with a tower and three bells. The living is rectorial and a peculiar, in the deanery of Frome; Rev. J. L. Gooch, incumbent; instituted 1816. Population, 1801, 324—1811, 321— 1821, 363.

BISHOP'S-HULL—a considerable parish in the hundred of Taunton and Taunton Dean, adjoining to Taunton on the west, and on the turnpike-road to Exeter. It contains 161 inhabited houses, and 213 families, 58 of whom are employed in agriculture, and 100 in trade, manufacture, or handicraft. The river Tone runs through the parish, on which are several mills. The church consists of a nave, chancel, and north and south aisles, with an octangular tower, sixty feet high, containing five bells. The living is a perpetual curacy, in the deanery of Taunton; Rev. Richard Codrington, incumbent; instituted 1790. Population, 1801, 683—1811, 844—1821, 928.

BISHOPS-LYDEARD—a parish of considerable extent, in the hundred of Kingsbury-West, 5 miles N. W. from Taunton, on the road to Minehead; containing 208 inhabited houses, and 225 families, 139 of whom are employed in agriculture. At an early period this was a town of considerable importance, having the advantage of a market and fairs, obtained by the interest of the bishops of the diocese, who were its ancient lords, and from whom it received the name by which it is distinguished. In the year 1666 a large urn was dug up by a labouring man, containing eighty pounds weight of Roman coins of the Emperors Claudius, Nero, Domitian, Nerva, Trajan, Antonine, Septimius-Severus, Tacitus, Gallienus, Tetricus, and some others. The division of this parish runs through *Sandhill-Park*, the seat of Sir T. B. Lethbridge, Bart. M.P. The church is a handsome structure, dedicated to St. Mary, consisting of a nave, chancel, and side aisles, with a noble tower at the west end, containing a clock and eight bells. The living is a vicarage and a peculiar, in the deanery of Taunton, belonging to the Dean and Chapter of Wells; Rev. S. Simmons, incumbent; instituted 1806. Population, 1801, 1068—1811, 1053—1821, 1016.

BLACKFORD—a parish in a detached part of the hundred of Whitley, surrounded by the hundreds of Horethorne, Catash and Norton-Ferrars, 4½ miles S. W. from Wincanton, and 5 miles nearly N. from Milborn Port. It contains 25 inhabited houses, and 38 families, 34 of whom are employed in agriculture. The church is dedicated to St. Michael, and consists of a nave, with a tower and three bells; over the entrance is a fine Saxon arch. This was formerly a chapelry to Maperton, an adjoining parish in the hundred of Catash; it is now a rectory, in the deanery of Cary; Rev. John Wooll, incumbent; instituted 1796. Population, 1801, 159—1811, 140—1821, 154.

BLAGDON—a parish in the hundred of Winterstoke, under the northern declivity of the Mendip-hills, 4½ miles S. E. from

Wrington; containing 211 inhabited houses, and 231 families, 143 of whom are employed in agriculture. The church is a handsome Gothic structure, consisting of a nave, chancel, north aisle, and chapel, with a tower containing five bells. The living is rectorial, in the deanery of Axbridge; Rev. D. G. Wait, incumbent; instituted 1819. Population, 1801, 797—1811, 918 —1821, 1068.

BLEADON—a parish in the hundred of Winterstoke, situated on the river Ax, 6 miles N. N. W. from Axbridge, under a ridge of hills lying to the north : it contains 102 inhabited houses, and 106 families, 71 of whom are employed in agriculture. The church is a large structure, consisting of a nave and chancel, with an embattled tower containing five bells. It is a rectory, in the deanery of Axbridge, in the gift of the Bishop of Winchester; Rev. David Williams, incumbent; instituted 1820. Population, 1801, 381—1811, 441—1821, 518.

BRADFORD—a parish in the hundred of Taunton and Taunton Dean, situated on the river Tone, 3 miles N. E. from Wellington, and 4 miles W. S. W. from Taunton; containing 62 inhabited houses, and 91 families, 58 of whom are employed in agriculture. *Heatherton-Park*, the residence of William Adair, Esq. lies to the south of the parish, adjoining the turnpike road. The church is dedicated to St. Giles, and consists of a nave, chancel, and two side aisles, with an embattled tower containing five bells. The living is a vicarage, in the deanery of Taunton; Rev. William Burridge is both patron and incumbent. Population, 1801, 447—1811, 436—1821, 525.

BRADLEY-WEST—a parish in the hundred of Glaston Twelve-Hides, 4 miles E. S. E. from Glastonbury; containing only 18 inhabited houses, and 21 families, 18 of whom are employed in agriculture. The chapel is a small structure, united to East-Pennard, in the deanery of Cary; Rev. Henry Gould, incumbent.

BRADON-SOUTH—a very small parish in the hundred of Abdick and Bulstone, 4 miles N. from Ilminster; containing, with the hamlet of North-Bradon, only 6 inhabited houses, and 7 families, the whole of whom are employed in agriculture. The living is a sinecure, there not being any church in the parish. It is a rectory, in the patronage of the Earl of Egremont; Rev. Robert Watson, incumbent. Population, 1801, no return—1811, 31— 1821, 32.

BRATTON, or BRATTON-SEYMOUR—a small parish in the hundred of Norton-Ferrers, 3 miles W. N. W. from Wincanton; containing 14 inhabited houses, and the same number of families, 13 of whom are employed in agriculture. The church consists of a nave, with a tower and three bells. The living is rectorial, in the deanery of Cary; Rev. John Messiter, incumbent; instituted 1789. Population, 1801, 62—1811, 79—1821, 80.

BREANE—a parish in the hundred of Bempstone, bounded on the west by the Bristol channel, and on the east by the river Ax; containing 14 inhabited houses, and 18 families, 14 of whom are employed in agriculture. The coast is composed of vast sand banks, forming a natural entrenchment against the fury of the tide, which, when the wind from the norsh-west sets in strong, beats against it with great violence. At the north-west point of the parish is Breane-down, a high peninsula, extending nearly a mile into the channel. The whole of it is a sharp ridge, very lofty, and secured on the sides by prodigious rocks, and on the sea-side totally inaccessible. The church consists of a nave and chancel, with a tower containing three bells. The benefice is a rectory, in the deanery of Axbridge; Rev. M. S. Smith, incumbent; instituted 1789. Population, 1801, 70—1811, 90—1821, 86.

BRENT with WRINGTON—these hundreds are generally coupled together, although situated several miles apart. The former lies on the west-side of the Mendip-hills, near the Bristol channel, the river Ax dividing it from Winterstoke hundred. The latter district is situated on the north-east side of the Mendip, and takes its name from the hundred town. The two divisions comprise the following parishes, viz. BERROW, EAST-BRENT, SOUTH-BRENT, BURRINGTON, LYMPSHAM, and the town of WRINGTON; and contain 719 inhabited houses, 902 families, 2195 males, and 2242 females. Total population, 4437.

BRENT-EAST—a parish in the hundred of Brent with Wrington, 6 miles W. S. W. from Axbridge, on the turnpike road from Bristol to Bridgewater; containing 122 inhabited houses, and 176 families, 134 of whom are employed in agriculture. At a short distance southward from the church stands Brent-Knoll. On the top of this hill, which is nearly 1000 feet above the level of the sea, there is a large double irregular intrenchment, in which brass and silver coins of the Roman empire have frequently béen found. The church is a handsome edifice, 114 feet in length, and 50 in breadth, consisting of a nave, chancel, and side aisles, with an embattled tower at the west end, supporting an elegant spire, rising to the height of sixty feet. The living is vicarial, in the deanery of Axbridge, and in the presentation of the Bishop of the diocese; Rev. Caleb Rocket, incumbent; instituted 1819. Population, 1801, 571—1811, 672—1821, 820.

BRENT-SOUTH—a parish adjoining the above, and in the same hundred; containing 116 inhabited houses, and 134 families, 105 of whom are employed in agriculture. The lands in this parish, except those on the ascent of Brent-Knoll, are a fine rich, well drained and cultivated marsh. The church consists of a nave, chancel, north aisle, and vestry room, with an embattled tower at the west end. The living is a vicarage, in the deanery of Axbridge; Rev. C. Johnson, incumbent; instituted 1799; patron, the Archdeacon of Wells. Population, 1801, 500—1811, 637—1821, 764.

BREWHAM-SOUTH—a parish in the hundred of Bruton, 3 miles
E. N. E. from Brewton ; containing 97 inhabited houses, and as
many families, the whole of whom are employed in agriculture.
The village is situated in a narrow vale by the side of the river
Brew, over which there is a stone bridge of one arch. The
church consists of a nave, chancel, north aisle, and porch, with a
tower containing three bells. The living is a curacy ; Rev. John
Dampier, incumbent ; instituted 1813. Population, 1801, 470
—1811, 508—1821, 600.

BREWHAM-NORTH—a parish separated from the above by the
river Brew, which rises about half a mile from Brewham-Lodge,
an extra-parochial place, the property of Sir Richard Hoare,
Bart. It contains 77 inhabited houses, and as many families,
68 of whom are employed in agriculture. At the Batts Farm,
near Brewham-common, was formerly a chapel, but there are no
remains of any ecclesiastical edifice at present. Population,
1801, no return—1811, no return—1821, 389.

BRIDGEWATER—a populous borough and market-town,
situated upon the river Parret, in latitude 51° 7′ 40″. 7 N. and
longitude 2° 59′ 38″. 7 W. 11 miles from Taunton, 35 from
Bristol, 40 from Bath, and 142 from London ; containing 1059
inhabited houses, and 1186 families, 132 of whom are employed
in agriculture, 817 in trade, manufacture, or handicraft, and 237
not included in either of the two preceding classes.

The surface of the country around Bridgewater is flat, but the
soil and climate are both favourable to agriculture, the interest
of which is studiously promoted by the noble Earl who derives
his title from this town. The river Parret is navigable by ships
of considerable tonnage, which enables the inhabitants to trade
directly with any part of the world ; but the rapidity and bold-
ness of the tide, which often rises two fathoms in one current,
occasions great damage to the smaller vessels, which is one reason
why Bridgewater enjoys little commerce, except in coals and
timber.

This town was first constituted a free borough by King John, in the year 1200, when its government was vested in a preapositus, or reeve; but upon the renewal of the charter by Edward the Fourth, that office was annulled, and a mayor and two bailiffs appointed. Henry the Eighth afterwards conferred additional privileges, and constituted it an independent county; hence the sheriffs of Somerset cannot send a process into this borough. It is now governed by a mayor, recorder, two aldermen (with the powers of justices of the peace) and twenty-four common council men. Besides these there are two bailiffs (chosen annually from the common council to act as sheriffs,) town-clerk, a water bailiff, and two serjeants at mace. Four sessions are held annually for trying all crimes, not capital, and a court of record weekly for the recovery of debts. The Midsummer county sessions are held here, and the assizes in turn with Wells and Taunton. The revenues of the corporation, arising from landed property and tithes, amount to upwards of £10,000 a year. The freemen are free of all the ports of England and Ireland, London and Dublin excepted. Bridgewater has been represented in parliament since the reign of Edward the First. The right of election is in all the inhabitants paying scot and lot, and the mayor is the legal returning officer. A short distance from the church is an excellent free-school, built with stone; likewise a spacious town-hall, and a good market-house. The market days are Tuesday, Thursday, and Saturday; and here are four fairs held annually, viz. at Christmas, Lent, Michaelmas, and St. Matthew's day, old style.

There was formerly a very large castle in this town, which formed the chief security to the inhabitants in times of danger, some remains of which are still to be seen on the west-side of the quay. The walls were 15 feet in thickness, with a moat 30 feet in breadth, and of great depth, which was filled with water at every tide; indeed, the fortifications were so strong, and its advantages both from nature and art so considerable, that it was thought impregnable; and in the civil war, in 1645, it became the depôt of all the treasure and valuable property in the town and county ; but the parliament army carried on the siege with such vigour, that the governor, Colonel Wyndham, notwithstanding he defended it with great bravery for a considerable time, was finally compelled to surrender, when the whole booty fell into the hands of the rebels, with upwards of 1000 prisoners, among whom were a great number of officers, gentlemen, and clergy. It was in the Castle Field that the unfortunate Duke of Monmouth encamped, after having been proclaimed king at Taunton, and previous to the battle of Sedgmoor, which terminated in the destruction of his army.

The church is a large handsome structure, dedicated to St. Mary, consisting of a nave, chancel, two side aisles, with a tower surmounted by a very fine spire, being together 174 feet in height. The living is a vicarage, in the gift of the King ; Rev. W. Woollen, D.D. incumbent ; instituted 1786. Population, 1801, 3634—1811, 4911—1821, 6155.

BRISLINGTON—a parish in the hundred of Keynsham, 2 miles S.E. from Bristol, in the lower turnpike road to Bath, bounded on the north and east by the river Avon ; it contains 173 inhabited houses, and 194 families, 84 of whom are employed in agriculture.

Dr. Fox has an establishment in this parish of a very extensive kind, for the admission of those labouring under mental derangement ; and it is so organized, that the patients enjoy every indulgence their situation will admit. The poor are employed in various branches of domestic labour, and the superior classes have engagements suitable to their former pursuits. The whole building is connected by inclosures with the doctor's residence, and so judiciously arranged that each person can enjoy the comforts of civilized and rational society, and yet be secure from doing injury either to himself or his fellows. Mr. Cumberland, of Bristol, has drawn up a detailed account of this institution, in the first volume of the County Annual Register, published in 1810.

The church is dedicated to St. Luke, and consists of a nave, chancel, and south aisle, with a tower containing five bells. The living is a donative, in the deanery of Redcliff and Bedminster ; Rev. Walter Kitson, incumbent.

BRISTOL—a city lying in latitude 51° 28′ 0″ N. and longitude 2° 21′ 30″ W. 112¾ miles from London, by Marshfield, and 119 by Bath; distance from the latter, 13 miles, and contains 13,474 inhabited houses, and 19,793 families, of whom 876 are employed in agriculture, 13,156 in trade, manufacture, or handicraft, and 3761 not comprised in either class. It is situated on the river Avon, being partly in the county of Gloucester and partly in Somerset, yet strictly not in either, being a county and city of itself: previous to its being so constituted, it was reckoned, in the parliament rolls, in Somersetshire; but in the late returns, under the Population Act, it is included in Barton-Regis hundred, in the county of Gloucester, and in fact the greater part may be considered as belonging to that county. Bristol, as a commercial city, is one of the most important in the empire, being the great emporium for the western counties. It was first constituted a county of itself by Edward the Third, when new boundaries were marked out on both sides of the Avon. Henry the Eighth made it a city and a bishop's see, and in the twenty-fourth year of Queen Elizabeth a new charter was granted for twelve Aldermen, and also for dividing the city into as many wards; after which the citizens procured a charter from Charles the First for the sum of nine hundred and fifty pounds, by which the castle and its precincts were finally separated from the county of Gloucester, and made part of the city, and an independent jurisdiction. During the civil-war, in the reign of Charles the First, the castle was alternately in the hands of the King and the Parliament, but it was at length totally demolished by Cromwell, and several handsome streets have been built upon the spot where it stood, one of which is called Castle-street. The civic government is administered by a mayor, twelve aldermen (all justices of the peace), two sheriffs, twenty-eight common-council men, town-clerk and deputy town-clerk, chamberlain, vice chamberlain, under-sheriff, assisted by a city marshal, and other inferior officers. The city is divided into twelve wards, having an alderman to preside over each. The mayor, &c. holds a quarter-sessions for the trial of offences, and a court of requests is held every Monday, for the recovery of debts. The more ancient streets of Bristol are in general narrow, and the greater part of the houses are built with the upper stories projecting beyond the lower; but the streets formed of late years are spacious, well paved, and contain very handsome buildings; and every opportunity of widening the streets is embraced, by pulling down the old houses, and erecting such as are both ornamental and useful in their place. In the suburbs are elegant and spacious buildings, principally inhabited by the gentry, merchants, and retired tradesmen, or houses for the accommodation of occasional visitors. The foot-ways are well paved with flag-stones, and the whole is well lighted; most of the houses are supplied with river water, and there is plenty of spring water, both from pumps and conduits.

The Quay is upwards of a mile in length, reaching from St. Giles's-bridge down to the mouth of the Frome, and up the old Avon to Bristol bridge, being one uninterrupted spacious wharf of hewn stone, having sufficient depth of water before it for ships of the greatest burden. On the western side of the Mud-dock is the great crane, erected on fourteen pillars, by the inge-nious Mr. Padmore, on a very curious and useful construction; others are erected in different situations, for loading and unload-ing, which are all numbered, for the convenience of finding the vessels. In 1803 the merchants applied to parliament for liberty to form the river Avon into a floating harbour, where the vessels might ride without being liable to sustain any damage from the revolution of the tides. This undertaking was begun in 1804, and completed in about five years, at an expense of nearly £100,000.

The cathedral, situated in College-green, was originally the collegiate church of the monastery of St. Augustine, and was founded by Robert Fitz-Harding, towards the latter end of the reign of King Stephen. At the time of the dissolution, in the reign of Henry the Eighth, it was changed into a cathedral, and dedicated to the Holy Trinity. The foundation consists of a bishop, dean, six prebends, one archdeacon, six minor canons, a deacon, sub-deacon, six lay clerks, six choristers, two masters of the Grammar School, and four alms-men, who were endowed with the site, church, and most of the lands belonging to the monastery. The diocese was taken from that of Salisbury, with part of Gloucestershire, which formerly belonged to Worcester, and three churches from that of Wells. It comprehends 221 churches and chapels, in the county of Dorset, two parishes in the archdeaconry of Bath, likewise seventeen churches and chapels in the county of Gloucester; subject to the jurisdiction of the Bishop and Chancellor of Bristol, but exempt from that of the archdeaconry. The see is charged in the King's books £294. 11s. The church is a venerable Gothic structure, in the form of a cross; the tower is square, 127 feet high, crowned with battlements, and four pinnacles: the abutments are of amazing strength, and project many feet from the walls. The church is remarkable for having the roof of each of the side-aisles of equal height with the nave and choir; these are uncommonly curious, having arches supporting arches. In the body of the church stands a stone pulpit, decorated with the arms of his Majesty, the Prince of Wales, the arms of the bishopric, and those of the city; likewise those of the Berkley family, and Bishop Wright's, by whom it was given to the church.

Exclusive of the cathedral, here are fifteen parish churches, and three episcopal chapels. That of St. Mary Redcliff is esteemed the finest parochial church in the kingdom, and is justly considered the chief architectural beauty of Bristol. It stands without the city-walls, and the whole building exhibits one of the most perfect specimens of Gothic architecture this country can boast. It is built in the form of a cross, having the nave raised above the aisles, in the manner of a cathedral: the roof, which is nearly sixty feet high, is arched with stone, and abounds with numerous carved devices and ornaments, and the pillars which support it are beautifully wrought into the most delicate mouldings: near the centre of the nave, on the south side, opposite the pulpit, is erected a throne, on which the mayor and corporation are seated when they attend in their robes of office to hear divine service, once every year, on Whit Sunday. The altar is very elegant, and richly decorated; over it are three capital paintings by Hogarth. The largest and middle picture represents Christ's ascension; the one on the left hand, is the High Priest with others sealing the tomb; and that on the right, the women coming to look for the body of Christ, and the angel, who tells them, "he is not here, but risen." In the centre compartment of the altar is a picture of our Saviour restoring to life the daughter of Jairus, painted by Mr. Tresham of the Royal Academy, at the request of his uncle, Sir Clifton Wintringham, Bart. who presented it to this church. The living is a vicarage, united with Bedminster; Rev. Martin Whish, incumbent.

Holy Cross, generally called Temple church, is remarkable for its tower, which leans towards the street, and is several degrees out of its perpendicular. It is 114 feet high, and contains a peal of eight bells. The living is a vicarage, in the gift of the corporation; Rev. F. Elwin, incumbent.

St. Stephen's, in Close-street, is a handsome church, and is much admired for the beauties of its ancient tower: it was built in the reign of Henry the Eighth. The pulpit and pews are of mahogany. The living is a rectory, in the gift of the King; Rev. E. C. Greville, incumbent.

All Saints, standing in Corn-street, is an ancient structure, with a modern tower, containing eight bells; on the top is a dome, supported by eight arches, with coupled Corinthian columns at each angle, and crowned with an octangular lanthorn, a gilded ball and cross. It is a vicarage, exempted from the jurisdiction of the archdeacon, in the gift of the Dean and Chapter of Bristol; Rev Henry Green, incumbent.

Christ Church, situate in the centre of the city, near the site of the old one, which was taken down in 1786, in order to widen Vine-street. It is built of free-stone, and on the stage above the church is a handsome tower, ornamented with sixteen Ionic pilasters, supporting four pediments. The stage above this contains ten bells, and has on each side four Corinthian pilasters, with a large vase at each corner of the tower: on the top is an obelisk of seventy feet, on which are elevated a ball and gilded dragon: the entire height of the steeple is 160 feet. The living is a curacy, united with St. Owen; in the presentation of the corporation; Rev. Robert Watson, incumbent.

St. Mark's Church, on College-green, usually called the Mayor's Chapel, is a light building, standing nearly north and south; it has a tower ninety-one feet high, with four pinnacles; it is a chapelry to St. Augustine.

St. Paul's is a new stone building, in the ancient style, and was opened on St. Paul's day 1794. It is a curacy, in the gift of the corporation; Rev. James Olive, incumbent.

St. Peter's, a rectory, in the gift of the corporation; Rev. Nathaniel Strutt, incumbent.

St. Augustine's, a vicarage, in the gift of the King; Rev. Luke Heslop, D.D. incumbent.

St. James's, a curacy, in the gift of the corporation; Rev. T. T. Biddulph, incumbent.

St. John's, a rectory, in the gift of the corporation; Rev. T. Johnes, incumbent.

St. Michael's, a rectory, in the gift of the corporation; Rev. William Knight, incumbent.

St. Philip and St. Jacob's, a vicarage, in the gift of the corporation; Rev. William Day, incumbent.

St. Mary's, a rectory, in the gift of the Duke of Chandos; Rev. John Neal, incumbent.

St. Thomas's, a chapelry, in the diocese of Bath and Wells united with St. Mary, Redcliffe.

St. Werburg's, a rectory, in the gift of the King; Rev. William Tandy, incumbent.

St. Leonard's, a vicarage, in the gift of the Dean and Chapter; Rev. John Eden, incumbent.

St. Nicholas's, a vicarage, united with St. Leonard; Rev. John Eden, incumbent.

Besides the above churches in the establishment, here are as many places of worship belonging to various denominations of protestant dissenters; likewise two meeting-houses for the Society of Friends, a Jew's synagogue, a Roman Catholic chapel, and a chapel in Orchard-street appropriated to the French protestants.

The charitable foundations in this city are very numerous; the principal ones are St. Peter's Hospital, for the reception of poor citizens in general, including superannuated persons, orphans, and idiots. An asylum for orphan girls, at Hook's mill. The Merchant's Hospital, for nineteen seamen and twelve seamen's widows. The Bristol Blind Asylum, in which the inmates are employed in various branches of manufacture. Colston's Hospital, founded for the education and maintenance of 100 boys, and endowed with lands in various parts of Somersetshire. The City Grammar-school, for instruction in Latin and Greek, which supports two masters. The Endowed College Grammar-school, founded by Henry Eighth. Queen Elizabeth's Grammar-school, and ten or twelve other public schools. Likewise the following alms-houses, viz. Colston's, St. Nicholas's, Forster's, Alderman Stephens's, Strange's, All Saints, Presbyterian, Spencer's, and Redcliff Hill. Besides these there are nearly twenty hospitals and poor houses, supporting upwards of 2000 persons.

The public buildings erected for the administration of justice, and for commercial purposes, are numerous. The Guildhall, standing in Broad-street, is a lofty building with a modern front, bearing the arms of Edward the First, and a Royal Statue. The Council-house is a stone building, erected in Corn-street, in the year 1703. The Mayor and Aldermen sit here daily, to administer justice. The Custom-house is a good building of brick, with a colonnade in front of free-stone pillars having Ionic capitals : the room in which business is transacted is about seventy feet in length. The Excise-office is also of brick, near the Custom-house, in Queen-square. The Post-office is of free-stone, near the Exchange ; its annual revenue is considered upwards of £10,000. The Exchange is a handsome and extensive building, and esteemed the most complete edifice of the kind in Europe : its front is 110 feet, and depth 148, and is capable of containing 1440 persons. The whole building throughout is of stone. The places between the capitals of the columns and pilasters in the front are filled with festoons, with representations of Great Britain and the four quarters of the world, with the chief products and manufactures of every country. It was opened for public business on the 23d of September 1743, and is said to have cost £50,000. The Merchant's hall is of free-stone, erected in 1701, but it may be said to have been almost rebuilt, in consequence of the many improvements it has received. On each side of the door are the merchants' arms cut in stone, and above is a good bust of his late Majesty. The Merchant Tailors'-hall, in Broad-street, is likewise a freestone building, nearly seventy feet long, and of proportionable breadth. The Cooper's-hall, in King-street, has a very superb front, with four noble columns of the Corinthian order. Here is also a commodious theatre, an assembly room, and various other places of public amusement. There are upwards of thirteen corporate bodies ; that of the Merchant Venturers is the most respectable, consisting of some of the principal gentlemen in the city and its environs, formed for the promotion of trade and commerce, and generally act in conjunction with the corporation, in promoting the mercantile interests of the city and the prosperity of its inhabitants.

Bristol returns two members to parliament; the right of election is in the freeholders of forty shillings a year, and the free burgesses. The freemen are those who are free by birth, freehold, servitude, purchase, donation, or those who obtain their freedom by marrying a freeman's daughter. This last singular privilege was granted by Queen Elizabeth, as an encouragement to matrimony. There are two principal and several other markets, which are plentifully supplied with all kinds of provisions, at a reasonable rate; and two fairs annually, viz. one on the first of March, in Temple-street, and the other on the first of September, in St. James's Church-yard, which continues several days.—Population, including the out-parishes of Clifton, Mangots-field, and Stapleton, on the north side of the Avon, in the hundred of Barton Regis, 1801, 63,645—1811, 67,516—1821, 87.779.

BROADWAY—a parish in the hundred of Abdick and Bulstone, 2½ miles W. N. W. from Ilminster; containing 63 inhabited houses, and 70 families, 39 of whom are employed in agriculture, and 38 in trade, manufacture, or handicraft. This village derives its name from having been built on a broad path cut through the woods which were at that time part of the forest of Neroche. The situation is flat, and the lands are nearly all pasture and meadow. A considerable manufacture of druggets, narrow cloths, &c. was carried on here, but of late years the trade has much declined. A fair is held here for cattle and toys on the 14th of September annually. The church consists of a nave, two side aisles, and chancel. The living is a rectory, in the deanery of Crewkerne; Rev. J. H. Mules, incumbent; instituted 1811. Population, 1801, 328—1811, 307—1821, 396.

BROCKLEY—a parish in the hundred of Chewton, 3 miles N. from Wrington; containing 19 inhabited houses, and as many families, 10 of whom are employed in agriculture. About a quarter of a mile eastward from the church is a fine romantic glen, called Brockley-Combe, belonging to Arthur Pigott, Esq. who resides at Brockley-Court; it is about half a mile in length, and very narrow. In the deepest part the rocks are almost inaccessible to the height of 300 feet. Along the bottom is a fine gravel walk, having on each side a deep slope formed of rugged rocks, having yews, forest and other shrubs, growing out of the crevices in a very picturesque manner. In the centre is a neat cottage. The church is a small structure, dedicated to St. Nicholas, and consists of a nave, two small aisles, and a porch, with a plain embattled tower at the west end. The south aisle belongs to Brockley-Court, under which is a vault of the Pigott family. The living is a rectory; Rev. J. Boak, incumbent; instituted 1795. Population, 1801, 111—1811, 109—1821, 173.

BROMPTON-RALPH—a parish in the hundred of Wellerton and Freemanners, 3 miles N. of Wiveliscombe; containing 53 inhabited houses, and 69 families, 57 of whom are employed in agriculture. It lies at the east end of Brendon-hill, full of ascents and deep narrow vales, well watered. The principal part of the lands are arable, and the crops, as well as the manures, are carried on horseback. The church is dedicated to St. Mary, and consists of a nave, chancel, and a small north aisle, with a tower containing four bells at the west end. The living is rectorial, in the deanery of Dunster; Rev. Thomas Sweet Escott, incumbent; instituted 1802. Population, 1801, 406—1811, 396—1821, 449.

BROMPTON-REGIS—a parish in the hundred of Willerton and Freemanners, 1½ mile S. from Dulverton; containing 140 inhabited houses, and 146 families, 109 of whom are employed in agriculture. At the southern extremity of this parish, between the turnpike-road and the river Ax, is *Baron-Downs*, the residence of S. T. Lucas, Esq. The church is dedicated to St. Mary, and consists of a nave, chancel, and north and south aisles, with an embattled tower containing four bells. The living is a vicarage, in the deanery of Dunster, in the patronage of Emanuel College, Cambridge; Rev. R. B. Boague, incumbent; instituted 1820. Population, 1801, 702—1811, 682—1821, 771.

BROOMFIELD—a parish in the hundred of Andersfield, 6 miles W. S. W. from Bridgewater; containing 66 inhabited houses, and 81 families, 70 of whom are employed in agriculture. The parish is very extensive, situated on high ground, and beautifully varied with swelling hills, commanding a great variety of pleasing prospects over the Bristol Channel and the Welch mountains. The lands are nearly divided between pasture and arable, and the soil is favourable to the growth of timber. Spanish chestnut trees, beech, firs, pines, and ash flourish here, and grow to a large size. An annual fair is held here on the 13th November, for coarse cloths and all kinds of cattle.

Near the church is the residence of Andrew Crosse, Esq. surrounded with beautiful grounds, and well-arranged plantations. The church consists of a nave, chancel, and north aisle, with a square tower at the west end containing five bells. The living is a donative and a peculiar, belonging to the Dean of Wells; Rev. John Blundell, incumbent; instituted 1785. Population, 1801, 369—1811, 362—1821, 489.

BRUSHFORD—a parish in the hundred of Willerton and Freemanners, 1½ mile S. from Dulverton, the river Barle dividing it from that parish : it contains 64 inhabited houses, and 67 families, 54 of whom are employed in agriculture. The church is dedicated to St. Nicholas, and consists of a nave, with a tower containing five bells. It is a rectory, in the deanery of Dunster; Rev. S. Nosworthy, incumbent; instituted 1811. Population, 1801, 303—1811, 291—1821, 311.

BRUTON—the name of a hundred lying to the south-east part of the county, between Shepton-Mallet and Wincanton, in-

cluding the following parishes, &c. viz. BREWHAM (NORTH and
SOUTH), BRUTON with the tything of REDLYNCH, and Chapelry of
WICK-CHAMPFLOWER, EASTRIP, MILTON-CLEVEDON, PITCOMBE
UPTON-NOBLE, and YARLINGTON; containing 801 inhabited
houses, 893 families, 1947 males, and 2341 females. Total
population, 4288.

BRUTON—a small market-town in the hundred of Bruton,
109 miles from London by Heytesbury, and 116 by Shaftsbury;
containing, with the tythings of Discove and Redlynch, 403 inhabited houses, and 452 families, 162 of whom are employed in
agriculture, 260 in trade, manufactures, or handicraft, and 30
not included in either class. The town is seated on the river
Brew, from which it derives its name. Its chief manufacture is
that of stockings, and there are three silk-mills; the latter employ
a great number of young people, particularly females. Here is an
excellent hospital for the support of a certain number of men,
women, and boys; the latter are boarded with the master. A
suit of clothes is given annually to each individual in the hospital,
and a nurse is kept to wait upon the sick. In the hospital, which
is built round a court, are 22 rooms, besides the master's, and a
small chapel. It was founded and endowed by Hugh Saxey,
Esq. auditor to Queen Elizabeth, who was born of poor parents
in this neighbourhood, and is said to have acted as stable-boy at
one of the inns in the town. Here is likewise a free grammar-
school, founded by Edward the Sixth, and endowed by Bishop
Fitzjames, and his brother Sir John Fitzjames, lord chief justice
of England. The master has an income of £80 per annum,
with a house and garden, and other conveniences.

At Discove, a tything in this parish, the remains of a Roman
tessellated pavement were found in the year 1711. Bruton has a
small market on Saturdays. Fairs, April 21 and September 19.
The church, which is dedicated to St. Mary, is a Gothic structure, consisting of a nave, chancel, side aisles, a vestry-room,
and two porches, with a fine embattled tower at the west end,

ornamented with pinnacles ninety-three feet high, containing a
clock and six bells. The living is a perpetual cure, in the
deanery of Cary, in the patronage of Sir R. C. Hoare, Bart.;
Rev. W. Cosens, incumbent; instituted 1800. Population, 1801,
1631—1811, 1667—1821, 1858.

BRYMPTON—a parish in the hundred of Stone, 2½ miles W.S.W.
from Yeovil, on the turnpike-road from that town to Taunton;
containing 20 inhabited houses, and 29 families, 15 of whom are
employed in agriculture. The manor-house is a large noble
building, approached by an avenue of trees, and sheltered on the
north and north-east by fine hills, planted with wood. The Earl
of Westmorland is lord of the manor. The church consists of a
nave, chancel, two side aisles, and two chapels, with a small
turret at the west end. The living is a rectory; Rev. Thomas
Williams, incumbent; instituted 1797. Population, 1801, 133
—1811, 124—1821, 125.

BUCKLAND-DENHAM—a parish in the hundred of Kilmersdon,
2½ miles N. W. from Frome; containing 93 inhabited houses,
and 96 families, 9 of whom are employed in agriculture, and
83 in trade, manufacture, or handicraft. The turnpike-road
from Bristol to Frome runs through the village, which consists
of a long street of indifferent houses. It formerly was a large
and very considerable place, having a market on Tuesdays, a fair
which continued three days, and a large manufacture of woollen
cloth; likewise a market cross, and town-hall wherein the
assizes were frequently held. It received its designation from
the Denhams, its ancient lords, who resided here in a large
mansion long since destroyed. The principal part of the population is employed in the cultivation of teasles, which are
used in the woollen manufactory. The church is dedicated to
St. Michael, and consists of a nave, chancel, and side aisles, with
a tower at the west end containing five bells. The living is a
vicarage and a peculiar, in the deanery of Frome, belonging to

the prebendary; Rev. R. A. Burney, incumbent; instituted 1817.
Population, 1801, 429—1811, 403—1821, 440.

BUCKLAND-ST. MARY—a parish so called from the dedication
of its church, situated in the several hundreds of Abdick and
Bulstone, South-Petherton, and Martock, 5 miles N. W. from
Chard; containing 101 inhabited houses, and 108 families, 98
of whom are employed in agriculture. On the top of that part
of Blackdown, which lies in this parish, on the road from Neroche
Castle to Chard, are immense quantities of flint stones lying in
vast heaps, upwards of sixty yards in circumference, and are
generally supposed to be the tombs of ancient warriors, who fell
during the severe contests between the Danes and Saxons in
these parts. An enclosure has lately taken place in this parish,
which accounts for the increase of population. A fair for cattle
and toys is held here on the Wednesday and Thursday after the
20th of September. The church is a neat structure, and consists of a nave, chancel, and two side aisles, being eighty feet
long and forty-four feet wide. The living is a rectory; Rev.
J. Templeman, incumbent; instituted 1788. Population, 1801,
418—1811, 454—1821, 565.

BUCKLAND-WEST—a parish in the hundred of Kingsbury-
West, 3 miles E. from Wellington; containing 160 inhabited
houses, and 171 families, 119 of whom are employed in agriculture. The lands are in general rich, and equally divided between arable and pasture; and the roads are deep, narrow, and
stony. The church is dedicated to St. Mary, and is partly of Saxon
and partly of Gothic architecture; it consists of a nave, chancel,
and side aisles, with a tower eighty-feet high containing five
bells. It is a chapelry to the parish of Wellington. Population,
1801, 676—1811, 689—1821, 750.

BURNET—a small parish in the hundred of Keynsham, 8 miles
S. E. from Bristol; containing only 10 inhabited houses, and 13

families, 11 of whom are employed in agriculture. John Whitson, Esq. alderman of Bristol, gave this manor in trust to the mayor and corporation of Bristol, for the endowment of his Redmaid's hospital in that city, and other charitable uses; they are the present feoffees and patrons of the living. The church is dedicated to St. Michael, and consists of a nave, and one small side aisle. The living is a rectory; Rev. J. F. Doveton, incumbent; instituted 1815. Population, 1801, 64—1811, 70 —1821, 75.

BURNHAM—a parish of considerable extent, on the coast of the Bristol channel, and bounded on the south by the river Brew, situate in the hundred of Bempstone, 10 miles W. S. W. from Axbridge; containing 143 inhabited houses, and 195 families, 103 of whom are employed in agriculture. The coast is a fine sandy beach, which, when the tide is at ebb, is nearly half a mile in breadth; the upper part of it rises in high sand banks, forming a strong entrenchment that the highest tides never break through. The lands in this parish are mostly pasture, and very rich. Henry Rogers, of Cannington, Esq. left the sum of £ 2350 to purchase lands, the clear profits thereof to be applied towards the maintenance of twenty poor people, two of the said poor to live within the manor of Burnham, and to have their proportions. The church consists of a nave, chancel, south aisle, and vestry-room, with a large plain tower and five bells. The living is a vicarage, in the gift of the Dean and Chapter of Wells; the Bishop of Rochester, incumbent. Population, 1801, 653—1811, 740—1821, 920.

BURRINGTON—a parish in the hundred of Brent with Wrington, 4 miles S. E. from Wrington, 6 miles N. E. from Axbridge, and 13 miles S. S. W. from Bristol; containing 103 inhabited houses, and 128 families, 66 of whom are employed in agriculture. In this parish is a place called Rickford, romantically situated one mile east, in the centre of a deep cove, almost surrounded by lofty projections, on the side of Mendip, covered with wood. In the centre of this cove is a beautifully transparent spring, which forms a shallow stream thirty yards wide, as many yards distance from its course, and winds through the vale to Wrington, in its way to the channel. The church is a neat struoture, consisting of a nave and side aisles, with a handsome turret, and an embattled tower containing six bells. The living is a perpetual curacy, annexed to Wrington; Rev. S. T. Wylde, incumbent. Population, 1801, 423—1811, 402—1821, 559.

BUTCOMBE—a parish in the hundred of Hartcliffe with Bedminster, 9 miles S. S. W. from Bristol; containing 34 inhabited houses, and 46 families, 45 of whom are employed in agriculture. Charles Gordon Ashley, Esq. resides at the Court-house in this parish. The church is dedicated to St. Michael, and consists of a nave, chancel, and a chapel on the south side, adjoining which is a strong embattled tower containing three bells. The living is a rectory; Rev. R. P. Hassell, incumbent; instituted 1818; patron, the Bishop of the diocese. Population, 1801, 133 —1811, 146—1821, 213.

BUTLEIGH—a parish in the hundred of Whitley, 4 miles S.S.E. from Glastonbury; containing 169 inhabited houses, and 176 families, 96 of whom are employed in agriculture. The manor and parish are the property of Lord Glastonbury, who has a handsome seat near the church. The church is a handsome structure, consisting of a nave, chancel, north aisle, and an embattled tower with five bells. The living is a vicarage, of which Lord Glastonbury is patron; Rev. Henry Gould, incumbent; instituted 1790. Population, 1801, 694—1811, 710 —1821, 809.

CADBURY-NORTH—a parish in the hundred of Catash, 3½ miles S. from Castle-Cary, and 6 from Wincanton; containing, with the hamlets of Galhampton and Woolston, 173 inhabited houses, and 210 families, 114 of whom are employed in agriculture. This parish is situated on high ground, well wooded and watered, and in a high state of cultivation. Here are two streams run through the parish, which turn several mills, one rising under Yarlington-hill, and the other at Blackford. The manor-house stands near the church, and is a large handsome building, the residence of James Bennett, Esq. The church is a large edifice, and was built by Lady Elizabeth Botreaux, about the year 1427; it consists of a nave, two side aisles, and a vestry, with a handsome tower at the west end, embattled and pinnacled, containing six bells. The living is a rectory, in the deanery of Cary, and in the patronage of Oriel College, Oxon; Rev. Samuel Blackhall, incumbent; instituted 1812. Population, 1801, 810—1811, 908 —1821, 1001.

CADBURY-SOUTH—a parish in the same hundred, five miles S. from Castle-Cary, containing 35 inhabited houses, and 54 families, 51 of whom are employed in agriculture. The neighbourhood of this place is uncommonly grand and picturesque, and is said to have been the seat of some great military action in ancient times. Near the village are the remains of one of the most famous fortifications in this or perhaps any other country. Leland, and other old topographers, call it Camalet, but by the inhabitants it is called Cadbury-castle. Dr. Stukeley says this place belonged to the Romans, and describes it as made in the solid rock, with three or four ditches quite round; its figure squarish, but conforming to the slope of the hill; the area upwards of thirty acres. A higher work within, ditched round, is called King Arthur's Palace, and might have been the Prætorium, and have served him too. The rampart is made of stones covered with earth, with only one entrance from the east, guarded by six or seven ditches. Many round stones, supposed for slings or cross-bows, have been discovered in this camp. Roman coins and other relics have been frequently found here,

and in the country round : the coins were chiefly those of
Antoninus and Faustina. Various camp-utensils and remains of
military equipage have been found at the top, and also near the
never-failing spring in the fourth ditch, called King Arthur's
Well. Leland asserts that a silver horse-shoe was found here,
within the memory of the people living in his time. The
church is a neat edifice, dedicated to St. Thomas-à-Becket, and
consists of a nave, chancel, south aisle, and porch, with an
embattled tower and stone spire. The living is a rectory, in
the deanery of Cary; Rev. James Rogers, D.D. incumbent;
instituted 1796. Population, 1801, 214—1811, 236—1821, 257.

CAMEL-WEST—a parish in the hundred of Somerton, four
miles E. N. E. from Ilchester, containing 43 inhabited houses,
and 66 families, 51 of whom are employed in agriculture. About
half a mile to the north, two catacombs were discovered some
few years since, in which were found several bodies, arranged in
rows, at the depth of about five feet, each in a small trench, the
intermediate space being filled up with small stones. The
church is dedicated to All Saints, and consists of a nave, chancel,
and north aisle, with a square tower on the south side, from
which rises a small steeple covered with lead. The living is a
rectory, in the deanery of Marston, in the patronage of the
Bishop of the diocese; Rev. Edward Willes, incumbent; instituted 1796. Population, 1801, 224—1811, 281—1821, 304.

CAMEL-QUEENS—See QUEEN'S-CAMEL.

CAMELEY—a parish in the hundred of Chewton, that receives
its name from a small brook, called the Cam, which rises in the
parish: the village is situated 10½ miles S. from Bristol, and
contains 111 inhabited houses, and 112 families, 51 of whom
are employed in agriculture: the country for some miles round is
agreeably varied with hills and vallies, and the lands are mostly
pasture : here are several quarries of excellent stone, used for

paving the footways in the cities of Bath and Bristol. The church is dedicated to St. James, and consists of a nave, with a handsome tower seventy feet high. The living is a rectory, in the deanery of Frome; Rev. Thomas Williams, incumbent; instituted 1810. Population, 1801, 454—1811, 498—1821, 604.

CAMERTON—a parish in the hundred of Wellow, seven miles S. W. from Bath, containing 181 houses, and 188 families, 32 of whom are employed in agriculture. The brook Cam, which rises at Cameley, likewise gives name to this parish, through which it passes, and continuing its course by Dunkerton, Combe, Hay, and Midford, discharges itself into the river Avon. North of the church is *Camerton-House*, the residence of Mrs. Jarrett. The church is a handsome Gothic structure, dedicated to St. Peter, and consists of a nave, chancel, and a chapel on the north side, with a large tower at the west end. The living is a rectory, in the deanery of Frome; Rev. John Skinner, incumbent; instituted 1800. Population, 1801, 594—1811, 786—1821, 1004.

CANNINGTON—the name of a hundred on the N. W. side of the county, bounded on the north by the Bristol Channel, and on the east it is divided from the hundreds of Huntspill and North Petherton by the river Parret. It contains ten parishes, viz. ASHOLT, CANNINGTON, CHARLINCH, FIDDINGTON, OTTERHAMPTON, OVER-STOWEY, SPAXTON, STOCKLAND-BRISTOL, STOKE-COURSEY and STRINGTON; containing 374 inhabited houses, 1040 families, 2578 males, and 2578 females. Total population, 5156.

CANNINGTON—a parish in the above hundred, 4 miles N. N. W. from Bridgewater; containing 213 inhabited houses, and 228 families, 159 of whom are employed in agriculture. The village is pleasantly situated on the turnpike-road from Bridgewater to Dunster, in a flat and woody country, but well cultivated. About half a mile to the west of this parish is an ancient seat called *Brymore*, which formerly was part of the manor of Radford : it is now the residence of Sir Philip Hales, Bart. The manor of Beer in this parish was purchased by Edward Colston, Esq. and by him appropriated towards the support of a hospital in Bristol, of his own foundation. The church is dedicated to St. Mary, and consists of a nave, chancel, and side aisles, with a handsome embattled tower at the west end, containing a clock and five bells. The living is a vicarage, and the Rev. C. H. Burt is both patron and incumbent. Population, 1801, 850—1811, 1001—1821, 1215.

CARHAMPTON—the name of a hundred, situated in the N. W. part of the county, and bounded on the north and north-west by the sea, and on the west by the county of Devon. This hundred has been very justly styled the Alps of Somersetshire, the whole being a picturesque assemblage of lofty hills succeeding each other, the steep sides of most of them being skirted with hanging woods, having deep romantic vallies winding between them, in which most of the towns and villages are situated; they are very fruitful, and are generally watered by small streams running through them. This hundred comprises the market towns of DUNSTER, MINEHEAD, and PORLOCK; and the following parishes, viz. CARHAMPTON, CULBONE, otherwise KITNOR, CUTCOMBE, EXFORD, LUCKHAM, LUXBOROUGH, OARE, SELWORTHY, STOKE-PERO, TIMBERSCOMBE, TREBOROUGH, WITHYCOMBE, and WOOTTON-COURTNEY; containing 1333 inhabited houses, 1499 families, 3613 males, and 3709 females. Total population, 7322.

CARHAMPTON—a parish in the above hundred, 1½ mile S.E. from Dunster, and 4½ W. from Watchet; containing 104 inhabited houses, and 123 families, 86 of whom are employed in agriculture. The church is dedicated to St. John, and consists of a nave, south aisle, and chancel, with a low stone tower containing four bells. The living is vicarial, in the deanery of Dunster, and a peculiar belonging to the Dean of Wells; Rev. Richard Bere, incumbent; instituted 1802. Population, 1801, 601— 1811, 532—1821, 587.

CASTLE-CARY—a parish, and formerly a market town in the hundred of Catash, 9 miles N. E. from Ilchester, and 115 from London; containing 299 inhabited houses, and 333 families, 158 of whom are employed in agriculture, 167 in trade, manufacture, or handicraft, and 8 not included in either class. On the east side of the principal street formerly stood the manorhouse, now almost entirely demolished, in which King Charles sheltered himself after the battle of Worcester, in his way to Lyme Regis; it was then inhabited by a Mr. William Kirton, who met him on the road and conducted him hither in disguise. The country around Castle-Cary is extremely beautiful, and the society in the town and neighbourhood is highly respectable, which, with the convenience of its situation, renders it a place of agreeable retirement. Here are three fairs annually, viz. Tuesday before Palm Sunday, May 1st, and Whit Tuesday.

The church is situated on rising ground, and has an interesting appearance : it is dedicated to All Saints, and consists of a nave, chancel, and side aisles, with an embattled tower at the west end fifty feet in height, surmounted by a spire thirty feet high from the battlements. In Cromwell's time many of its ornaments were defaced, and the organ entirely destroyed. The living is a vicarage, in the deanery of Cary, and in the patronage of the Bishop of the diocese; Rev. William Hunt, incumbent; instituted 1801. Population, 1801, 1281—1811, 1406—1821, 1627.

CATASH—a hundred on the east side of the county, which takes its name from an Ash tree in the road from Castle-Cary to Yeovil, where the hundred court was usually held; it comprises the following parishes, viz. ALFORD, ALMSFORD, BABCARY, BAR-

ROW (NORTH and SOUTH,) BARTON ST. DAVID, CADBURY (NORTH and SOUTH,) CASTLE-CARY, COMPTON-PAUNCEFOOT, KENTON-MANSFIELD, KINGS-WESTON, LOVINGTON, LYDFORD-WEST, MAPERTON, QUEEN-CAMEL, SPARKFORD, SUTTON-MONTIS or MONTAGUE, and WESTON-BAMPFYLD; containing 1231 inhabited houses, 1464 families, 3498 males, and 3677 females. Total population, 7175.

CATCOT—a chapelry in the parish of Moorlinch and hundred of Whitley, 7 miles E. N. E. from Bridgewater; containing 111 inhabited houses, and 131 families, 115 of whom are employed in agriculture. The church consists of a nave, with a tower at the west end, and is united with Moorlinch. Population, 1801, 391—1811, 445—1821, 579.

CHAFFCOMBE—a small parish in the hundred of South Petherton, 2½ miles E. N. E. from Chard; containing 47 inhabited houses, and 56 families, 51 of whom are employed in agriculture. About three-quarters of a mile to the South of this parish is *Avishays*, the residence of J. Inglett Fortescue, Esq.. The church is dedicated to St. Michael, and consists of a nave, chancel, and north aisle or chapel, with a tower at the west end. The living is rectorial, in the deanery of Crewkerne; Rev. B. Abraham, incumbent; instituted 1792. Population, 1801, 165—1811, 195—1821, 225.

CHARD—a market town at the southern extremity of the county, in the hundred of Kingsbury-East, 12 miles S. from Taunton, and 8 miles W. from Crewkerne; containing 511 inhabited houses, and 641 families, 128 of whom are employed in agriculture, 312 in trade, manufacture, or handicraft, and 201 not included in either class. The town principally consists of two streets, intersecting each other, in which are several well-built houses. At the west end of the principal street rises a spring, the water from whence is conveyed by leaden pipes to four conduits, from which the inhabitants receive an excellent supply : the surplus forms small streams, about two feet wide on each side of the street, and may be turned either north or south into the Severn or South Sea ; hence it appears that this town is situated on the highest ground between the North and South Seas. At the intersection of the two streets stands an ancient Gothic building, which was formerly a chapel, but is now used as a Town-hall ; and in one of them stood the Assize-hall, which of late years has been used occasionally as a market-house.

Chard was formerly a borough, and from the 28th of Edward the First, till the 2nd of Edward the Third, sent members to parliament, which privilege was lost in consequence of some public dispute. The town is now governed by a portreve, and two bailiffs, annually chosen from among the burgesses. An hospital for the benefit of old infirm parishioners, was endowed with two very considerable estates by a Mr. Hervey, the government of which is vested in the hands of the portreve, *ex officio.* The market is held here on Monday, and is said to be the largest in England for potatoes ; considerable quantities of corn and cattle are also brought here. The fairs are the first Wednesday in May, August, and September.

The church is a large handsome edifice, dedicated to St. Mary, being 120 feet in length, and 46 in breadth, consisting of a nave, chancel, north and south aisles, north and south transept, and a tower at the west end containing a clock and five bells. The great tythes are leased out under the Dean of Wells, being annexed to that dignity. The benefice is vicarial, and is in the patronage of the Bishop of the diocese ; Rev. Warre S. Bradley, incumbent ; instituted 1819. Population, 1801, 2784—1811, 2932—1821, 3096.

CHARLCOMBE—a parish in the liberty of Hampton and Claver-ton, and locally in the hundred of Bath-Forum, 1½ mile N. from Bath ; containing only 16 inhabited houses, and 17 families.

The church, though small, is a curious ancient fabrick, consisting of a nave and chancel, with a square embattled turret. The benefice is rectorial, in the deanery of Bath, and was conveyed to the corporation of Bath by the patron, the Rev. Walter Robins, to be annexed to the mastership of the free Grammar School for ever; Rev. T. Wilkins, incumbent; instituted 1811. Population, 1801, 75—1811, 100—1821, 124.

CHARLINCH—a parish in the hundred of Cannington, 4 miles E. from Bridgewater; containing 35 inhabited houses, and 41 families, 35 of whom are employed in agriculture. The church, which stands upon an eminence, consists of a nave, chancel, and south aisle or chapel, with a tower at the west end containing four bells. The living is a rectory, in the deanery of Bridgewater; Rev. J. Starkey, incumbent; instituted 1808. Population, 1801, 183—1811, 198—1821, 251.

CHARLTON-ADAM—a parish in the hundred of Somerton, 3 miles E. from Somerton, on the ancient Fosse road from Bath to Ilchester: it contains 62 inhabited houses, and 79 families, 67 of whom are employed in agriculture. The church is dedicated to St. Peter and St. Paul, and consists of a nave, chancel, and south aisle, with a tower containing five bells. The living is a vicarage, in the deanery of Ilchester; Rev. Thomas Strangways is both patron and incumbent. Population, 1801, 254—1811, 252—1821, 377.

CHARLTON-HORETHORNE—a parish in the hundred of Horethorne, 3 miles N. N. W. from Milborn Port; containing 103 inhabited houses, and 110 families, 80 of whom are employed in agriculture. This village is pleasantly situated in a rich vale, on the turnpike-road between Wincanton and Sherbourn. The lands are enclosed and well cultivated. The church is dedicated to St. Peter and St. Paul, and consists of a nave, chancel, and side aisles, with a tower at the west end contain-

ing four bells. The living is a vicarage, in the deanery of
Marston; Rev. John Peddle, incumbent; instituted 1784. Population, 1801, 512—1811, 526—1821, 489.

CHARLTON-MACKEREL—a parish in the hundred of Somerton,
2½ miles E. from Somerton, and 3½ miles N. from Ilchester;
containing 48 inhabited houses, and 62 families, 51 of whom
are employed in agriculture. The river Cary, which divides this
parish from Somerton on the west, and Kingsdown on the south,
runs under a stone bridge of two arches on the Roman Fosse
road, and gives name to a very ancient manor in this parish,
called Cary-Fitzpaine. The church, which is a handsome Gothic
structure, is dedicated to St. Mary, and is built in the form of a
cross, with a large embattled tower rising from its centre, containing four bells. The living is a rectory, in the deanery of
Ilchester; Rev. W. T. P. Brymer, incumbent; instituted 1821.
Population, 1801, 268—1811, 239—1821, 309.

CHARLTON-MUSGRAVE—a parish in the hundred of Norton-
Ferrers, 1½ mile N. N. E. from Wincanton; containing 57 inhabited houses, and 64 families, 55 of whom are employed in
agriculture. The church consists of a nave, chancel, and tower
at the west end, and is dedicated to St. Michael. The benefice
is rectorial, in the deanery of Cary; Rev. Paul Leir, incumbent;
instituted 1812. Population, 1801, 383—1811, 385—1821, 366.

CHARLTON-QUEEN—See QUEEN-CHARLTON.

CHEDDER—a parish in the hundred of Winsterstoke, 2 miles
E. S. E. from Axbridge; containing 314 inhabited houses, and
393 families, 239 whereof are employed in agriculture. The
bounds of this parish extend from the middle of the summit of
Mendip, a considerable way into the Moors, and the soil and
surface are as various as can well be imagined. The situation
is rendered exceedingly fine by the contrast between the lofty

brow of the Mendip on the one hand, and the extensive level of the Moors on the other; the slopes of the hills are every where diversified. Here the spectator is lost in astonishment at the immence caverns, enormous chasms, and bold protuberances which are mixed together in awful variety. The chasm, called Chedder-cliffs, is certainly the most remarkable object of its kind in England; Dr. Collinson describes it as running across the south-west ridge of the hill from top to bottom, extending in a north-east winding direction more than a mile in length, and then branching off by two passages, in the form of a Y, by an easy ascent to the top of the Mendip. At the entrance from the town, nine small springs, pure as crystal, burst from the foot of the cliffs, all within the space of about thirty feet, and joining together within forty yards of their source, form a broad rapid river, of the clearest and finest water in the world. The bed of this river is sand, mixed with shingles, and in many places is almost covered with broken fragments of stone, and small rocks rising above the surface of the water. On these are many curious aquatic plants, polypodies, aspleniums, and confervas, which being kept in continual motion by the stream, broken by many little falls from ledges of natural rocks, render the scene uncommonly beautiful. This river contains trout, eels, and roach, and in its course turns several paper and other mills. Proceeding in this winding passage, the cliffs rise on either hand in the most picturesque forms, some of them being near 800 feet high, and terminate in craggy pyramids. On the right hand several of them are perpendicular to the height of 400 feet, and resemble the shattered battlements of vast castles. On the left hand, or west side, are two also of this form, which lean over the valley with a threatening aspect; and the tops of many others, at the height of several hundred feet, project over the heads of the spectators with terrific grandeur; in general, the projections on the one side stand opposed to corresponding hollows on the other, which is a strong indication that this immense gap was formed by some dreadful convulsion of the earth. Stupendous however as these cliffs are, the top of Mendip is some hundred feet higher, sloping upwards with a gentle ascent, and affording a most extensive prospect over the southern and western parts of this county, a considerable part of Wilts and Dorset, the Bristol Channel, and a long range of the coast of Wales.

The town stands upon the slope of the Mendip, and consequently somewhat above the level of the Moors. It had formerly a considerable market, which has been discontinued more than a century; but the market-cross, which is of a hexagonal shape, is still standing, and in good preservation. A paper manufactory has been established here, and a number of the poor are employed in spinning and knitting hose. The cheese in this neighbourhood has been esteemed superior to that of any other part of the county, and indeed equal to any in England. Chedder has two fairs annually, viz. May 4, and October 29. The church is a large handsome building, dedicated to St. Andrew, and consists of a nave, chancel, north and south aisles, with a small chapel on the south side; at the west end is a noble Gothic tower ornamented with pinnacles, containing a clock and six bells. The living is a vicarage and a peculiar, belonging to the Dean and Chapter of Wells; Rev. John Cobley, incumbent; instituted 1804. Population, 1801, 1150—1811, 1276—1821, 1797.

CHEDDON-FITZ-PAINE—a parish in the hundred of Taunton and Taunton-Dean, 3 miles N. N. E. from Taunton; containing 44 inhabited houses, and 65 families, 44 of whom are employed in agriculture. This parish derived its appellation from the surname of one of its ancient possessors. The church consists of a nave, chancel, and south aisle, with a tower containing five bells. The living is rectorial, in the deanery of Taunton; Rev. Francis Warre, incumbent; instituted 1800. Population, 1801, 260—1811, 255—1821, 272.

CHEDZEY—a parish in the hundred of North Petherton, 3 miles E. from Bridgewater; containing 84 inhabited houses, and 97 families, 77 of whom are employed in agriculture. This parish contains 1406 acres. The lands are in general rich, and the soil a sandy loam. Roman coins have frequently been found here, and in 1701 several earthen urns, and a fibula, were discovered near the church. The church is a large Gothic structure, consisting of a nave, chancel, transept, and north and south aisles, with a large tower at the west end containing five bells. The living is a rectory, in the deanery of Bridgewater; Rev. T. Coney, L. L. D. is both patron and incumbent; instituted 1811. Population, 1801, 457—1811, 462—1821, 472.

CHELVEY—a parish in the hundred of Hartcliff with Bedminster, 8 miles from Bristol; containing only 9 inhabited houses, and as many families, 7 of whom are employed in agriculture. The lands in this parish are good, and mostly applied to pasture. The manor-house is a large old structure, formerly inhabited by the Tyntes family; some of the rooms are spacious and lofty, with elegant ceilings; a part of it is now occupied by a farmer. The church is dedicated to St. Bridget, and consists of a nave, chancel, and south aisle, with a tower containing one bell. The living is a rectory, in the deanery of Redcliff and Bedminster; Rev. William Shaw, D. D. incumbent; instituted 1795, Population, 1801, 43—1811, 62—1821, 62.

CHELWOOD—a parish in the southern part of the hundred of Keynsham, 8 miles S. S. E. from Bristol; containing 42 inhabited houses, and 45 families, 40 of whom are employed in agriculture. The church is a small neat building, dedicated to St. Leonard, and consists of a nave, chancel, and south aisle, with a tower at the west end, built in 1772. The living is a rectory, in the deanery of Redcliff and Bedminster, and in the patronage of the Bishop of the diocese; Rev. John Turner,

incumbent; instituted 1817. Population 1801, 192—1811,
205—1821, 222.

CHERITON-NORTH—a parish in the hundred of Horethorne, 2¼
miles S.W. from Wincanton; containing 43 inhabited houses,
and 55 families, 54 of whom are employed in agriculture. The
church is dedicated to St. John, and consists of a nave only,
with a tower at the west end containing four bells. The living
is rectorial, in the deanery of Marston; Rev. R. Gatehouse,
incumbent; instituted 1809. Population, 1801, 233—1811,
232—1821, 216.

CHEW—a hundred in the N.E part of the county, which
takes its name from Chew, its chief town, as that also is denominated from the river Chew on which it stands: it contains the following parishes, &c. viz. CHEW-MAGNA, CHEW-
STOKE, CLUTTON, DUNDRY, NORTON-HAWFIELD, NORTON-
MARLEWARD, STOWEY, and TIMSBURY; containing 1064 inhabited houses, 1161 families, 2866 males, and 2818 females.
Total Population, 5684.

CHEW-MAGNA—a parish in the hundred of Chew, 6½ miles
S. from Bristol; containing 368 inhabited houses, and 403
families, 177 of whom are employed in agriculture, 140 in trade,
manufacture or handicraft, and 86 not included in either class.
This town stands on the river from which it derives its name,
over which is a stone bridge of two arches; and it is denominated Chew-Magna, on account of its being larger than other
places of a similar name. This place was formerly a borough,
and a considerable market-town, which privileges have been lost
long since; its only manufactures at present are a few edge-tools
and stockings. A short distance from the town are the vestiges
of a Roman encampment, called from its shape Bow-ditch,
being of a circular form, with triple ramparts. The church

consists of a nave and side aisles, 106 feet in length and 60 in breadth, with a tower at the west end 103 feet high, containing a clock and six bells. The living is a vicarage, and one presentation with Dundry; Rev. John Hall, incumbent; instituted 1787. Population, 1801, 1345—1811, 1527—1821, 1884.

CHEW-STOKE—a parish adjoining the above, and in the same hundred, 7 miles and a half from Bristol, on the turnpike-road from that city to Wells; it contains 108 inhabited houses, and 126 families, of whom 72 are employed in agriculture. The church is dedicated to St. Andrew, and was built by the family of St. Loe, whose arms are cut in stone on the south wall of the church. The benefice is a rectory, in the deanery of Redcliff and Bedminster; Rev. W. P. Wait, incumbent; instituted 1819. Population, 1801, 517—1811, 524—1821, 681.

CHEWTON—the name of a hundred, divided into three parts; the first is situated S.S.E. from the hundred of Chew, and contains the parishes of CAMELEY, CHEWTON-MENDIP, CHILCOMPTON, COMPTON-MARTIN, EMBORROW, FARRINGTON-GOURNEY, HINTON-BLEWETT, LITTLETON-HIGH, MIDSOMER-NORTON, PAULTON, STONEASTON, UBLEY, WEST-HARPTREE, and the tything of WIDCOMBE; the second, containing only one parish, viz. BROCKLEY, is surrounded by the hundreds of Wrington, Hartcliff with Bedminster, and Winterstoke; and the last contains the parish of KINGSTONE-SEYMOUR, which is bounded by the Bristol Channel; the whole hundred containing 2966 inhabited houses, 3309 families, 8188 males, and 7878 females. Total population, 16,066.

CHEWTON-MENDIP—a parish additionally styled Mendip, from its situation being under that mountain, and to distinguish it from Chewton-Keynsham. It is situated in the hundred of Chewton, 6 miles N. N. E. from Wells, and lies on the turnpike-road from that city to Bristol; it contains 225 inhabited houses, and 260 families, 231 of whom are employed in agriculture This parish is very extensive, and in that part which lies on the Mendip-hills there are many pits where lead ore and lapis-calaminaris have been dug in large quantities. About 5 miles northward, in a detached part of the parish, is the hamlet of North-Widcombe, containing 31 inhabited houses, and 36 families. Chewton-Mendip has a fair for horses, cattle, and sheep, on All Saints day. The church, which stands upon an eminence on the west side of the village, consists of a nave, chancel, and south aisle, with a noble Gothic tower 126 feet high, surmounted with beautiful Gothic pinnacles at the angles. The living is a vicarage, in the deanery of Frome; Rev. H. H. Mogg, incumbent; instituted 1814. Population, 1801, 1015—1811, 1225 —1821, 1327.

CHILCOMPTON—a parish in the hundred of Chewton-Mendip, on the turnpike-road between Bath and Wells, being 11 miles S.W. from the former, and 9 miles N.E. from the latter: it contains 87 inhabited houses, and 112 families, 29 of whom are employed in agriculture, 78 in trade, manufacture, or handicraft, and 5 not comprised in either class. A considerable proportion of the population is employed in the coal-works, which abound in this neighbourhood. The church is an ancient structure, consisting of a nave, chancel, south aisle and porch, with a large embattled tower at the west end 60 feet high, containing six bells. The living is a perpetual curacy, in the deanery of Frome, and a peculiar belonging to the Dean of Wells; Rev. A. Amesley, incumbent; instituted 1802. Population, 1801, 348—1811, 402—1821, 474.

CHILLINGTON—a parish in a detached part of the hundred of South-Petherton, 4 miles W. N. W. from Crewkerne; containing 54 inhabited houses, and 62 families, 60 of whom are employed

in agriculture. The church is a small structure, dedicated to
St. James, consisting of a nave, with a turret at the west
end. The living is a curacy, in the deanery of Crewkerne,
united with Seavington. Population, 1801, 216—1811, 251—
1821, 270.

CHILTHORNE-DOMERE—a parish in the hundred of Stone and
Yeovil, 2 miles S. S. E. from Ilchester, and 3 from Yeovil; containing 26 inhabited houses, and 43 families, 40 of whom are
employed in agriculture. This place obtained its adjunct appellation from the family of Domer, who were lords of the manor
in the 9th of Edward the Third. The church consists of a
nave, with a turret at the west end. The living is a vicarage,
in the deanery of Ilchester; the Rev. John Bayley is both patron
and incumbent. Population, 1801, 167—1811, 213—1821, 234.

CHILTON-CANTILO — a parish in the hundred of Hounds-
borough-Berwick and Coker, 6 miles N. from Yeovil; containing 25 inhabited houses, and 33 families, 26 of whom are
employed in agriculture. This parish is detached from its proper
hundred, and locally situated in a nook between the hundreds of
Somerton and Horethorne; the lands are in general good and
well cultivated. A small stream rising at Sandford-Occas, runs
under a stone bridge of one arch through this parish. The
church, which is dedicated to St. James, is built in the form of
a cross, with a tower at the west end. The living is a rectory,
in the deanery of Marston; Rev. J. Tomkins, incumbent; instituted 1788. Population, 1801, 129—1811, 138—1821, 140.

CHILTON-TRINITY—a parish in the hundred of North Petherton, 1½ mile from Bridgewater; containing only 9 inhabited
houses, and as many families, the whole of whom are employed
in agriculture. This parish was anciently a hundred of itself,
and was called *Chilton-Trinitatis*, on account of the dedication of its church, which consists of a nave, with a tower

at the west end, and is dedicated to the Holy Trinity. The living is a rectory, consolidated with Bridgewater, in the gift of the Crown; Rev. W. Wollen, D.D. incumbent; instituted 1786. Population, 1801, 50—1811, 46—1821, 49.

CHINNOCK-EAST—a parish in the hundred of Houndsborough Berwick and Coker, 4 miles S. W. from Yeovil, and on the turnpike-road between that town and Crewkerne : it contains 97 inhabited houses, and 120 families, 72 of whom are employed in agriculture. In a meadow about a mile to the west of the church is a salt spring, which never fails in dry, nor overflows in wet seasons ; the proportion of salt it contains is about one-fortieth part. The church is small, and the benefice is vicarial, in the patronage of the King ; Rev. Henry Gould, incumbent; instituted 1780. Population, 1801, 505—1811, 519—1821, 581.

CHINNOCK-MIDDLE—a parish adjoining the above on the north side, in the same hundred, 7 miles S. W. from Yeovil, and 4 from Crewkerne : it contains 29 inhabited houses, and 38 families, 20 of whom are employed in agriculture. The church is an ancient structure, of Saxon architecture, and the living is a rectory, in the deanery of Ilchester ; Rev. Charles Digby, incumbent; instituted 1807. Population, 1801, 129—1811, 124—1821, 173.

CHINNOCK-WEST—a parish within half a mile of the above, and in the same hundred ; containing 86 inhabited houses, and 104 families, 48 of whom are employed in agriculture. It is a chapelry to the adjoining parish of Chisleborough. Population, 1801, 327—1811, 388—1821, 477.

CHIPSTAPLE—a parish in the hundred of Willerton and Freemanners, 2½ miles W. from Wiveliscombe, being in the southern part of the hundred and county, in a romantic spot, varied with hills and dales ; it contains 70 inhabited houses, and as many families, 58 of whom are employed in agriculture. The church is dedicated to All Saints, and consists of a nave, chancel, and south aisle, with an embattled tower at the west end containing four bells. The living is rectorial, in the deanery of Dunster; the Rev. J. S. Richards is both patron and incumbent; instituted 1809. Population, 1801, 301—1811, 288—1821, 337.

CHISLEBOROUGH—a parish in the hundred of Houndsborough Berwick and Coker, 6 miles W. S. W. from Yeovil; containing 84 inhabited houses, and 100 families, 73 of whom are employed in agriculture. This village is nearly surrounded by lofty and well-cultivated hills, commanding extensive prospects over the Bristol Channel and the Welch coast. Here is a large fair on the 29th October, for horses, cattle, and toys. The church, which is dedicated to St. Peter and St. Paul, consists of a nave and chancel, with a tower in the centre containing four bells. The living is a rectory, in the deanery of Ilchester; Rev. Charles Digby, incumbent; instituted 1807. Population, 1801, 298—1811, 355 —1821, 434.

CHRISTON—a small parish in the hundred of Winterstoke, 5½ miles N. W. from Axbridge, at the east end of Bleadon-hill; containing 13 inhabited houses, and as many families, the whole of whom are employed in agriculture. The church is a small structure, consisting of a nave and chancel, with a tower in the centre containing three bells. The living is a rectory, in the deanery of Axbridge; Rev. William Truman, incumbent; instituted 1806. Population, 1801, no return—1811, 57—1821, 55.

CHURCHILL—a parish in the hundred of Winterstoke, 5 miles N. from Axbridge; containing 153 inhabited houses, and 179 inhabitants, 161 of whom are employed in agriculture. This village lies in a pleasant valley; the turnpike-road from Bristol to Bridgewater divides it from the Mendip, which rises with a steep ascent. On the summit, between this parish and Rowbarrow, is an ancient encampment, called Doleberry-castle, containing within its area upwards of thirty acres, and fortified with a double vallum; its form is a parallelogram, open at each end. It has been generally supposed to have been the work of the Britons, but Roman and Saxon coins have frequently been found in it, likewise numerous warlike weapons. The church is dedicated to St. John, and consists of a nave, chancel, and two side aisles, with an embattled tower at the west end containing five bells. The living is a perpetual curacy, in the deanery of Axbridge, and a peculiar belonging to the Dean and Chapter of Bristol; Rev. John Manby, incumbent; instituted 1804. Population, 1801, 599—1811, 740—1821, 842.

CLAPTON in GORDANO—a parish in the hundred of Portbury, 9 miles W. from Bedminster; containing 25 inhabited houses, and 30 families, 18 of whom are employed in agriculture. It received its adjunctive name from Emerick de Gardino, or Gordein, one of its ancient possessors, who likewise held Easton, Weston, and Walton, each of which received the same appellation. The lands in this parish are mostly pasture, and on the slope of the hill southward, is a fine wood of oak and hazel. Coal has been worked here for upwards of a century. The church is dedicated to St. Michael, and consists of a nave, chancel, and north aisle, with a tower and three bells. The living is a rectory, in the deanery of Redcliff and Bedminster; Rev. W. H. Colston, D.D. incumbent; instituted 1811. Population, 1801, 123—1811, 131—1821, 157.

CLATWORTHY — a parish in the hundred of Williton and Freemanners, 3 miles from Wiveliscombe; containing 36 inhabited houses, and 49 families, 39 of whom are employed in agriculture. The river Tone rises in this parish, on a hill called Beverton, and runs under a stone bridge between Huish Campflower and Wiveliscombe. The lands are in general meadow and pasture; the manure is carried on horseback, the roads not admitting of carriages. The church consists of a nave and tower, and is dedicated to St. Mary. The living is a rectory, in the deanery of Dunster; Rev. William Bernard, incumbent; instituted 1810. Population, 1801, 197—1811, 238—1821, 280.

CLAVERTON—a parish in the liberty of Hampton and Claverton, and locally in the hundred of Bath-Forum, 2½ miles E. from Bath; containing 26 inhabited houses, and 33 families, 21 of whom are employed in agriculture. This parish is bounded on the east by the river Avon, and on the west by Claverton-down, which rises to a great height above the level of the river. The top is a fine smooth plain, commanding most delightful prospects on every side. On the N.W. brow, fronting the city, is an extensive plantation of firs, and immediately under them is the shell of a castle erected by the late Mr. Allen, which forms a pleasing object, not only from Bath, but from the other side of the Severn. The church is a small Gothic structure, consisting of a nave, chancel, and north aisle, with a tower at the west end. The living is a rectory, in the deanery of Bath; Rev. Henry Marriott, incumbent; instituted 1808. Population, 1801, 123—1811, 123—1821, 137.

CLEVEDON—a parish in the hundred of Portbury situated 8 miles N.W. from Wrington at the south-west point of a chain of rocky mountain that bounds the greater part of this hundred. It contains 103 inhabited houses, and 107 families, 89 of whom are employed in agriculture. The church stands to the west of the village, near the edge of the Cliff, and is built in the form of a cross, with a tower in the centre. The living is vicarial, in the deanery of Redcliff and Bedminster; Rev. E. C. Grenville, incumbent; instituted 1789; patron the Bishop of Bath and Wells. Population, 1801, 334—1811, 455—1821, 581.

CLOFORD—a parish in the hundred of Frome, and part of Hillhouse liberty, situate 4½ miles S.W. from Frome, on a brook that rises in the parish of Wanstraw: it contains two hamlets, Leighton and Holwell; the latter is romantically situated in a deep and narrow valley, to the south-west of the parish of Nunney; it is called in old writings Holy-waters, from a well there, over which was a chapel formerly visited by pilgrims. On the east-side of Cloford-common is a very extensive wood, called Postle-bury, the remaining vestige of a considerable Roman villa. The church is dedicated to St. Mary, and consists of a nave, chancel, and side aisle or chapel. The living is a vicarage, in the deanery of Frome; Rev. Thomas Williams, incumbent; instituted 1801. Population, 1801, 257—1811, 308—1821, 312.

CLOSWORTH—a parish in the hundred of Houndsborough Berwick and Coker, 4½ miles S. from Yeovil, and bounded on the south and east by the county of Devon: it contains 40 inhabited houses, and 43 families: only 6 families are returned as being employed in agriculture, and 3 in trade, &c. but this must have been an erroneous return, as 34 families are mentioned as not comprised in either class. The river Ivel passes this parish on the east, and runs under Boarden bridge, along the borders of the county to Yeovil. The church is dedicated to All Saints, and consists of a nave, chancel, and tower containing five bells. The living is a rectory, in the deanery of Marston; Rev. Nath. Bartlett, incumbent; instituted 1790. Population, 1801, 195 —1811, 188—1821, 187.

CLUTTON—a parish in the hundred of Chew, 9 miles S. S. E. from Bristol; containing 253 inhabited houses, and 260 families, 25 of whom are employed in agriculture, 222 in trade, manufacture, or handicraft, and 13 not comprised in either class. The principal part of the population is employed in working of coal, with which the neighbourhood abounds: in one stratum wrought here some years since, the coal was so strongly impregnated with sulphur, that all its joints appeared to be covered with leaf-gold. The church is situated about half a mile east from the turnpike-road, and consists of a nave, chancel, and porch, with a tower at the west end, which was rebuilt in 1728. The living is a rectory, in the deanery of Redcliff and Bedminster; Rev. T. B. Johnson, incumbent; instituted 1815. Population, 1801, 935—1811, 998—1821, 1206.

COKER-EAST—a parish in the hundred of Houndsborough Berwick and Coker; containing, with the hamlet of North Coker, 210 inhabited houses, and 220 families, 63 of whom are employed in agriculture, 135 in trade, manufacture, or handicraft, and 22 not comprised in either class. Several vestiges of Roman antiquity have been discovered here at different periods. In the year 1753, in a field belonging to a Mr. Forbes, the foundation of a Roman dwelling-house was found, consisting of several apartments, one of which was floored with beautiful tessellated pavement, representing a variety of figures. In the hamlet of North-Coker was formerly a chapel, which was taken down about half a century since, and a workhouse erected upon its site. A short distance to the south of the church is *Coker-House*, the residence of William Helyer, Esq. The church is a handsome edifice, dedicated to St. Michael, and is built in the form of a cross, with a tower in the centre containing a clock and eight musical bells. The living is a vicarage, in the deanery of Marston, and in the gift of the Dean and Chapter of Exeter; Rev. James Carrington, incumbent; instituted 1791. Population, 1801, 859—1811, 1007—1821, 1103.

COKER-WEST—a parish in the hundred of Houndsborough Berwick and Coker, about 2 miles W. N. W. from the above, on the turnpike-road leading from Yeovil to Crewkerne, and 3 miles S. W. from the former. Several small streams run through this and the adjoining parish, which turn a number of mills in their way to the river Ivel. The church is dedicated to St. Martin, and consists of a nave, chancel, and a south aisle, which is now used as a vestry-room, with a tower containing six bells. The living is a rectory, in the deanery of Marston; Rev. George Jekyell, incumbent; instituted 1802. Population, 1801, 758—1811, 782 —1821, 928.

COMBE-FLOREY—a parish in the hundred of Taunton and Taunton-Dean, 7 miles N. W. from Taunton; containing 58 inhabited houses, and 65 families. The church is dedicated to St. Peter and St. Paul, and consists of a nave, chancel, and north aisle, with a tower containing five bells. The living is a rectory, in the deanery of Taunton; Rev. James Bernard, incumbent; instituted 1821. Population, 1801, 249—1811, 289—1821, 306.

COMBE-HAY—a parish in the hundred of Wellow, 2½ miles S. S. W. from Bath; containing 41 inhabited houses, and as many families, 34 of whom are employed in agriculture. The ancient Roman Fosse road passes on the west side of the village, and forms part of the parish boundary. For nearly two miles it is seen in its original perfect form, with a deep fosse, or ditch, on either side. The lands in this parish are highly cultivated, and the scenery is beautifully varied with hill and dale. Two springs, rising on the hills, form a rivulet which runs through the village, and pursues its course by Midford to the Avon. The church is a small handsome edifice, consisting of a nave, rebuilt about half a century since. It has a tower at the west end, containing a clock and three bells. The living is a rectory, in the deanery of Frome; Rev. Fredrick Gardiner, incumbent; instituted 1806. Population, 1801, 232—1811, 278—1821, 237.

COMBE-INGLISH, or INGLISH-COMBE—a parish in the hundred of Wellow, adjoining to the above on the north-west, 2½ miles S. W. from Bath; it contains 52 inhabited houses, and 66 families, 42 of whom are employed in agriculture. About 1½ mile south-west is a considerable hamlet, called Inglishbatch. On the opposite side of the turnpike-road from Bristol to Frome, on a high ridge of hills, is one of the most remarkable barrows in this country, called Barrow-hill. This tumulus is, at its base, 800 yards in circumference; its apex is 36 yards in diameter, from east to west, and 28 yards from north to south, and the perpendicular height upwards of 100 feet. A copper coin, of Antoninus Pius, was found in 1786, in the road near the foot of the hill. The church is an ancient structure, and consists of a nave, chancel, and small chapel on the south side; in the centre is an embattled tower containing five bells. The living is a vicarage, in the deanery of Bath; Rev. D. Hughes is both patron and incumbent; instituted 1808. Population, 1801, 226—1811, 249—1821, 311.

COMBE-ST. NICHOLAS—an extensive parish in the hundred of Kingsbury-East, 2½ miles N.N.E. from Chard; containing 197 inhabited houses, and 211 families, 92 of whom are employed in agriculture, 70 in trade, manufacture, or handicraft, and 49 not included in either class. The church is a large handsome building, 114 feet in length and 50 in breadth, consisting of a nave, chancel, and side aisles, with a square embattled tower at the west end. The living is a vicarage and a peculiar, in the deanery of Crewkerne; Rev. J. L. Warren, incumbent; patron, the Dean of Wells. Population, 1801, no return—1811, 941—1821, 1048.

COMBE-MONKTON—See MONKTON-COMBE.

COMPTON-BISHOPS—a parish in the hundred of Winterstoke, 2 miles N.W. from Axbridge, situated under the southern ridge of Mendip, by which the village is almost surrounded; it contains 76 inhabited houses, and 97 families, 56 of whom are employed in agriculture. This parish extends eastwardly to the town of Axbridge, part of the west street being within its limits; and on the south it is bounded by the river Ax. Previous to its sequestration in the reign of Edward the Fourth it was in possession of the Bishop of this see, from whom it received its distinctive name. The church, which is dedicated to St. Andrew, consists of a nave, with an embattled tower at the east end. The living is a vicarage and a peculiar, in the deanery of Axbridge, belonging to the prebendary; Rev. Edward Foster, incumbent; instituted 1783.

COMPTON-DANDO—so denominated from one of its ancient possessors, is situated in the hundred of Keynsham, 7 miles W. from Bath, and an equal distance from Bristol; containing 67 inhabited houses, and 76 families, 52 of whom are employed in agriculture. The lands are mostly applied to pasture, and the slopes of the hill are covered with woods and coppices. The river Chew forms the boundary of this parish on the north-west, in its way to Keynsham. The church is dedicated to St. Mary, and consists of a nave, chancel, and north aisle, with a tower at the west end containing five bells. The living is a vicarage, in the deanery of Redcliffe and Bedminster, and in the gift of the Bishop of the diocese; Rev. R. Boodle, incumbent; instituted 1818. Population, 1801, 330—1811, 346—1821, 344.

COMPTON-DUNDON—a parish in the hundred of Whitley, 3 miles N. from Somerton; containing 37 inhabited houses, and 101 families, 79 of whom are employed in agriculture. In the 17th of Edward the Second, Cecilia, the widow of Sir John Beauchamp, of Hatch, obtained the grant of a weekly market to be held here on the Thursday, and a fair yearly on the eve, day, and morrow after the feast of St. Mary Magdalen, but this charter has long since been lost. The church is dedicated to St. Andrew, and consists of a nave, with a tower at the west end containing three bells. The living is a vicarage and a peculiar, in the deanery of Ilchester, belonging to the prebendary thereof; Rev. William Mitchell, incumbent; instituted 1821. Population, 1801, 446—1811, 476—1821, 493.

COMPTON-MARTIN—a parish in the hundred of Chewton, 8½

miles N. from Wells ; containing 88 inhabited houses, and 103 families, 82 of whom are employed in agriculture. Moreton, a tything in this parish, about 3 miles N. N. E. was formerly a place of very considerable note, and gave name to a very ancient family. The church of Compton Martin is a handsome edifice, consisting of a nave, and two side aisles, with a good tower at the west end containing six bells. The living is a rectory, in the deanery of Redcliff and Bedminster ; Rev. J. Royle, incumbent ; instituted 1816. Population, 1801, 404—1811, 498—1821, 534.

Compton-Pauncefoot—a parish in the hundred of Catash, 5 miles W. S. W. from Wincanton ; containing 41 inhabited houses, and 45 families, 38 of whom are employed in agriculture. This place is pleasantly situated in the centre of a number of small villages, on the edge of a fruitful vale, under a range of hills to the south and south-east. A small stream that rises near Maperton, runs through this village, and after dividing the parishes of North and South Cadbury, pursues its course by Sparkford, and Queen and West-Camel to Yeovilton, where it falls into the river Yeo, or Ivel. About three-quarters of a mile south-east from the church is Compton-Lodge, the residence of J. H. Hunt, Esq. The church, which is dedicated to St. Mary, is a small Gothic structure, and consists of a nave, chancel, and south aisle, with a tower at the west end surmounted with a stone spire. The living is a rectory, in the deanery of Cary ; Rev. John Harlin, incumbent ; instituted 1820. Population, 1801, 207—1811, 211—1821, 228.

Congresbury—a parish in the hundred of Winterstoke, 2½ miles W. from Wrington ; containing 211 inhabited houses, and 221 families. It is said to have derived its name from St. Congar, son of one of the eastern emperors, who retired here from the persecution of his father's court, A. D. 711, where he built himself an habitation, and an oratory, which he dedicated to the

Holy Trinity; and Ina, King of the West Saxons, bestowed upon him the little territory lying round his cell, wherein he instituted twelve canons, after which he made a pilgrimage to Jerusalem, where he died, but his body was brought back and buried here. Congresbury was formerly a market-town, and had a fair on the 14th September, which is still held. The river Yeo passes through the village to the north of the principal street, and falls into the Bristol Channel below Wick-St. Lawrence. The manor of Congresbury, with the advowson of the church, was given by John Carr, Esq. alderman of Bristol, to the mayor and corporation of that city in 1583, to the use of the Orphans' Hospital which he had founded there. The church is dedicated to St. Andrew, and consists of a nave, chancel, and side aisles, with an embattled tower at the west end, surmounted with a neat spire, and contains a clock and five bells. The living is a vicarage, in the deanery of Axbridge, and in the presentation of the mayor and corporation of Bristol'; Rev. H. Bevan, incumbent; instituted 1818. Population, 1801, 827—1811, 913 —1821, 1202.

COPELAND—a hamlet and chapelry in the parish of Beer-crocomb, and hundred of Abdick and Bulston, 10 miles S. W. from Langport. Population returned with Beer-crocomb.

CORFE—a parish in the hundred of Taunton and Taunton-Dean, 3 miles S. from Taunton; containing 50 inhabited houses, and 59 families, 47 of whom are employed in agriculture. The lands are equally applied to arable and pasture. The church consists of a nave, chancel, and a small aisle on the south side, with a tower at the west end containing four bells. It was formerly a chapel to St. Mary Magdalen, Taunton; Rev. M. Dickson, incumbent; Population, 1801, no return—1811, no return—1821, 232.

CORSTON—a parish in the hundred of Wellow, 4 miles W.

from Bath; containing 78 inhabited houses, and 84 families, 54 of whom are employed in agriculture. The lands are mostly arable, and produce excellent crops of wheat and barley. The church is dedicated to All Saints, and consists of a nave, with a small tower on which is a low conical spire. The living is a vicarage, in the deanery of Redcliff and Bedminster, and in the patronage of the Bishop of the diocese; Rev. John Turner, incumbent; instituted 1821. Population, 1801, 268—1811, 278—1821, 368.

CORTON-DENHAM—a parish in the hundred of Horethorn, 3½ miles N. W. from Milborn Port, situated under a ridge of high hills, which extend several miles from north to south, and from which there is an extensive prospect over the middle part of the county and the Bristol Channel: it contains 77 inhabited houses, and 85 families, 52 of whom are employed in agriculture. In 1772 an urn, containing about two quarts of Roman coins, was found by some labouring men who were digging in a common field, for the purpose of making an inclosure. They consisted principally of Valerian, Gallienus, Aurelian, Tacitus, Florianus, and Probus, in good preservation. The church is dedicated to St. Andrew, and stands on an eminence; it consists of a nave, chancel, and north aisle, with an embattled tower at the north side containing five bells. The living is a rectory, in the deanery of Marston; Rev. J. H. Wyndham, D. D. incumbent; instituted 1813. Population, 1801, 377—1811, 422—1821, 469.

COSSINGTON—a parish in the hundred of Whitley, 4 miles N. E. from Bridgewater; containing 46 inhabited houses, and 65 families, 42 of whom are employed in agriculture. The church consists of a nave only, with a tower at the west end containing five bells. The living is rectorial, in the deanery of Pawlet; Rev. T. Hobbs, incumbent; instituted 1801; patron, the Bishop of Bath and Wells. Population, 1801, 237—1811, 254—1821, 268.

COTHELSTON—a parish in the hundred of Taunton and Taunton-Dean, 7 miles N. N. W. from Taunton ; containing 21 inhabited houses, and 22 families, 18 of whom are employed in agriculture. *Cothelston-House,* which till lately has been designated Terhill-House, is now the residence of Edward Jeffries Esdaile, Esq. The prospect from this spot is very extensive, commanding a view over fourteen counties. The church consists of a nave, chancel, and south aisle, with a tower at the west end containing six bells. The living is a curacy, in the deanery of Taunton ; Rev. J. Townsend, incumbent ; instituted 1821. Population, 1801, 103—1811, 118—1821, 108.

CRANMORE-EAST—a small parish in the liberty of Cranmore, and locally in the hundred of Frome, 5 miles E. from Shepton-Mallet, and 6 miles S. W. from Frome ; containing 10 inhabited houses, and 11 families, the whole of whom are employed in agriculture. It is a chapelry to Doulting, but the inhabitants generally have their burials at West Cranmore. The chapel is a small structure, dedicated to St. James. Population, 1801, 53 —1811, 47—1821, 68.

CRANMORE-WEST—a parish in the same liberty, but within the confines of Wells-Forum hundred, 3½ miles E. from Shepton-Mallet, and 7½ miles S. W. from Frome ; containing 59 inhabited houses, and as many families, 46 of whom are employed in agriculture. It lies in a vale, and is watered by several streams from springs rising in the parish. On an eminence south of the church is *South-hill House,* a handsome seat, the residence of Colonel Strode. The church consists of a nave, chancel, and north aisle, with a tower at the west end. The living is a curacy, in the deanery of Cary, and is likewise a chapelry to Doulting. Population, 1801, 229—1811, 268—1821, 270.

CREECH-ST. MICHAEL—an extensive parish in the hundred of Andersfield, 3 miles E. from Taunton ; containing 166 inhabited houses, and as many families, 140 of whom are employed in agriculture. The church, which stands upon an eminence, is dedicated to St. Michael, and gives the additional name to the parish; it consists of a nave, chancel, and side aisles, with a square tower on the north side, containing five bells. The living is a vicarage, in the deanery of Taunton; Rev. Henry Creswell, incumbent; instituted 1813. Population, 1801, 628—1811, 714—1821, 812.

CREWKERNE—the name of a hundred in the southern part of the county, bordering on Dorsetshire; it derived its name from Crewkerne, its chief town, and comprises the following parishes; viz. CREWKERNE, HINTON-ST. GEORGE, MERRIOT, MISTERTON, SEABOROUGH, and WAYFORD, and contains 1033 inhabited houses, 1115 families, 2878 males, and 3183 females. Total population, 6061.

CREWKERNE—a market town and parish, in the hundred to which it gives name, 8 miles from Ilminster, 9 from Yeovil, and 132 from London; containing 536 inhabited houses, and 580 families, 284 of whom are employed in agriculture, and 296 in trade, manufacture, or handicraft. It is pleasantly situated in a valley, watered by the rivers Ax and Parret, and sheltered by cultivated hills, which command extensive prospects over the adjoining country. Its name signifies in Saxon, the Cottage of the Cross. Leland mentions a cross having stood there in his time, environed with slender pillars. The manufactures of Crewkerne consist of sail-cloth, dowlas, and stockings. Here is a market on Saturdays, plentifully supplied with provisions of every description; likewise an annual fair on the 4th of September, for linen, cheese, and pedlery. In the town are two charity-schools, one of which received a considerable endowment from Dr. Hody; and here are likewise two alms-houses.

The church is a Gothic structure, built in the form of a cross, with a lofty embattled tower rising from its centre, supported by

four massive pillars ; on each side of the communion table is a
door leading to a small room, formerly used for auricular confession ; over that by which the devotees entered, are carved
the figures of two swine, to represent their impure state previous to confession, and over the other by which they came out,
are two angels, to signify their purity after absolution. The
living is a perpetual curacy, united with Misterton ; Rev. R. H.
Ashe, D. D. incumbent ; instituted 1775. Population, 1801,
2576—1811, 3021—1821, 3434.

CRICKET-MALHERBE—a parish in the hundred of Abdick and
Bulstone, 2½ miles S. from Ilminster, containing 9 inhabited
houses, and 16 families, 12 of whom are employed in agriculture.
The church is dedicated to St. Mary, and consists of a nave with
a small turret, in which are two bells. The living is a rectory,
in the deanery of Crewkerne ; Rev. John Colmer, incumbent ;
instituted 1801.   Population, 1801, 64—1811, 60—1821, 73.

CRICKET ST. THOMAS—a small parish in the hundred of South
Petherton, 4 miles E. from Chard ; containing 15 inhabited
houses, and 16 families, 13 of whom are employed in agriculture.
The church consists of a nave, chancel, and south aisle, with a
turret, containing two bells. The living is a rectory ; Rev.
J. Templeman, incumbent ; instituted 1821. Population, 1801,
69—1811, 74—1821, 75.

CROSCOMBE—a parish in the hundred of Whitestone, 2 miles
W.S.W. from Shepton Mallet ; containing 168 inhabited houses,
and 174 families, 64 of whom are employed in agriculture, 71
in trade, manufacture, or handicraft, and 39 not included in
either class. The village is pleasantly situated in a valley, watered
by a rivulet, which runs on to the river Brew.   Edward the First
granted it a charter for a weekly market, which was confirmed by
Edward the Third and Henry the Fourth ; but having lost this
privilege, another charter was procured by Hugh Fortescue, Esq.

for its renewal, which has also been suspended some years; it still retains a fair, held annually on Lady-day. The church is dedicated to St. Mary, and consists of a nave, chancel, and side aisles, with an embattled tower, containing a clock and five bells, supported by a handsome spire. The living is a rectory, in the deanery of Cary; Rev. Francis Blackburn is both patron and incumbent; instituted 1814. Population, 1801, 705—1811, 668—1821, 742.

CROWCOMBE—a parish in the hundred of Williton and Free-manners, 3 miles E. from Stogumber; containing 119 houses, and as many families, 63 of whom are employed in agriculture, 48 in trade, manufacture, or handicraft, and 8 not comprised in either class. The village is situated to the S.W. of the Quantock Hills, and was formerly a place of considerable note, having been an incorporated borough; and in the reign of Henry III. had a weekly market; it is still governed by a portreeve, annually chosen at a court-leet held at Michaelmas; but the market has been discontinued long since. The parish contains about 3500 acres of land, watered by springs rising on the hills in the upper part of the parish, which unite and form a rivulet, that runs into the sea; one of these springs has been observed to ebb and flow at equal periods with the sea, although several hundred feet above its level. *Crowcombe-Court,* the residence of George Henry Carew, Esq. is situated near the church, surrounded by beautiful and well-arranged plantations. Here is a charity-school, endowed by Thomas Carew, Esq. who gave an estate at Cove, in Devonshire, for the clothing and educating 15 poor chiidren. The church consists of a nave, chancel, and side aisles, with an embattled quadrangular tower at the west end, containing a clock and five bells; it was formerly surmounted by an octagonal spire, which was destroyed by lightning December 21, A.D. 1725. The living is a rectory; Rev. W. H. Harvey, incumbent; instituted 1821. Population, 1801, 575—1811, 611—1821, 742.

CUCKLINGTON—a parish in the hundred of Norton-Ferrars, 3 miles E. from Wincanton; bounded on the west by Stoke-Trister, and on the east by Dorsetshire; it contains 53 inhabited houses, and 64 families, 54 of whom are employed in agriculture. In the reign of Edward the First a market on Tuesdays, and a fair which continued 10 days, was held here by charter, neither of which remain at present. About a mile south of the church is *Shanks-House*, the residence of Nathaniel Dalton, Esq. The church is a Gothic structure, dedicated to St. Lawrence; consisting of a nave, chancel, and two side aisles, with an embattled tower on the south side, terminated with a pinnacle. The living is rectorial, in the deanery of Cary, united with Stoke-Trister; Rev. William Phelips, incumbent. Population, 1801, 358—1811, 297—1821, 320.

CUDWORTH—a parish in the hundred of South-Petherton, 4 miles nearly N. E. from Chard; containing 31 inhabited houses, and 30 families, 29 of whom are employed in agriculture. The church is dedicated to St. Michael, and consists of a nave, chancel, north aisle, and porch, with a turret containing two bells. The living is a curacy, in the deanery of Crewkerne, and a peculiar belonging to the prebendary of Cudworth and Knowle; Rev. J. Cabel, incumbent; instituted 1808. Population, 1801, 163—1811, 140—1821, 144.

CULBONE, anciently KITNOR—a very small parish, in the hundred of Carhampton, 3 miles W. N. W. from Porlock; containing only 10 inhabited houses, and 11 families, 6 of whom are employed in agriculture. This parish is environed on every side by mountains, which rise so high as to render the sun invisible nearly three months in the year, and for the same reason it is not possible to approach it on horseback without considerable danger. The church is a neat Gothic building, consisting of a nave, chancel, and aisle, of a size proportioned to the limited population of the place. It is situated in a narrow cove, at an elevation of 400 feet from the sea, surrounded with hills, ascending almost perpendicular to the height of 1200 feet, and covered with trees, consisting of oaks, beech, ash, poplars, pines and firs, mingled together by the hand of nature in the most picturesque manner; a beautiful rivulet rushes through a narrow channel in the interior of this cove, and passing the church, forms a succession of cascades as it flows down the rocks into the sea. The living is a rectory, in the deanery of Dunster; Rev. J. Boyce, incumbent; instituted 1821. Population, 1801, 56—1811, 44—1821, 45.

CURLAND—a parish in the hundred of Abdick and Bulstone, 7 miles S. S. E. from Taunton; containing 31 inhabited houses, and 39 families, 23 of whom are employed in agriculture. The church is small, and was formerly a chapelry to Curry-Mallet; it is now a rectory, in the deanery of Crewkerne; Rev. J. H. Cardew, incumbent. Population, 1801, 157—1811, 163—1821, 168.

CURRY-MALLET—a parish in the hundred of Abdick and Bulstone, 8 miles S. W. from Langport; containing 69 inhabited houses, and 89 families, 54 of whom are employed in agriculture. The inhabitants had a right of common on West Sedge Moor, which is now enclosed, and a portion of it is allotted to this parish. This manor forms part of the Dutchy of Cornwall, and is the property of the King, as Prince of Wales, who likewise presents to the living. The church is dedicated to St. James, and consists of a nave, chancel, north aisle, chapel, and porch, with a plain embattled tower at the west end, containing five bells. It is a rectory, in the deanery of Crewkerne; Rev. J. H. Cardew, incumbent; instituted 1797. Population, 1801, 353—1811, 379—1821, 461.

CURRY-NORTH—a hundred, situated in the southern part of the county, east of Taunton; consisting of five parishes; viz. NORTH-CURRY, WEST-HATCH, STOKE-ST. GREGORY, THORNE-FALCON, and THURLBEAR; containing 713 inhabited houses,

748 families, 1937 males, and 1880 females. Total population, 3817.

CURRY-NORTH—a parish in the hundred to which it gives name. It is situated 6 miles E. from Taunton, and contains 323 inhabited houses, and as many families, 228 of whom are employed in agriculture. This was formerly a place of considerable note, having had a weekly market, and a fair annually, the latter of which continues to be held on the first of August. The church is a large Gothic structure, dedicated to St. Peter and St. Paul, built in the form of a cross, with an hexagonal embattled tower, containing a clock and five bells. The living is a vicarage, (with Stoke-St. Gregory and West-Hatch annexed,) in the deanery of Taunton, and a peculiar belonging to the Dean and Chapter of Wells ; Rev. W. K. Coker, incumbent ; instituted 1820. Population, 1801, 1194—1811, 1344—1821, 1645.

CURRY-RIVEL—a parish in the hundred of Abdick and Bulstone, 2 miles W.S.W. from Langport ; containing 218 inhabited houses, and 251 families, 162 of whom are employed in agriculture. To the westward of this parish is *Burton-Pynsent*, formerly the seat of the Earl of Chatham ; the estate has lately been sold, and the mansion-house pulled down. The church is a handsome structure, consisting of a nave, chancel, and two side aisles, with a large embattled tower at the west end, containing a clock and five bells. The living is a vicarage ; Rev. Jas. Sedgwick, incumbent ; instituted 1799. Population, 1801, 974— 1811, 1030—1821, 1192.

CUTCOMBE---a parish in the hundred of Carhampton, 6 miles S.W. from Dunster ; containing 112 inhabited houses, and 122 families. To the north-west of this village is Dunkery, the highest mountain in the west of England, being 1770 feet above the sea, at high-water mark ; on the top is a large collection of rough stones, and among them the ruins of three large fire-hearths, about eight feet square; these form an equilateral triangle, and in the centre is another considerably larger; these are the remains of those beacons which were formerly erected for the purpose of alarming the country, in case of invasion. The church of Cutcombe is dedicated to St. Lawrence, and consists of a nave, chancel, and north aisle, with a tower, containing five bells. The living is a rectory, in the deanery of Dunster; Rev. George Nibbs, incumbent; instituted 1791; patron, the King. Population, 1801, 594—1811, 602—1821, 664.

SAINT DECUMAN'S — a parish of considerable extent, in the hundred of Williton and Freemanners, 8 miles E. from Minehead, 21 N.W. from Taunton, and the same distance from Bridgewater; it includes the sea-port town of WATCHET, and contains 360 inhabited houses, occupied by 385 families, 177 of whom are employed in agriculture, 190 in trade, manufacture, or handicraft, and 18 not included in either class. The town of WATCHET stands on the verge of the Bristol Channel, situated in a delightful and well-cultivated vale; it was formerly a place of considerable trade, having a large herring-fishery, but, like other ports in this neighbourhood, the trade is now principally confined to the freightage of coal, kelp, and limestone. Here is a small market on Saturday, and an annual fair on August 25, for cattle. About two miles to the south-west is the hamlet of Williton, which gives name to the hundred, and has a small chapel, united to St. Decuman's. A mile further to the south is *Orchard-Wyndham*, now the residence of Henry Tripp, Esq. The church of St. Decuman's is a handsome structure, 108 feet in length and 48 in breadth, consisting of a nave, two side aisles, and a chapel, with a castellated tower at the west end, containing eight bells. The living is a vicarage, in the deanery of Dunster, and a peculiar belonging to the prebendary. Rev. Henry Poole, incumbent; instituted 1798. Population, 1801, 1602—1811, 1659—1821, 1865.

DINDER—a parish in the hundred of Wells-Forum, 2 miles S. E. from Wells, containing 43 houses, and as many families, 26 of whom are employed in agriculture. The church is dedicated to All-Saints, and consists of a nave, chancel, and north aisle, with a tower at the west end 60 feet high, containing a clock and five bells. The living is a rectory, in the deanery of Cary, and a peculiar belonging to the bishop of the diocese. Rev. John Jenkins, incumbent; instituted 1797. Population, 1801, 185—1811, 215—1821, 175.

DINNINGTON—a hamlet and chapelry to the parish of Seavington-St. Michael, in the hundred of South Petherton, 3 miles E.S.E. from Ilminster, containing 41 inhabited houses, and 44 families, 35 of whom are employed in agriculture. The church is a small building, consisting of a nave, with a turret at the west end. It is a chapel to Seavington-St. Michael. Population, 1801, 219—1811, 219—1821, 208.

DITCHEAT—a parish in the hundred of Whitestone, 5 miles S. from Shepton-Mallet, containing 230 inhabited houses, and 262 families, 115 of whom are employed in agriculture. This parish extends over 6000 acres of land, in general good, and mostly applied to pasture and meadow. In the year 1765, a woman in this parish, of the name of Kingston, was delivered of a stout boy without arms or shoulders; he was baptized by the name of William, and a short time since continued to reside at Ditchet, in the occupation of a farmer; he performed the usual business of the field, saddled and bridled his own horses with his feet and toes, wrote out his own bills, and exercised every function of life in a most astonishing manner, having all the strength, power, and dexterity of the most regularly made man. The church is dedicated to St. Mary, and is built in the form of a cross, with a tower 60 feet high, containing a clock and six bells. The living is a rectory, in the deanery of Cary; Rev. W. Leir, incumbent; instituted 1812. Population, 1801, 1010—1811, 1236—1821, 1223.

DODDINGTON—a parish in the hundred of Williton and Free-mannors, 2 miles W.N.W. from Nether Stowey; containing only 13 houses, and 19 families, 15 of whom are employed in agriculture. The church is a small building, consisting of a nave, chancel, and a chapel on the south side, with a tower at the west end, containing four bells. The living is a rectory, in the deanery of Bridgewater; Rev. C. R. Ashfield, incumbent; instituted 1821. Population, 1801, 71—1811, 75—1821, 113.

DONYATT—a parish in the hundred of Abdick and Bulstone, 2½ miles W. S. W. from Ilminster; containing 107 inhabited houses, and 109 families, 87 of whom are employed in agri-culture. The river Ile runs through this parish, over which is a stone bridge of one arch. *Park-Farm*, about half a mile from the church, was formerly a seat belonging to one of the Dukes of Somerset. The church is dedicated to St. Mary, and consists of a nave, chancel, north and south aisles, and a porch, with a quadrangular embattled tower at the west end, contain-ing a clock and four bells. The living is a rectory, in the deanery of Crewkerne; Rev. Edward Combe, incumbent; in-stituted 1821. Population, 1801, 417—1811, 465—1821, 518.

DOULTING—a parish in the hundred of Whitestone, 2 miles E. from Shepton-Mallet; containing 130 inhabited houses, and as many families, 100 of whom are employed in agriculture. The church stands upon the site of an oratory, which was erected by the monks of Glastonbury, and dedicated to the honour of St. Aldhelm; near it is a well, called St. Aldhelm's Well. The church is a large structure, built in the form of a cross, with an octagonal tower in the centre, surmounted by a spire, and containing six bells. The living is vicarial, in the deanery of

Cary; Rev. John Bishop, D.D. incumbent; instituted 1782.
Population, 1801, 539—1811, 524—1821, 633.

DOWLISH-WAKE—a parish in the hundred of South-Petherton,
2 miles S.E. from Ilminster; containing 46 inhabited houses,
and 72 families, 56 of whom are employed in agriculture.
Several springs, rising in this neighbourhood, form a little rivulet,
and running through West-Dowlish, joins the river Ile, at the
foot of Sea-Mill, in the parish of Ilminster. The church stands
upon an eminence, and commands a good view of the country
to the south-west. It is dedicated to St. Andrew, and consists
of a nave, chancel, north aisle, and chapel, with a quadrangular
tower between the chancel and the nave. The living is a
rectory, in the deanery of Crewkerne; Rev. S. Collinson, D.D.
incumbent; instituted 1778. Population, 1801, 241—1811,
251—1821, 319. The increased population of this parish is
accounted for by an additional quantity of land having been
allotted for the cultivation of potatoes.

DOWLISH WEST—a very small parish adjoining the above, but
situated in the hundred of Abdick and Bulstone, nearly 2 miles
S.S.W. from Ilminster; containing only 6 inhabited houses, and
7 families, 6 of whom are employed in agriculture. The church
of Ilminster was built of stone, cut out of a quarry in this parish.
The living is a rectory, and now a sinecure, the church having
been in ruins more than a century; Rev. S. Collinson, D.D.
incumbent; instituted 1778. Population, 1801, 40—1811, 40—
1821, 32.

DOWNHEAD—a small parish in the hundred of Whitestone,
6 miles W.S.W. from Frome; containing 40 inhabited houses,
and 53 families, 50 of whom are employed in agriculture. The
living is a curacy, and the chapel, which consists of a nave, with
a tower containing three bells, belongs to the church of Doult-

ing; it was rebuilt in the year 1751. Population, 1801, 225—
1811, 172—1821, 208.

DRAYTON—a parish in the hundred of Abdick and Bulstone,
2 miles S. S. W. from Langport; containing, with the tything of
Middleney, 78 inhabited houses, and 99 families, 83 of whom
are employed in agriculture. The river Parret passes to the
eastward of this parish, and divides it from Muchelney. The
church is very ancient, consisting of a nave, north aisle, chancel,
and porch, with an embattled tower at the west end containing
a clock and five bells. The living is a rectory; Rev. Edward
Combe, incumbent. Population, 1801, no return—1811, no
return—1821, 469.

DULVERTON—a market-town and parish in the hundred of
Williton and Freemanners, 14 miles S. from Dunster, and 13
W. from Wiveliscombe; containing 206 inhabited houses, and
232 families, 115 of whom are employed in agriculture, 104 in
trade, manufacture, or handicraft, and 13 not included in either
class. The town consists of two streets, having channels of
water running through them. The chief manufactures are coarse
woollen cloths and blankets. It has a market on Saturdays, and
two fairs annually, viz. July 10 and November 8. The river
Barle, which rises in Exmoor Forest, passes through the town
under a stone bridge of five arches, and unites with the river
Ex near Brushford. The Ex runs about a mile and a half
eastward of the town, under a stone bridge, called Hele-bridge,
on the turnpike-road to Dunster. Both these rivers are broad
shallow streams, clear and rapid, flowing over a rough rocky
bed, and forming in their course a continual succession of water-
falls. An act of parliament has lately been obtained for opening
a new line of road, by the side of the river Ex to Cutcombe, and
from thence to Minehead by Dunster, which will probably be
completed in the course of a few years. About a mile to the
south-east of the town is *Pixton*, the seat of the Earl of Caer-

narvon. The church of Dulverton is a neat Gothic edifice, consisting of a nave, chancel, and two side aisles, with an embattled tower 60 feet high, containing a clock and five bells. The living is a vicarage, in the deanery of Dunster ; Rev. Roger Frankland, incumbent; instituted 1799. Population, 1801, 1049—1811, 1035—1821, 1127.

DUNDRY—a parish in the hundred of Chew, 4½ miles S.S.W. from Bristol ; containing 82 inhabited houses, and 92 families, 83 of whom are employed in agriculture. The church stands on the top of a very high hill, and is seen at a great distance both by sea and land ; it consists of a nave, north aisle, and chancel, with a remarkable fine embattled tower, crowned with open turretted pinnacles, and containing a clock and six bells. The living is a curacy annexed to Chew-Magna. Population, 1801, 366—1811, 417—1821, 454.

DUNKERTON—a parish in the hundred of Wellow, 4½ miles S.S.W. from Bath ; containing 72 inhabited houses, and 78 families, of whom 13 are returned as being employed in agriculture, 5 in trade, manufacture, or handicraft, and 60 not included in either class ; a considerable proportion of the latter number of families are employed in the coal works, which abound in this neighbourhood. Its name is derived from Dun, a hill, Carn, a monument of stones, and Ton, a town, there being a remarkable eminence about a mile from the church, whereon once stood a carned, or hill of stones, to commemorate some victory. The parish is bounded on the east by the old Roman Fosse-way, which divides it from the parishes of Combe-Hay and Wellow. The church is dedicated to All Saints, and consists of a nave, with a tower at the west end containing five bells. The living is a rectory, in the deanery of Frome ; Rev. C. T. Bampfylde, incumbent ; instituted 1820. Population, 1801, 238—1811, 305—1821, 365.

DUNSTER—a market-town in the hundred of Carhampton, situated on an eminence about a mile S. from the Bristol Channel, and 3 miles S. E. from Minehead; containing 179 inhabited houses, and 183 families, 84 of whom are employed in agriculture, 78 in trade, manufacture, or handicraft, and 21 not included in either class. The town is small, consisting chiefly of two streets; in the centre of the principal one stands an old market-cross, and a range of shambles. The market is on Friday, and here is an annual fair on Whit Monday. A rapid stream, formed from springs rising on Dunkery-hill, runs through a deep vale on the south and east sides of the town, turning several mills in its course, and passing under a stone bridge of three arches, it empties itself into the sea. The castle is a noble edifice, situated on a steep hill to the south of the town, and commands a most extensive prospect over the sea, and the mountains of South Wales; it is now the seat of John Founes Luttrell, Esq. whose ancestors came into the possession of this estate in the reign of Edward the Third. The church is one of the largest Gothic structures of the kind in England, and was built by Henry the Seventh as a mark of his gratitude for the assistance he received from the inhabitants of the town in the famous battle of Bosworth field, which terminated the disputes between the houses of York and Lancaster. It is 168 feet long, and 55 feet wide, with a tower in the centre, embattled and pinnacled, 90 feet in height, and contains a clock and eight bells. Only that part west of the tower is now used for divine service, which consists of a nave, chancel, and north and south aisles. The living was formerly vicarial, but is now a perpetual curacy, in the deanery of Dunster; Rev. T. F. Luttrell, incumbent; instituted 1821. Population, 1801, 772—1811, 868—1821, 895.

DURLEIGH—a parish in the hundred of Andersfield, 1½ mile W. S. W. from Bridgewater; containing 25 inhabited houses, and 26 families, the whole of whom are employed in agriculture. The church is a small structure, consisting of a nave, chancel, and porch, with a square embattled tower at the west end containing four bells. The living is a vicarage, in the deanery of Bridgewater; Rev. Henry Parsons, incumbent; instituted 1820. Population, 1801, 104—1811, 124—1821, 127.

DURSTON—a parish in the hundred of North Petherton, 5 miles N.E. from Taunton; containing 39 inhabited houses, and 45 families, 35 of whom are employed in agriculture. The church is a small building, and the living a curacy, in the deanery of Bridgewater; Rev. T. T. Biddulph, incumbent. Population, 1801, 169—1811, 167—1821, 211.

EARNSHILL—a very small parish in the hundred of Abdick and Bulstone, 6 miles N.N.E. from Ilminster; containing only 1 inhabited house, and 1 family. It formerly had a chapel belonging to Curry Rivel, but was afterwards made parochial, or rather extra-parochial. It is the property of Richard Thomas Combe, Esq. who resides in a very pleasant modern-built house in the centre of the park. It is a rectory, and a sinecure, the church having been destroyed; Rev. Edward Combe, incumbent; instituted 1821. Population, 1801, 20—1811, 16—1821—13.

EASTON-ST. GEORGES, or EASTON IN GORDANO—a parish in the hundred of Portbury, 6 miles W.N.W. from Bristol; containing 395 inhabited houses, and 440 families, 16 of whom are returned as being employed in agriculture, 62 in trade, manufacture, or handicraft, and 362 not included in either class. The latter number of families are chiefly those of mariners, &c. who under the regulation of the master and wardens of the Merchant Adventurers of Bristol, have the charge of vessels up and down the river, and who principally reside at Crockerne-Pill, a hamlet in this parish, on the bank of the river Avon. The church of Easton consists of a nave, chancel, south aisle, and a vestry-room on the north side, with a handsome tower at the west end containing a clock and six bells. The living is a vicarage, in the deanery of Redcliff and Bedminster, and a peculiar belonging to the prebendary; Rev. T. H. Morehouse, incumbent; instituted 1818. Population, 1801, 1688—1811, 1820—1821, 2109.

EDINGTON—a chapelry to the parish of Moorlinch, in the hundred of Whitley, 6½ miles E. N. E. from Bridgewater; containing 65 inhabited houses, and 69 families, 62 of whom are employed in agriculture. Near the church is a spring, the water of which contains sulphur and steel; it is very cold, and previous to a change of the weather, smells like the foul barrel of a gun: it has been found efficacious in scorbutic cases. The living is a curacy, united with Moorlinch; it has a small chapel, consisting of a nave, with a turret at the west end containing two bells. Population, 1801, 284—1811, 284—1821, 341.

ELM—a parish in the hundred of Frome, 2½ miles W. N. W. from Frome; containing 66 inhabited houses, and 70 families, 20 of whom are employed in agriculture, and 47 in trade, manufacture, or handicraft. Some extensive iron-works have been lately established here, which has increased the population considerably. The church is a small structure, dedicated to St. Mary, and consists of a nave and chancel, with a tower containing three bells. The living is a rectory, in the deanery of Frome; Rev. R. Blakeney is both patron and incumbent. Population, 1801, 331—1811, 368—1821, 449.

ELWORTHY—a parish in the hundred of Williton and Freemanners, 5 miles N. from Wiveliscombe; containing 28 inhabited houses, and 33 families, 29 of whom are employed in agriculture. The village is situate on the left of the turnpike-road leading from Taunton to Minehead; and on the opposite side is *Hartrow*, the residence of the Rev. Thomas Sweet Escott; a mile from which is *Willet-House*, belonging to Daniel Francis Blommart, Esq. To the eastward of that part of Brendon-hill that lies within this parish, is a lofty smooth knoll, on which

the neighbouring gentry, about half a century since, erected an
hexagonal embattled tower, 80 feet high; it is called Willet Tor,
and is a fine object to the country for many miles round. The
church consists of a nave, with an embattled tower at the west
end containing four bells. The living is a rectory, in the deanery
of Dunster; Rev. Thomas Roe, incumbent; instituted 1818.
Population, 1801, 150—1811, 196—1821, 187.

EMBORROW—a parish in the hundred of Chewton, 6½ miles
N. E. from Wells; containing 38 inhabited houses, and 43 families, 40 of whom are returned as being employed in agriculture.
On the south side of the turnpike-road is a very fine lake, called
Lechmere-waters; it extends over ten acres in a line from S. W.
to N. E.: and on the south-east side is a beautiful plantation of
firs, beeches, and sycamores, with pleasant walks cut through it.
The church is dedicated to St. Mary, and consists of a nave,
chancel, and north aisle, with a small neat tower in the centre
containing two bells. The living is a curacy, in the deanery of
Frome, annexed to Chewton-Mendip. Population, 1801, 241—
1811, 220—1821, 250.

ENMORE—a parish in the hundred of Andersfield, 4 miles
W. S. W. from Bridgewater; containing 55 inhabited houses,
and as many families, 27 of whom are employed in agriculture.
Enmore-Castle, the seat of the Earl of Egremont, is a very singular
structure; its figure is quadrangular, embattled on every side,
with a semicircular bastion at each corner, having in the interior
a spacious court. It is surrounded by a dry ditch, 16 feet deep
and 40 wide. The entrance is from the east, through a gateway
defended by a drawbridge. The stables and out-offices are all
under ground; the principal way into them is at some distance
from the castle: the whole was designed and erected by the late
Earl. The castle stands on a gentle eminence, and commands
an extensive prospect over the surrounding country, which is
finely cultivated, and adorned with neat villas on every side. The

church is a Gothic structure, 80 feet long and 20 feet wide, consisting of a nave and chancel, with a square embattled tower at the west end, having a clock and five bells. The living is a rectory, in the deanery of Bridgewater; Rev. John Poole, incumbent; instituted 1796. Population, 1801, 254—1811, 254 —1821, 287.

EVERCHREECH—a parish in the hundred of Wells Forum, 4 miles N.W. from Bruton; containing, with the chapelry of Chesterblade, which is in this parish, 266 inhabited houses, and 275 families, 40 of whom are returned as being employed in agriculture, 74 in trade, manufacture, or handicraft, and 161 as not included in either class. It appears from this return, that the families of the labouring poor employed in the cultivation of the land, have been included in the third class, whereas they ought to have been returned among those employed in agriculture. To the south of the hamlet of Chesterblade, on the summit of a high hill, is a Roman encampment, distinguished by the name of Small Down; and near the hamlet of Southwood is a spring strongly impregnated with salt. The church of Everchreech is dedicated to St. Peter, and consists of a nave, chancel, and two side aisles, with a richly ornamented Gothic tower 130 feet high, terminated with 28 elegant pinnacles; it contains a clock and six bells. The living is a vicarage, in the deanery of Cary, with Chesterblade chapel annexed, and is a peculiar belonging to the Dean of Wells; Rev. Richard Jenkins, incumbent; instituted 1821. Population, 1801, 918—1811, 1105 —1821, 1253.

EXFORD—a parish in the hundred of Carhampton, 7 miles S.S.W. from Porlock, and 9 W.N.W. from Dulverton; containing 68 inhabited houses, and 106 families, 54 of whom are employed in agriculture. The river Ex, which rises about 8 miles to the westward, gives name to this parish, and runs through it in its way to the ancient city of Exeter. The church is dedicated to

St. Mary, and is a Gothic structure, consisting of a nave, chancel, and south aisle, with an embattled tower at the west end, 70 feet high, and contains four bells. The living is a rectory, in the deanery of Dunster, and in the patronage of Peter-House College, Cambridge ; Rev. William Bevill, incumbent ; instituted 1789. Population, 1801, 375—1811, 316— 1821, 373.

EXMOOR—an extra-parochial place, at the western extremity of the county, situated in the hundred of Williton and Freemanners, containing 9 inhabited houses, and as many families, 7 of whom are employed in agriculture. Exmoor was formerly a forest, and it is said that most of the wood was consumed in some iron works near Exford, where the pits from which the ore was dug still remain : a considerable part of this wild romantic waste has lately been brought into cultivation by John Knight, Esq. of Wolverley, in the county of Worcester. This forest was in the time of the Druids dedicated to religious rites, and here are several circular entrenchments, which it is supposed were thrown up for the celebration of their ceremonies. From the late return in 1821, the population of this place appears to be 101 males and 12 females ; total, 113.

EXTON—a parish in the hundred of Williton and Freemanners, 5 miles N. from Dulverton ; containing 43 inhabited houses, and 60 families, 56 of whom are employed in agriculture. The village stands on an eminence, overlooking the river Ex, from which it derives its name. The new road from Dulverton to Minehead (for which an Act of Parliament has lately been obtained) will pass through this place. The church is dedicated to St. Peter, and consists of a nave, chancel, and north aisle, with a tower at the west end, containing four bells. The living is a rectory, in the deanery of Dunster ; Rev. John Jeffrey, incumbent ; instituted 1801. Population, 1801, 251—1811, 225 —1821, 301.

FARLEY-HUNGERFORD—a parish in the hundred of Wellow, 7 miles S.S.E. from Bath; containing 28 inhabited houses, and 34 families, 26 of whom are employed in agriculture. It is situated in a very rich and beautiful tract, and is said to have derived its name from the *fairness* of its *leys*, or meadows. It formerly had a castle, and was for several years in the possession of the Saxon Thanes; it received its adjunctive name from Thomas Lord Hungerford, who purchased the estate about the time of Richard the Second, from whom it descended to Sir Richard Hungerford, the famons spendthrift, who sold it in 1686, with thirty-six other manors. This gentleman was a representative in Parliament thirty-three years, and though at one time possessed of £30,000 per annum, he was supported by charity the last thirty years of his life, and died at the advanced age of 116. Joseph Houlton, Esq. is the present owner of the estate, and resides at Farley-House. The chapel of the castle continues nearly perfect, and contains a number of ancient monuments, in memory of the Hungerfords. The parish church consists of a nave, with a small tower containing five bells. The living is a rectory, in the deanery of Frome; Rev. B. Richardson, incumbent; instituted 1796. Population, 1801, no return—1811, 149—1821, 174.

FARMBOROUGH—a parish in the hundred of Keynsham, 7 miles S. W. from Bath; containing 166 inhabited houses, and as many families, 138 of whom are employed in agriculture. The land in this parish is chiefly pasture, and is watered by a small stream, formed by a spring that rises on Barrow-Hill, which after turning Priston-Mill, pursues its course by Inglishcombe, Newton St. Loe, and Tiverton, into the river Avon. The church is dedicated to All Saints, and consists of a nave, chancel, vestry-room, and porch, with a tower at the west end, containing six bells. The living is a rectory, in the deanery of Redcliff and Bedminster; Rev. P. Gunning, D. D. incumbent; instituted 1785; patron, the Bishop of Bath and Wells. Population, 1801, 532—1811, 621—1821, 752.

FARRINGTON-GOURNEY—a parish in the hundred of Chewton, 9 miles N.E. from Wells; containing 103 inhabited houses, and 113 families, 42 of whom are employed in agriculture, 48 in trade, manufacture, or handicraft, and 23 not included in either class; the latter number probably comprehends those engaged in working the coal-mines, which abound in this neighbourhood. The church is dedicated to St. John, and consists of a nave, with a tower at the west end. The living is a vicarage, annexed to Chewton-Mendip. Population, 1801, 344—1811, 359— 1821, 526.

FIDDINGTON—a parish in the hundred of Cannington, 7 miles W.N.W. from Bridgewater, and about 4 S. from the Bristol Channel; it contains 36 inhabited houses, and 40 families, 33 of whom are employed in agriculture. The church, which is dedicated to St. Martin, consists of a nave and chancel, with a tower at the west end, containing four bells. The living is a rectory, in the deanery of Bridgewater; Rev. H. W. Rawlings, incumbent; instituted 1821. Population, 1801, 147—1811, 173—1821, 185.

FITZHEAD—a parish in the hundred of Kingsbury-West, 3 miles E. from Wiveliscombe; containing 54 inhabited houses, and 63 families, 48 of whom are employed in agriculture. The church is a small Gothic edifice, dedicated to St. Mary, consisting of a nave, with a tower at the west end containing a clock and five bells. The living is a curacy, in the deanery of Dunster with Runnington annexed, and is a peculiar belonging to the prebendary thereof; Rev. H. Davis, incumbent; instituted 1808. Population, 1801, 236—1811, 304—1821, 300.

FIVEHEAD—a parish in the hundred of Abdick and Bulstone, 5 miles W. S. W. from Langport; containing 59 inhabited houses, and 74 families, 64 of whom are employed in agriculture. The inhabitants had formerly a right of common on West Sedgemore, which is now enclosed, and that part allotted to this parish joins it on the north. The church is a neat building, consisting of a nave, chancel, south aisle, and porch, with an embattled tower at the west end, containing a clock and five bells. The living is a vicarage, in the deanery of Crewkerne; Rev. Thomas Price, incumbent; instituted 1782; patrons the Dean and Chapter of Bristol. Population, 1801, 280—1811, 307 —1821, 326.

FLAX-BOURTON—a parish in the hundred of Portbury, 6 miles W.S.W. from Bristol; containing 31 inhabited houses, and 36 families, 13 of whom are employed in agriculture. The living is a curacy, in the deanery of Redcliff and Bedminster, and is a chapel to Wraxall, where the rites of baptism and burial are performed. Population, 1801, 161—1811, no return—1821, 192.

FORSCOTT—a parish in the hundred of Wellow, 8 miles N.W. from Frome; containing 10 inhabited houses, and as many families, the whole of whom are employed in agriculture. A small rivulet runs through this parish, under a stone bridge, and pursues its course to the river Avon, by Wellow, turning several mills in its way. The church is a small neat edifice, dedicated to St. James, consisting of a nave and chancel, with a tower at the west end in which are two bells. The living is a rectory, in the deanery of Frome; Rev. Israel Lewis, incumbent; instituted 1806. Population, 1801, 100—1811, 129—1821, 115.

FRESHFORD—a parish in a detached portion of the hundred of Bath-Forum, 5 miles S.S.E. from Bath; containing 131 inhabited houses, and 136 families, 18 only of whom are employed in agriculture. The river Frome divides this parish from the county of Wilts on the east, and is joined by the river Avon on the north-east. The church is a Gothic structure, dedicated to St. Peter, consisting of a nave, chancel, south aisle and porch, with a tower at the west end, embattled and pinnacled, containing a clock and four bells. The living is a rectory, in the deanery of Bath; Rev. George Bythsea, incumbent; instituted 1818. Population, 1801, 624—1811, 571—1821, 587.

FROME—the name of a hundred on the E. side of the county, bordering on the county of Wilts; comprising the following parishes, viz. BECKINGTON, BERKLEY, CLOFORD, CRANMORE-EAST, ELM, FROME, LAVERTON, LULLINGTON, MARSTON-BIGOT, NUNNEY, ORCHARDLEIGH, ROAD, RODDEN, STANDERWICK, WANSTRAW, WHATLEY, WITHAM-FRIARY, and WOOLVERTON; containing 3729 inhabited houses, 4077 families, 9810 males, and 10,755 females. Total population, 20,565.

FROME—a large populous market-town, in the hundred to which it gives name. It derives its appellation from the river Frome, which passes through the lower part of the town, under a bridge of five arches, and pursues its course through Becking-ton to Road, and then forms the boundary of the county to Freshford, where it joins the river Avon. This town was for-merly called Frome-Selwood, from its vicinity to Selwood-Forest. It lies in latitude 51° 13′ 49″ 9. N. and longitude 2° 18′ 41″ 6. W. 12 miles from Bath, 24 from Bristol, 15 from Wells, and 107 from London; and contains 2307 inhabited houses, and 2526 families, 106 of whom are employed in agriculture, 1576 in trade, manufacture, or handicraft, and 844 not comprised in either class. It is irregularly built, and consists of a great number of streets, very narrow, and indifferently paved, but most of them being on a declivity renders the town tolerably clean. A new opening has lately been made through the town, forming a very hand-some street, with well-built houses on each side. The chief manufacture is that of woollen cloth; it has likewise an exten-sive trade in card making for the woolcombers, and on the river are several mills for fulling, &c. The town was formerly governed by a bailiff, but is now under the direction of con-stables chosen at the courts-leet of the Marquis of Bath, and Earl of Cork and Orrery. Here is a free-school, founded by

Edward the Fourth; a good charity-school, an alms-house for widows, and several meeting-houses for various denominations of dissenters. The church is extremely neat and spacious, being 152 feet long, and 54 feet wide, consisting of a nave, chancel, north and south aisles, four chapels, a vestry-room, and two porches, with a quadrangular tower supporting a handsome spire; the tower contains a clock, chimes, and eight bells. The living is a vicarage, in the deanery of Frome; Rev. C. Phillott, incumbent; instituted 1813. Within that part of Frome called the Woodlands, to the north of Bramble Forest, stands another church, called the new church, which was built by Thomas Lord Viscount Weymouth, in the year 1712, and endowed with £60 per annum out of an estate at Pennard, in this county, in compliance with the last will and testament of his deceased brother, the Hon. Henry Frederick Thynne. His lordship also augmenting the stipend with £30 per annum, and £500, the greater part of which has since been applied to the purchase of an estate, called Codrington, within the parish of Frome, the net proceeds of which are also settled upon the minister of this church. The church is a handsome building, 68 feet long and 34 feet wide, with a square tower at the west end, surmounted by an octangular spire 70 feet high. Frome has two weekly markets, viz. Wednesday and Saturday (the former is the principal one for cattle and corn); also four fairs annually, February 24, July 22, September 14, and November 25. Population, 1801, 8748—1811, 9493—1821, 12,411.

GLASTON-TWELVE-HIDES—the name of a hundred in the centre of the county; comprising the following parishes, viz. BALTONSBOROUGH, BRADLEY-WEST, GLASTONBURY (ST. JOHN and ST. BENEDICT), MEARE, NYLAND (with *Batcombe* tything) PENNARD-WEST, and WOOTTON-NORTH, containing 1015 inhabited houses, 1149 families, 2820 males, and 2952 females. Total population, 5772.

GLASTONBURY—a market-town in the above hundred, comprising two parishes, St. Benedict and St. John the Baptist; it is situated in the centre of the county, 6 miles from Wells, 26 from Bath and Bristol, and 130 from London, and contains 533 inhabited houses, occupied by 690 families, 362 of whom are employed in agriculture, 118 in trade, manufacture, or handicraft, and 88 not included in either class. This town is indebted for its origin to its monastic institutions, and was first built by King Ina, about the year 708, and in 873, it was entirely demolished by the Danes, but shortly after rebuilt by King Edmund, the ninth Saxon Monarch, who exempted its inhabitants from all civil impositions, and made it entirely subject to, and dependant upon the abbey. In this state it continued till the year 1184, when both the town and the abbey were consumed by fire. It was again rebuilt by Henry the Third, and on the 11th of September 1276, it was again destroyed by an earthquake, which laid the whole town in ruins, and precipitated the church of St. Michael from the top of Tor-hill. Glastonbury at present consists of two streets, intersecting each other at the cross; several of the houses are built of stone, taken from the ruins of the abbey. It was once a parliamentary borough, but was disfranchised on the execution of Abbot Whiting, who, at the dissolution, refused to surrender his abbey to Henry the Eighth, for which he was tried at Wells, and with two of his monks, was drawn on a hurdle to the Tor, near the town, and there hanged; after which his head was set on the gate of the abbey, and his quarters were sent to Bath, Wells, Bridgewater, and Ilchester. The abbey, from which this town derived its celebrity, surpassed in value and authority every other in England, except that of Westminster; the abbot sat in the upper house as a spiritual Lord, and lived in all the state of regal splendour, having an income of £40,000 per annum. The abbey, according to the Monkish annals, was first instituted by Joseph of Arimathea, who, with twelve others, were sent by Philip, the Apostle of Gaul, to preach the gospel in Britain. It was afterwards liberally endowed by King Ena, who built the great church and erected a chapel, the silver embellishments of which weighed upwards of 2640 pounds; and on the altar were 260 pounds weight of solid gold, exclusive of the church-plate, which was incredibly magnificent. He likewise granted to the abbey a great extent of territory, and confirmed to the monks all the civil and religious privileges they had hitherto enjoyed : besides other immunities he rendered this monastery independent of the episcopal authority, and annexed to its jurisdiction seven of the neighbouring parishes, which afterwards composed the archdeaconry, and are still called the jurisdiction of Glastonbury. The only parts of this once magnificent structure that now remain, are some fragments of the church, St. Joseph's chapel, and the Abbot's kitchen. A short distance from the town, on the summit of a high hill, is the Tor, or tower of St. Michael, the only remains of a splendid church and monastery, built on the site of a former one that was destroyed by an earthquake, in the year 1271 : it is much admired for its architectural beauty: at the west end of it there is a carved figure of St. Michael, holding in his hand a pair of scales, in one of which is the Bible, and in the other a devil, assisted by an imp endeavouring to bear down the scale, but they are represented as too light to weigh down the sacred volume.

Sharpham-Park, the residence of William Gould, Esq. is situated about 3 miles to the S. W. of the town, well known as the birth-place of Henry Fielding, the author of several novels, entitled, Tom Jones, Joseph Andrews, Amelia, and several others, which acquired him deserved celebrity. The church of St. John the Baptist is a neat handsome building, situated in the high-street, and preserves many marks of its former embellishments; in its lower division are a number of niches, which appear to have been filled with statues at large as life; some of them are now remaining on the south and west sides of the tower. The church of St. Benedict stands in the west-street, and is supposed to have been built by Abbot Beer, towards the latter end of the fourteenth century. The living is a curacy, and St. John's a donative, both in the patronage of the Bishop of the diocese; Rev. Thomas Parfit, incumbent; instituted 1812. Population, 1801, 2035—1811, 2331—1821, 2630.

GOATHILL—a small parish in the hundred of Horethorne, 1½ mile S. from Milbourn-Port, and bounded on the east, south, and west, by the county of Dorset; it contains only 4 inhabited houses, and as many families, 3 of whom are employed in agriculture; near the church are two springs, one of which is a chalybeate, strongly tinctured with iron; the other, about three yards distant, is considered serviceable in topical inflammation of the eyes. The church consists of a nave, dedicated to St. Peter, and is a rectory, in the deanery of Marston; Rev. Robert Frome, incumbent; instituted 1797. Population, 1801, 24—1811, 17—1821, 20.

GOATHURST—a parish in the hundred of Andersfield, 3½ miles S.W. from Bridgewater, containing 58 inhabited houses, and 67 families, 30 of whom are employed in agriculture. About half a mile westward, is the hamlet of Andersfield, from which this hundred received its name, and was formerly a place of considerable note.

Halswell-Park, the residence of Charles Kemeys Tynte, Esq. M. P. is situated to the north of the church: the mansion-house is a noble and elegant building, and the inclosures around exhibit the finest scenery in this part of England. A spring, that rises in the park, runs through the parish, and falls into the river Parret, near Bridgewater. The church is dedicated to St. Edward, and consists of a nave, chancel, and side aisles, with an embattled tower, containing a clock and six bells. The living is rectorial, in the deanery of Bridgewater; Rev. H. Parsons, incumbent; instituted 1789. Population, 1801, 296 — 1811, 318—1821, 342.

GOSE-BRADON—a small parish in the hundred of Abdick and Bulstone, 4 miles N. from Ilminster. It is now quite depopulated, having neither church, house, or inhabitant. It is a rectory, and a sinecure, in the gift of Mr. Uttermare; now vacant.

GREINTON—a parish in the hundred of Whitley, 9 miles E. from Bridgewater, 7 miles W.S.W. from Glastonbury; containing 34 inhabited houses, and 41 families, 32 of whom are employed in agriculture. The church is dedicated to St. Michael, and consists of a nave, with a tower at the west end containing four bells. The living is a rectory, in the deanery of Pawlet; Rev. John Brice, incumbent; instituted 1800. Population, 1801, 128—1811, 155—1821, 237.

HALSE—a parish in the hundred of Williton and Freemanners, 2 miles N.E. from Milverton; containing 75 inhabited houses, and 31 inhabitants, 57 of whom are employed in agriculture. The church is dedicated to St. James, and consists of a nave, chancel, and north aisle, with a tower at the west end containing a clock and five bells. The living is a vicarage, in the deanery of Taunton; Rev. N. Spencer, incumbent; instituted 1793. Population, 1801, 383—1811, 425—1821, 447.

HAMPTON and CLAVERTON—a liberty locally situated in the hundred of Bath-Forum: it comprises the parishes of Charlton, Claverton, and Hampton, and contains 79 inhabited houses, 97 families, 232 males, and 272 females. Total population, 504.

HARDINGTON—a small parish in the hundred of Kilmersdon, 4 miles N.N.W. from Frome, containing only 4 inhabited houses, and as many families, 2 of whom are employed in agriculture. *Hardington-Park*, a short distance to the north-west of the church, near which the manor-house stood, was formerly well stocked with deer. It is the property of Sir C. W. Bampfylde, Bart.

The church is a small structure, with a tower at the west end. The living is a rectory, in the deanery of Frome; Rev. C. F. Bampfylde, incumbent; instituted 1814. Population, 1801, no return—1811, 26—1821, 31.

HARDINGTON-MANDEVILLE—a parish in the hundred of Houndsborough, Berwick, and Coker, 4 miles S. W. from Yeovil; containing 95 inhabited houses, and 116 families, 58 of whom are employed in agriculture. The church consists of a nave, chancel, and north aisle, with a tower at the west end, containing five bells. The living is a rectory, in the deanery of Ilchester; Rev. John Helyer is both patron and incumbent; instituted 1802. Population, 1801, 489—1811, 532—1821, 537.

HARPTREE-EAST—a parish in the hundred of Winterstoke, 8 miles N. from Wells, and 11 S. from Bristol; containing 130 inhabited houses, and 139 families, 20 of whom are returned as being employed in agriculture, 19 in trade, manufacture, or handicraft, and 100 not included in either class. Richmond-castle, situate about a mile S. W. from the village, was not entirely demolished till the time of Henry the Eighth, when Sir John Newton dug up the foundations for the purpose of erecting a new house near it. At a short distance to the east of the church, is *Harptree-Court*, the residence of Captain Waldegrave. The church is dedicated to St. Lawrence, and consists of a nave, chancel, and north aisle, with a tower at the west end, containing a clock and five bells. The living is a vicarage, and a peculiar in the deanery of Frome, belonging to the prebendary; Rev. John Parsons, incumbent; instituted 1811. Population, 1801, 467—1811, 502—1821, 627.

HARPTREE-WEST—a parish in the hundred of Chewton, 10 miles S. from Bristol, and 9 N. from Wells; containing 98 inhabited houses, and 109 families, 20 of whom are employed in agriculture, 21 in trade, manufacture, or handicraft, and 68 not included in either class. The church is dedicated to St. Mary, and consists of a nave, chancel, and south aisle, with a small tower at the west end, containing five bells, surmounted by a spire. The living is a vicarage, in the deanery of Redcliff and Bedminster; Rev. James Roquett, incumbent; instituted 1789, patron, the King, as Prince of Wales. Population, 1801, no return—1811, 297—1821, 529.

HARTCLIFF with BEDMINSTER—the name of a hundred, situated in the northern part of the county, comprising the following parishes; viz. Ashton Long, Backwell, Barrow-Gourney, Bedminster, Butcombe, Chelvey, and Winford; containing 1962 inhabited houses, 2320 families, 5462 males, and 5957 females. Total population, 11,419.

Hasleborough—a parish in the hundred of Houndsborough Berwick and Coker, 2½ miles E. N. E. from Crewkerne, from which it is divided by the river Parret; it contains 155 inhabited houses, and 177 families, 60 of whom are employed in agriculture, 96 in trade, manufacture, or handicraft, and 21 not included in either class. The church is dedicated to St. Michael, and consists of a nave, chancel, and north aisle, or chapel, with a tower at the west end, containing five bells. The living is a vicarage, in the deanery of Wells, and a peculiar belonging to the prebendary; Rev. Thomas Wyndham, incumbent; instituted 1797. Population, 1801, 677—1811, 664—1821, 768.

Hatch-Beauchamp—a parish in the hundred of Abdick and Bulstone, 6½ miles E. S. E. from Taunton; containing 35 inhabited houses, and 46 families, 36 of whom are employed in agriculture. Here was formerly a weekly market on Thursdays, and an annual fair, procured by John de Beauchamp, lord of this manor, 29 Edward the First, 1301, both of which have long been discontinued: the parishioners had a right of common on West-Sedgemoor, which is now enclosed, and a portion allotted to

this parish. Near the church is a handsome house, built of free-
stone, well shaded by thriving plantations, which till lately was
the residence of Henry Powell Collins, Esq. but now occupied
by John Clifton, Esq. The church is dedicated to St. John the
Baptist, and is a neat edifice, consisting of a nave, chancel,
north aisle, and porch, with an embattled tower, adorned with
eight Gothic pinnacles, and containing a clock and four bells. The
living is a rectory, in the deanery of Crewkerne; Rev. Henry
Adams, incumbent; instituted 1789. Population, 1801, 196—
1811, 227—1821, 245.

HATCH-WEST—a parish in the hundred of North Curry, 5 miles
E. S. E. from Taunton ; containing 59 inhabited houses, and 52
families, 57 of whom are employed in agriculture. The church
consists of a nave, chancel, and porch, with a tower and three
bells. The living is appendant to the adjoining parish of North
Curry. Population, 1801, no return—1811, 297—1821, 367.

HAWKRIDGE—a small parish in the hundred of Williton and
Freemanners, 4½ miles W. N. W. from Dulverton, on the confines of Exmoor-forest, and bounded on the south by the county
of Devon ; it contains 10 inhabited houses, and as many families,
8 of whom are employed in agriculture. The village stands on
a lofty hill, to the south of which is a deep narrow vale, watered
by a rivulet called Dines-brook, that falls into the river Barle,
at Castle-bridge, and divides this parish from Dulverton :
near this spot is an ancient fortification, called Mountsey, or
Mounceaux Castle. The church is a small building, consisting
of a nave, with a tower at the west end, containing three bells.
The living is a rectory, in the deanery of Dunster; Rev. Brian
Beauchamp, incumbent; instituted 1801. Population, 1801,
72—1811, 75—1821, 50.

HEATHFIELD—a parish in the hundred of Taunton and Taunton-
Dean, 5 miles W. N. W. from Taunton ; containing 21 inhabited

houses, and 25 families, 23 of whom are employed in agriculture.
The church consists of a nave, chancel, and a small south aisle,
with a tower, containing two bells. The living is a curacy, in
the deanery of Taunton ; Rev. Thomas Cornish, incumbent ; instituted 1787. Population, 1801, 120—1811, 122—1821, 131.

HEMINGTON—a parish in the hundred of Kilmersdon, 6 miles
N.W. from Frome ; containing 72 inhabited houses, and as
many families, 65 of whom are employed in agriculture. North-
east from the village is a place called High-Church, formerly a
considerable hamlet, and the site of the original parish church ;
it is now depopulated, having only one house remaining, called
High-Church Farm. The church consists of a nave, chancel,
and south aisle, with a tower at the west end. The living is a
rectory, in the deanery of Frome, united with Hardington ; Rev.
C.M. Bampfyld, incumbent ; instituted 1814. Population, 1801,
357—1811, 339—1821, 323.

HENSTRIDGE—a parish in the hundred of Horethorne, 3½ miles
E. N. E. from Milbourn-Port, bounded on the east and south by
the county of Dorset; the parish is very extensive, including
within its limits the hamlets of Whitchurch, Yeanston, and
Bowden, and contains 184 inhabited houses, and as many families,
159 of whom are employed in agriculture. The church is dedicated to St. Nicholas, and consists of a nave, chancel, and north
aisle, with an embattled tower at the west end, containing a
clock and six bells. The living is a vicarage, and a peculiar belonging to the prebendary ; Rev. N. Bridges, D.D. incumbent ;
instituted 1813. Population, 1801, 827—1811, 875—1821, 911.

HIGH-HAM—a parish in the hundred of Whitley, 3 miles N.
from Langport ; containing 181 inhabited houses, and as many
families, 148 of whom are employed in agriculture. The village
is situated on the top of a hill, which is skirted on the west and
north-west by a fine wood extending to Aller. About a mile

S. S. E. is the chapelry of Low-Ham, so denominated in contra-distinction to the former, from its situation; the chapel was built in the year 1669. The church of High-Ham is dedicated to St. Andrew, and consists of a nave, chancel, and two side aisles, with a large embattled tower at the west end containing five bells : it is said to have been built in the year 1476, by Abbot Selwood, with the joint contributions of Lord Paulet and other noblemen. It is a rectory; Rev. Joseph Shaw, incumbent; instituted 1803. Population, 1801, no return—1811, 783—1821, 953.

HILL-FARRANCE—a parish in the hundred of Taunton and Taunton-Dean, 4 miles W. from Taunton; containing 94 inhabited houses, and 98 families, 63 of whom are employed in agriculture. The church is dedicated to the Holy Cross, and consists of a nave, chancel, and a south aisle or chapel, with a tower containing five bells. The living is a curacy, in the deanery of Taunton, and in the gift of Trinity College, Cambridge; Rev. James Ford, incumbent; instituted 1820. Population, 1801, 438—1811, 425—1821, 483.

HINTON-BLEWETT—a parish in the hundred of Chewton, 12 miles S. from Bristol; containing, with the hamlet of South Widcombe, 53 inhabited houses, and 71 families, 51 of whom are employed in agriculture. The church, which is dedicated to All Saints, consists of a nave, chancel, and north aisle, with a neat tower at the west end. The living is a rectory, in the deanery of Redcliff and Bedminster; Rev. James Johnson, incumbent; instituted 1807. Population, 1801, 255—1811, 252—1821, 264.

HINTON-CHARTERHOUSE—a parish, in the liberty of Hinton and Norton, and locally in the hundred of Wellow, 5½ miles S.S.E. from Bath, containing 85 inhabited houses, and 97 families, 18 of whom are employed in agriculture, 75 in trade.

manufacture, or handicraft, and 4 not included in either class. A priory, for Carthusian monks, was founded here in 1227, and endowed the manors of Hinton and Norton, the ruins of which are surrounded by a grove of venerable oaks. Near the church, at the extremity of an avenue of trees, stands a modern free-stone mansion, the residence of Mrs. Day. The church is dedicated to St. John the Baptist, consisting of a nave, chancel, and south aisle, with a tower at the west end, containing three bells. It is a curacy, in the deanery of Frome, annexed to Norton St. Philip. Population, 1801, 619 — 1811, 677—1821, 640.

HINTON ST. GEORGE — a parish so called from the dedication of its church. It is situated in the hundred of Crewkerne, 3 miles N. N. W. from Crewkerne, containing 144 inhabited houses, and 161 families, 82 of whom are employed in agriculture. Here is a very extensive park, the seat of Earl Pawlet, who receives the title of Baron from this place. The church is dedicated to St. George, and consists of a nave, chancel, and side aisles, with a tower at the west end, containing five bells; the living is a rectory, in the deanery of Crewkerne ; Rev. H. Stamberry, incumbent; instituted 1789. Population, 1801, 575 — 1811, 611—1821, 737.

HOLCOMBE—a parish in the hundred of Kilmersdon, 7½ miles W. N. W. from Frome, containing 112 inhabited houses, and as many families, the principal number of whom are employed in the coal-works, there being only 20 returned as occupied in the cultivation of the land, which is chiefly pasture. The church is a small ancient edifice, dedicated to St. Andrew, having a fine Saxon arch over the south entrance. The living is a rectory, in the deanery of Frome ; Rev. Thomas Tordiffe, incumbent; instituted 1805. Population, 1801, 619—1811, 509—1821, 527.

HOLFORD — a parish in the hundred of Whitley, 3 miles

W.N.W. from Nether-Stowey, containing 44 inhabited houses, and as many families, 21 of whom are employed in agriculture. The church is a small structure, dedicated to St. Mary, consisting of a nave, with a tower containing three bells; the living is a rectory, in the deanery of Bridgewater, and in the gift of Eton College; Rev. George Buxton, incumbent; instituted 1788. Population, 1801, 125—1811, 180—1821, 240.

HOLTON—a parish in the hundred of Whitley, 2 miles S.W. from Wincanton, containing 46 inhabited houses, and 47 families, 35 of whom are employed in agriculture. The church is dedicated to St. Nicholas, and consists of a nave, with a tower at the west end containing three bells. The living is a rectory, in the deanery of Cary; Rev. Jos. Legge, incumbent; instituted 1785. Population, 1801, 179—1811, 201—1821, 235.

HOLWELL—a parish in the hundred of Horethorne, 4½ miles S. from Milbourn-Port, containing, with the hamlet of Buckshaw, 70 inhabited houses, and as many families, 61 of whom are employed in agriculture. This parish is entirely surrounded by Dorsetshire. The church is dedicated to St. Lawrence, and is within the jurisdiction of the Bishop of Bristol; it consists of a nave, chancel, north aisle, and a chapel on the south side, with a tower containing five bells. The living is a rectory, in the deanery of Shaston, Dorset, and in the patronage of Queen's College, Oxford; Rev. Isaac Monkhouse, incumbent; instituted 1797. Population, 1801, 293—1811, 344—1821, 342.

HORETHORNE—the name of a hundred in the S.E. part of the county, on the borders of Dorsetshire; it derived its name from a down, near Milbourn-Port, called Horethorne-Down, there having been a remarkable thorn on the spot where the hundred courts were formerly held. It comprises the town of MILBOURN-PORT, and the following parishes, viz. CHARLTON-HORETHORNE, CHERITON-NORTH, CORTON-DENHAM, GOATHILL, HENSTRIDGE,

HOLWELL, HORSINGTON, MARSTON-MAGNA, POINTINGTON, SANDFORD-ORCAS, STOWELL, TEMPLE-COMBE, and TRENT, containing 1260 inhabited houses, 1370 families, 3227 males, and 3442 females.—Total population, 6669.

HORNBLOTTON—a parish in the hundred of Whitestone, 7 miles S. from Shepton-Mallet; containing 20 inhabited houses, and 24 families, the whole of whom are employed in agriculture. The church is dedicated to St. Peter, and is a small structure, consisting of a nave, with a tower at the west end containing three bells. The living is a curacy, annexed to Doulting. Population, 1801, 96—1811, 88—1821, 111.

HORSINGTON—a parish in the hundred of Horethorne, 4 miles S. from Wincanton, and 4 N. N. W. from Milbourn-Port; containing 154 inhabited houses, and 196 families, 105 of whom are employed in agriculture. About a mile N. N. W. from the village is the hamlet of South Cheriton, which formerly had a chapel, but there are no remains of it at present. The church of Horsington is dedicated to St. John the Baptist; it is a Gothic structure, consisting of a nave, chancel, side aisle and porch, with an embattled tower 60 feet high, containing a clock and five bells. The living is a rectory, in the deanery of Marston; Rev. T. W. Wickham, incumbent; instituted 1798. Population, 1801, 833—1811, 880—1821, 925.

HOUNDSBOROUGH BERWICK AND COKER—formerly three distinct hundreds, but now united in one; it lies in the southern part of the county, bordering on Dorsetshire, and comprises the following parishes, viz. BERWICK, CHILTON-CANTILOE, CHINNOCK-EAST, CHINNOCK-MIDDLE, CHINNOCK-WEST, CHISLEBOROUGH, CLOSWORTH, COKER-EAST, COKER-WEST, HARDINGTON-MANDEVILLE, HASLEBOROUGH, NORTON under HAMDON, ODCOMBE, PENDOMER, PERROT-NORTH, and SUTTON-BINGHAM, containing 1269 inhabited houses, 1547 families, 3516 males, and 3716 females. Total Population, 7285.

HUISH-CHAMPFLOWER—a parish on the confines of the hundred of Williton and Freemanners, 2 miles W. N. W. from Wiveliscombe; containing 53 inhabited houses, and as many families, 45 of whom are employed in agriculture. This parish received its additional name from the family of Champflower, who held this manor with that of Wick-Campflower, near Bruton, for some time previous to the reign of Richard the Third. The church consists of a nave, chancel, and north aisle, with a tower at the west end containing five bells. The living is a rectory, in the deanery of Dunster; Rev. George Trevelyan, incumbent; instituted 1803. Population, 1801, 321—1811, 317—1821, 317.

HUISH-EPISCOPI—a parish in the hundred of Kingsbury-East, half a mile E. from Langport; containing 75 inhabited houses, and 94 families, 87 of whom are employed in agriculture. The church is dedicated to St. Mary, and consists of a nave, chancel, and side aisles, with a lofty tower, ornamented with eight Gothic pinnacles, each surmounted with a spear-head. The living is a vicarage, and a peculiar belonging to the Archdeacon of Wells; Rev. E. Wells, incumbent; instituted 1802. Population, 1801, 367—1811, 437—1821, 472.

HUISH-ROAD—a chapelry in the parish and hundred of Carhampton, 4 miles S. E. from Dunster, and 2 miles S. from its own parish, in which the population is included.

HUNTSPILL AND PURITON—the name of a hundred lying on the river Parret, near its influx into the Bristol Channel; it comprises the parishes of HUNTSPILL, PURITON, and WOOLLAVINGTON (the two latter are united), and contains 340 inhabited houses, 359 families, 844 males, and 843 females. Total population, 1687.

HUNTSPILL—a parish in the hundred of Huntspill and Puriton,

8 miles N. from Bridgewater; containing 274 inhabited houses, and 283 families, 214 of whom are employed in agriculture. The parish is about fifteen miles in circumference, and the lands are nearly all pasture and meadow. The town had formerly the privilege of a market, which has been discontinued long since : it has still a fair for cattle and sheep on the 29th of June, toll free. The church is dedicated to All Saints, and is a handsome structure, consisting of a nave, chancel, and side aisles, with a tower at the west end. The living is a rectory, in the deanery of Paulet, and in the gift of Baliol College, Oxford; Rev. T. C. Rogers, incumbent; instituted 1819. Population, 1801, 1012—1811, 1119—1821, 1337.

HUTTON—a parish in the hundred of Winterstoke, 7 miles N. W. from Axbridge; containing 44 inhabited houses, and 58 families, 35 of whom are employed in agriculture. The church is dedicated to St. Mary, and is a neat building, standing on rising ground, near the ascent of a hill south of the village; it consists of a nave and chancel, with a tower at the west end containing five bells. The living is a rectory, in the deanery of Axbridge; Rev. Joseph Smith, incumbent; instituted 1820. Population, 1801, 244—1811, 243—1821, 325.

ILCHESTER—a borough and market-town, in the hundred of Tintenhull, situated on the river Ivel, which bounds it on the north, being 18 miles S. from Wells, 24 E. from Taunton, 35 S. from Bristol, and 125 from London; containing 157 inhabited houses, and 184 families, 55 of whom are employed in agriculture, 87 in trade, manufacture, or handicraft, and 42 not comprised in either class. This town, in point of antiquity and ancient importance, has a superiority over most others in the county. The British name of it was *Cairpensavelcoit*, signifying the city at the head of the river's mouth in the wood; and it is ranked by Ptolemy as the first town in the territory of the Belgæ. When the Romans possessed these parts, this was one of their most eminent stations, and was fortified by a strong wall and deep ditch, vestiges of which still remain ; the fosse-road, now forming one of the principal streets, passed through it from north-east to south-west ; and the ditch, which formed the road called Yard-lane, crosses the fosse and the gardens at the back part of the town, where the wall has often been discovered by the gardeners. This town is celebrated in electioneering contests ; when the borough belonged to Mr. Harcourt, the electors drank sixty hogsheads of cider at one election. It It now belongs to Lord Huntingtower, who, after the election in 1818, pulled down the houses of all those who voted contrary to his interest ; others have since been built by Lord Darlington, upon a spot of ground within the borough, called Ilchester-Mead ; there are likewise two piles of buildings within the town, built by his lordship, each containing from twenty to thirty tenements, all inhabited by persons opposed to the interests of Lord Huntingtower. This borough first returned members to parliament in 1297, but in 1359 this privilege was rescinded, nor was it restored till 1471 ; it was soon afterwards again taken away, and once more restored by James the First, in 1621 ; it now sends two members, who are returned by the bailiff and twelve burgesses ; the right of election is in all the inhabitants, paying scot and lot. In the reign of Edward the Third the assizes were directed to be held here, but they are now alternately held at Taunton, Wells, and Bridgewater. In the centre of the town, near the cross, stands the Town-Hall, where the county-court is held ; and to the west of the principal street, near the river Ivel, stands the county-gaol, which will probably be pulled down, the magistrates having it in contemplation to enlarge the gaol at Shepton-Mallet, for the reception of the prisoners. There were formerly a considerable number of churches in this town ; the only one remaining is that of St. Mary's, which consists of a nave, chancel, and north aisle, or chapel ; at the west end is a large octagonal tower, built of Roman stone ; it is 50 feet in height, and contains a clock and five bells. The living is rectorial, in the deanery of Ilchester, and in the patronage of the Bishop of the diocese ; Rev. R. T. Whalley, incumbent ; instituted 1821. Here is a market on Wednesdays, which has existed ever since the conquest, but is now little attended ; here were also three fairs, one of which is still held on the last Wednesday in August. The celebrated Roger Bacon was born at the Friary-house in this town, A.D. 1214 ; his superiority in genius and science over most of his contemporaries, caused him ten years imprisonment, the monks fearing that their order would fall into contempt, if their pretensions to magic were exposed to the world, and their miracles explained, as depending upon the simple universal principles inherent in the system of nature; yet notwithstanding the bigotry and ignorance by which he was surrounded, his knowledge and intellectual acquirements were such as in a more fortunate age might have rivalled the glory of a Locke or a Newton ; he died in the year 1294, at the age of 80, and was buried in the house of Grey Friars, at Oxford. The pious and accomplished Mrs. Elizabeth Rowe was likewise a native of Ilchester ; she was the daughter of Mr. Singer, a dissenting minister, who possessed a small family estate in the neighbourhood of Frome, to which place Mrs. Rowe retired after the death of her husband, and where she wrote most of those literary productions which have given her deserved celebrity. Population, 1801, 867—1811, 745—1821, 994—the latter return includes 152 male and 40 female prisoners in the county gaol.

ILMINSTER—a market-town and parish in the hundred of Abdick and Bulstone, on the turnpike-road leading from Somerton to Chard, being 16 miles from the former, and 5 from the latter; it contains 348 inhabited houses, and 410 families, 137 of whom are employed in agriculture, 234 in trade, manufacture, or handicraft, and 39 not included in either class. The town principally consists of two streets, intersecting each other, one of which is more than a mile in length ; the greater part of the population is employed in the manufacture of narrow cloths, which formerly flourished here to a very great degree. Here is a good market-house, and a range of shambles ; the market, which is on Saturday, was established previous to the Norman conquest, and has continued ever since ; it has likewise an annual fair, kept the last Wednesday in August. In the town is a good free school, founded in the year 1550, by Humphrey Walrond and Henry Greenfield, of Sea, in this parish, and endowed with lands in Cricket-Malherbe, Donyat, Ashill, Isle-Abbots, Cudworth, &c. in this county; and likewise the fee simple of the manor of Sandwich, in the Isle of Purbeck, in Dorsetshire. The river Ile runs through this parish, to the west of the town, and crosses the turnpike-road to Taunton, under a stone bridge of 4 arches, which is kept in repair by the trustees of the above school. The neighbourhood of Ilminster is extremely populous, having no less than thirty parishes within five miles round the town ; the whole of the churches may be seen from an eminence in its vicinity. A short distance north of the town is *Dillington-House,* the residence of William Hanning, Esq. The church is a Gothic structure, built in the form of a cross, and consists of a nave, chancel, transept, north and south aisles, vestry-room, and porch, with a handsome tower in the centre, crowned with twelve pinnacles, and contains a clock and five bells. The living is a vicarage, and a peculiar in the gift of the King ; Rev. J. H. Mules, incumbent; instituted 1820. Population, 1801, 2045—1811, 2160—1821, 2156.

ILTON—a parish in the hundred of Abdick and Bulstone, 3 miles N. N. W. from Ilminster; containing 67 inhabited houses, and 109 families, 90 of whom are employed in agriculture. The river Ile, from which this parish is named, bounds it on the east. The church consists of a nave, chancel, and two side aisles; on the south side, over the porch, is a tower, surmounted by a wooden spire, and contains a clock and four bells. The living is a vicarage, and a peculiar belonging to the Prebendary; Rev. William Palmer incumbent; instituted 1807. Population, 1801, 363—1811, 390—1811, 460.

ISLE-ABBOTS—a parish in the hundred of Abdick and Bul-stone, 4 miles N. from Ilminster, and 5 S.W. from Langport; it contains 67 inhabited houses, and 109 families, 90 of whom are employed in agriculture. The ancient appellation of this parish was Ile, derived from a river of that name, which bounds the parish on the east, and it received its additional name from having formerly belonged to the abbots of Muchelney. The church is dedicated to St. Mary, and consists of a nave, chancel, north aisle, and porch, with a handsome tower, ornamented with pinnacles and several statues; it is 70 feet high, and has a clock and five bells. The living is a vicarage, in the gift of the Dean and Chapter of Bristol; Rev. J.H. Mules, incumbent; instituted 1820. Population, 1801, 254—1811, 330—1821, 460.

ISLE-BREWERS—a parish in the hundred of Abdick and Bul-stone, divided from the above by the river Ile, from which it received its designation, and additionally called Brewers, from having been the property of a family of that name. It con-tains 23 inhabited houses, and 26 families, 16 of whom are employed in agriculture. The church is dedicated to All Saints, and consists of a nave and chancel, with an embattled tower at the west end containing four bells. The living is vicarial, in the deanery of Crewkerne; Rev. James Mitchell, incumbent; instituted 1799. Population, 1801, 181—1811, 181—1821, 219.

INGLISH-COMBE—*See* COMBE-INGLISH.

KATHERINE, ST.—a parish in the hundred of Bath-Forum, 4 miles N.N.E. from Bath; containing 18 inhabited houses, and 20 families, 16 of whom are employed in agriculture. It is denominated from the patron Saint to which the church is dedi-cated. The village stands on the declivity of a hill, and a small rivulet winds through the vale below, which is composed of rich verdant meadows. The church consists of a nave and chancel, with a tower at the west end containing four bells. It was built by the Abbots of Bath. The living is a vicarage, annexed to Bath Hampton, to which it was formerly a chapelry. Population, 1801, no separate return—1811, no separate return—1821, 127.

KELWESTON, generally pronounced KELSTON—a parish in the hundred of Bath-Forum, 3 miles N. W. from Bath, on the upper turnpike-road from that city to Bristol; it contains 50 inhabited houses, and as many families, 24 of whom are employed in agriculture. Between this village and the river Avon is the seat of Sir J. C. Hawkings, Bart. The church is dedicated to St. Nicholas, and consists of a nave, chancel, and two porches, one of which is walled up, and is now used as a vestry-room; at the west end is a tower containing four bells. The living is a rectory, in the deanery of Bath; Rev. C. Hawkings, incumbent; instituted 1806. Population, 1801, 221—1811, 248—1821, 248.

KENN—a parish in the hundred of Winterstoke, 5½ miles N. W. from Wrington; containing 47 inhabited houses, and 49 families, 16 of whom are employed in agriculture. The church is a small building, consisting of a nave, with a turret at the west end. The living is a curacy, in the deanery of Redcliff and Bedminster, annexed to Yatton. Population, 1801, 160—1811, 195—1821, 276.

KENTON-MANDEVILLE—a parish in the hundred of Catash, 4 miles E. from Somerton; containing 70 inhabited houses, and 77 families, 6 of whom are employed in agriculture, and 69 in trade, manufacture, or handicraft. The houses are built of stone raised in the parish, and is of a very peculiar kind. The church, which stands at the southern extremity of the village, is dedicated to St. Mary, and consists of a nave and chancel. From

the north-side of the nave is an arched passage, 8 feet long and
4 feet wide, that leads to the tower, which is octagonal, and is
terminated by a conical roof, tiled, and contains four bells.
The living is a rectory, in the deanery of Cary; Rev. W. H.
Colston, D.D. incumbent; instituted 1810. Population, 1801,
206—1811, 261—1821, 349.

KEWSTOKE—a parish in the hundred of Winterstoke, 10 miles
N.W. from Axbridge, under the northern brow of Worle-hill:
it contains 54 inhabited houses, and 87 families, 70 of whom
are employed in agriculture. At Woodspring, a hamlet in this
parish, was formerly a priory of Augustine Monks, the ruins of
which still remain, some part having been converted into a farm-
house. The church of Kewstoke is dedicated to St. Paul, and
consists of a nave, chancel, and south aisle, with a tower at the
west end containing five bells. The living is a vicarage, in the
deanery of Axbridge, and in the gift of the Crown; Rev. Thomas
H. Hume, incumbent; instituted 1799. Population, 1801, no
return—1811, 379—1821, 429.

KEYNSHAM—the name of a hundred on the N.E. side of
the county, divided from the county of Gloucester by the river
Avon; it comprises the following parishes, viz. BRISLINGTON.
BURNETT, CHELWOOD, COMPTON-DANDO, FARMBOROUGH, KEYN-
SHAM, MARKSBURY, NEMPTNETT-TRUBWELL, PENSFORD, PRISTON,
PUBLOW, QUEEN-CHARLETON, SALTFORD, STANTON-DREW, STAN-
TON-PRIOR, and WHITCHURCH, otherwise FELTON, containing
1498 inhabited houses, 1648 families, 4003 males, and 4083
females. Total population, 8086.

KEYNSHAM—a small market-town in the hundred to which
it gives name, 5 miles S.E. from Bristol, and 7 miles W.N.W
from Bath, on the turnpike-road between those two cities: it
contains 340 inhabited houses, and 385 families, 138 of whom
are employed in agriculture, 158 in trade, manufacture, or handi-

craft, and 89 not included in either class. The town principally consists of one street, nearly a mile in length : it had formerly a considerable woollen manufacture, now entirely dropt. Here are a number of wire, brass, and other mills, on the banks of the river Avon, which winds round close to the town, and receives the river Chew at the county-bridge, which is built of stone, and extends over fifteen arches. A number of the poor are employed in spinning for the Bradford and other clothiers ; and the herb woad, which is used for the purposes of dying, is raised here in considerable quantities. Keynsham has a small market on Thursdays, and two fairs annually, viz. March 25, and August 15, for cattle, cheese, &c. William Earl of Gloucester, at the request of his son Robert, founded an abbey of Black Canons, and endowed it with the whole property of the manor and hundred of Keynsham, to which many other donations were afterwards added : it is reported to have been a very magnificent building ; there are no remains of it at the present time. The church, which was appropriated to the abbey, is a large handsome building, situated near the centre of the town, and consists of a nave, chancel, and two side aisles, with a lofty tower at the west end containing eight bells. The living is a vicarage, in the deanery of Redcliff and Bedminster ; Rev. C. R. Ashfield, incumbent; instituted 1819. Population, 1801, 1591—1811, 1748—1821, 1761.

KILMERSDON—the name of a hundred lying on the E. side of the county, between the hundreds of Frome and Chewton ; comprising the parishes of Ashwick, Babington, Buckland-Denham, Hardington, Hemington, Holcombe, Kilmersdon, Radstock, Stratton on the Fosse, and Writhlington, containing 1156 inhabited houses, 1212 families, 2832 males, and 2900 females. Total population, 5732.

Kilmersdon—a parish in the centre of the above hundred, 7 miles N.W. from Frome, and 10 miles S.S.W. from Bath ;

containing 369 inhabited houses, and 388 families, 71 of whom
are employed in agriculture, 64 in trade, manufacture, or handicraft, and 253 not included in either class. A considerable proportion of the latter number of families is employed in the coal
mines, which has occasioned a great increase in the population
of this parish. About a mile eastward from the village is *Am-
merdown*, the seat of T. S. Jolliffe, Esq. The church is a handsome edifice, dedicated to St. Peter and St. Paul, and consists of
a nave, chancel, and north aisle, with a tower at the west end.
The living is a vicarage, in the deanery of Frome, and in the
gift of the Crown; Rev Charles Neve, incumbent; instituted
1806. Population, 1801, 1721—1811, 1780—1821, 1991.

KILMINGTON—a parish in the hundred of Norton-Ferrars, 7
miles E. N. E. from Bruton; containing 119 inhabited houses,
and 121 families, 64 of whom are employed in agriculture. This
parish extends eastward a considerable distance, being bounded
on the north by Maiden-Bradley, and on the south by Stourton,
both in the county of Wilts. On an eminence about 2 miles
south-west from the church, is a monument erected to the
memory of King Alfred, by the late Henry Hoare, Esq.; its form
is triangular, and is 155 feet in height, having a turret at each
angle : round one of them is a railed gallery, which is ascended
by 121 steps, and commands one of the most beautiful inland
prospects in the kingdom. On a tablet over the entrance is the
following inscription : "Alfred the Great, A.D. 879, on this
summit erected his standard against Danish invaders; to him
we owe the origin of juries, and the creation of a naval force.
Alfred, the light of a benighted age, was a philosopher, and a
Christian; the father of his people, and the founder of the English
monarchy and liberties." *Stourhead*, the seat of Sir Richard
Colt Hoare, adjoins this parish on the Wiltshire side. The
church of Kilmington is dedicated to St. Mary, and consists of a
nave, chancel, and north and south aisle, with a handsome tower
at the west end. The living is rectorial, in the deanery of Cary;

Rev. and Hon. C. R. Strangways, incumbent; instituted 1811 Population, 1801, 504—1811, 528—1821, 556.

KILTON—a parish in the hundred of Williton and Freemanners, 6½ miles E. from Watchet; containing 18 inhabited houses, and 28 families, 27 of whom are employed in agriculture. The church is a small building, dedicated to St. Nicholas, and consists of a nave, with a tower containing four bells. The living is a vicarage, in the deanery of Dunster, and in the gift of the Crown; Rev. W. Wollen, D.D. incumbent; instituted 1815. Population, 1801, 114—1811, 126—1821, 149.

KILVE—a parish in the hundred of Williton and Freemanners, 5½ miles E. from Watchet, bounded on the North by the Bristol Channel: it contains 44 inhabited houses, and 48 families, 30 of whom are employed in agriculture. The church is dedicated to St. Mary, and consists of a nave, with a tower at the west end containing three bells. The living is rectorial, in the deanery of Bridgewater; Rev. J. Mathew, incumbent; instituted 1797. Population, 1801, 176—1811, 218—1821, 263.

KINGSBURY-EAST— the name of a hundred, divided into four unequal parts, and situated in different parts of the county. That part which contains the parish from which it receives its name with East-Lambrook, lies between the hundreds of Bulstone and Martock: a small portion, containing the parish of Huish-Episcopi, adjoins the town of Langport; and the two other parts, divided by a strip of South-Petherton hundred, and containing the remaining parishes, are situated at the extreme part of the county, southward, on the borders of Devonshire— the whole hundred contains the following parishes, viz. CHARD, COMBE-ST. NICHOLAS, HUISH-EPISCOPI, KINGSBURY-EPISCOPI, EAST-LAMBROOK, and WINSHAM; containing 1219 inhabited houses, 1433 families, 3417 males, and 3555 females.—Total population 6972.

KINGSBURY-WEST — the name of a hundred, lying W. of the preceding, in two parts; one between the hundred of Taunton and Taunton-Dean, on the west, and the hundred of Milverton, on the east; and the other on the north-west side of Milverton, adjoining to the hundred of Williton and Freemanners. It comprises the parishes of ASH-PRIORS, BISHOP'S-LIDEARD, BUCKLAND-WEST, FITZHEAD, WELLINGTON, and WIVELISCOMBE; containing 1844 inhabited houses, 2003 families, 4340 males, 4888 females.—Total population, 9228.

KINGSBURY-EPISCOPI — a parish in the east division of the hundred to which it gives name, 3 miles N. from South-Petherton, containing, with the chapelry of East-Lambrook, 280 inhabited houses, and 303 families, 263 of whom are employed in agriculture. This parish obtained the additional title of Episcopi from having, at an early period, belonged to the see of Wells. The church, which is dedicated to St. Martin, is a noble Gothic structure, consisting of a nave, chancel, two aisles, porch, and vestry-room, with an elegant tower at the west end, 120 feet in height, crowned with twenty Gothic pinnacles, and ornamented with several statues of kings, &c. placed in Gothic niches; but many of them are much mutilated. The living is a rectory and a peculiar, belonging to the Chancellor of Wells; Rev. James Crowther, incumbent; instituted 1820. Population, 1801, 1134—1811, 1181—1821, 1470.

KINGSDON—a parish in the hundred of Somerton, 2½ miles N. from Ilchester, and 2½ S. S. E. from Somerton, containing 94 inhabited houses, and 111 families, 79 of whom are employed in agriculture. The church is dedicated to All-Saints, and is built in the form of a cross, with a tower at the west end, containing a clock and six bells. The living is a rectory, in the deanery of Ilchester, Rev. John Tucker, incumbent; instituted 1794. Population, 1801, 455—1811, 489—1821, 536.

KINGSTON—a parish in the hundred of Taunton and Taunton-

Dean, 3½ miles N. from Taunton, containing, with the hamlet of Hestercombe, 144 inhabited houses, and 162 families, 111 of whom are employed in agriculture. About a mile and a half to the south-east of the village is *Hestercombe-House,* the residence of Miss Warre, in whose family this estate has continued for several centuries. *Pyrland-House,* the residence of Mrs. Yew, is nearly the same distance to the south, on the turnpike-road to Taunton. The church is a handsome Gothic structure, dedicated to St. Mary, and consists of a nave, chancel, and side aisles, with an elegant tower at the west end, crowned with twenty-four pinnacles, and containing a clock and six bells. The living is a rectory, in the deanery of Taunton, and in the gift of the Dean and Chapter of Bristol; Rev. A. Foster, incumbent; instituted 1791. Population, 1801, 834—1811, 847—1821, 954.

KINGSTON — a parish in a detached part of the hundred of Tintinhull, 1½ mile S. E. from Ilminster, containing 48 inhabited houses, and 58 families, 42 of whom are employed in agriculture. Allownshays, a hamlet, 1 mile eastward from the village, is a place of great antiquity, and was formerly a chapelry. The church of Kingston consists of a nave and chancel, with a large embattled tower in the centre, containing four bells; the living is a rectory, in the deanery of Crewkerne; Rev. John Harbin, incumbent; instituted 1817. Population, 1801, 197—1811, 227 —1821, 192.

KINGSTON-SEYMOUR—a parish in the hundred of Chewton, 5½ miles N. W. from Wrington; containing 43 inhabited houses, and 55 families, 53 of whom are employed in agriculture. It is bounded on the west by the Bristol Channel, and on the south by the river Yeo. On January 20, 1606, this and several other parishes were inundated by the sea; the banks were broken down, a great number of persons drowned, and the cattle and goods were carried away with the violence of the waves; a tablet was put up in the church, relating the particulars of the event. November 27, 1701, the inhabitants again suffered a great loss of property from the same cause, but it does not appear that any lives were lost upon this occasion. The church consists of a nave, chancel, and south aisle, with a tower and spire at the west end, containing a clock and five bells. The living is a rectory, in the deanery of Redcliff and Bedminster; Rev. D. Williams, incumbent; instituted 1820. Population, 1801, 267—1811, 290—1821, 320.

KING-WESTON—a parish in the hundred of Catash, 3½ miles N. E. from Somerton : containing 23 inhabited houses, and as many families : it is a place of great antiquity, having belonged to some of the Saxon kings. The houses are built of stone, and have a very neat appearance : here is a very handsome seat, adjoining the turnpike-road, the residence of William Dickinson, Esq. M. P. The church is situated on high ground, and consists of a nave, chancel, and small aisle, or chapel, with an embattled tower, containing a clock and three bells. The living is a vicarage, in the deanery of Cary, and in the patronage of the Lord of the Manor; Rev. C. H. Pulsford, incumbent; instituted 1819. Population, 1801, 90—1811, 111—1821, 111.

KITTISFORD—a parish in the hundred of Milverton, 4 miles S. from Wiveliscombe; containing 32 inhabited houses, and as many families. The church is dedicated to St. Nicholas, and consists of a nave, chancel, and side aisles, with a tower containing three bells. The living is a rectory, in the deanery of Taunton; Rev. Thomas Sweet Escott, incumbent; instituted 1802. Population, 1801, 143—1811, 143—1821, 175.

KNOWLE-ST.-GILES—a parish in the hundred of South Petherton, 2½ miles N. N. E. from Chard; containing 19 inhabited houses, and as many families. The church is dedicated to St. Giles, which gave the additional name to the village, and consists of a nave, with a turret and two bells. The living is a

donative and a peculiar, in the deanery of Crewkerne, belonging
to the Chancellor of Wells ; Rev. L. Evans, incumbent. Population, 1801, 61—1811, no return—1821, 91.

LAMBROOK-EAST—a parish in the hundred of Kingsbury-East,
1½ mile N. from South Petherton. The population for 1821 has
been included in the return of Kingsbury Episcopi. The church
is a small structure, and the living is a rectory, and a peculiar
in the deanery of Crewkerne ; Rev. William Marsh, incumbent ;
instituted 1817 ; patrons, the Dean and Chapter of Wells.

LAMYAT — a parish in the hundred of Whitestone, 2 miles
N. W. from Bruton ; containing 36 inhabited houses, and 53
families, 50 of whom are employed in agriculture. The church
is dedicated to St. Mary and St. John, and consists of a nave,
with a tower containing three bells. The living is rectorial, in
the deanery of Cary ; Rev. G. L. Uphill, incumbent ; instituted
1780. Population, 1801, 206—1811, 220—1821, 243.

LANGFORD-BUDVILLE—a parish in the hundred of Milverton,
2 miles S. from Milverton, and 2½ N. W. from Wellington ; containing 99 inhabited houses, and 116 families, 95 of whom are
employed in agriculture. It is called Langford, from its having formerly had a ford over the river Tone, which bounds the parish on
the south ; and additionally Budville, from a family of that name,
who possessed an estate here for many generations. The church
is dedicated to St. James, and consists of a nave, chancel, and
south aisle, with a large tower at the west end, containing five
bells. The living is a curacy, and a peculiar in the deanery of
Taunton, annexed to Milverton. Population, 1801, 524—1811,
503—1821, 564.

LANGPORT—a market-town and parish in the hundred of
Pitney, situated on the river Parret, which is navigable for
barges, and has over it a stone bridge of nine arches : the fall

of this river to Burrowbridge is only one inch in a mile, and from thence to Bridgewater one inch and a half. The town is governed by a portreeve and twelve burgesses, who have the royalty of the river. The principal articles of commerce are timber, stone, iron, salt, and corn. Langport contains 132 inhabited houses, and 185 families, 2 of whom are employed in agriculture, 169 in trade, manufacture, or handicraft, and 14 not included in either class; it has a market on Saturday, and four annual fairs. The church, which stands upon an eminence at the east end of the town, consists of a nave, chancel, north and south aisles, and two chapels, with a tower at the west end containing five bells. The living is a vicarage, united with Huish-Episcopi, and both form a peculiar, belonging to the Archdeacon of Wells; Rev. Edward Wells, incumbent; instituted 1802. Population, 1801, 754—1811, 861—1821, 1004.

LANGRIDGE—a parish in the hundred of Bath-Forum, 3½ miles N. from Bath; containing 16 inhabited houses, and 17 families, 16 of whom are employed in agriculture. This village is situated on the eastern declivity of Lansdown-hill, with a beautiful vale below it, watered by a small rivulet in its course to the river Avon. In the year 1643 a warmly contested battle was fought on Lansdown-hill, between the Royal and the Parliament armies, the former commanded by the Marquis of Hertford and Prince Maurice, and the latter by Sir William Waller. Of the king's cavalry, which came into the field 2000 strong, only 600 were left alive; yet notwithstanding this great slaughter they came off victorious. The number of gentlemen killed in this engagement exceeded that of the private soldiers; among them was Sir Bevill Grenville, to whose conduct the success of the royal party in Cornwall was chiefly owing. A very superb monument of free-stone has been erected to his memory, on the spot where he fell, about a mile and a half north-west from Langridge church, on the boundary which divides this parish from the county of Gloucester. The church is dedicated to St. Nicholas, and consists of a nave, chancel, and two porches (one of which is walled up and now used as a vestry-room.) It has a tower at the west end containing four bells. The living is a rectory, in the deanery of Bath; Rev. George Swaine, incumbent; instituted 1814. Population, 1801, 86—1811, 96—1821, 103.

LAVERTON—a parish in the hundred of Frome, 4½ miles N. from Frome; containing 36 inhabited houses, and 38 families, 25 of whom are employed in agriculture. A small rivulet runs through the village, and falls into the river Frome, which passes through the adjoining parish. The church is a small structure, dedicated to St. Bartholomew, with a tower containing three bells. The living is rectorial, in the deanery of Frome; Rev. George Rogers, incumbent; instituted 1817; patron, the Bishop of the diocese. Population, 1801, 134—1811, 133—1821, 189.

LEIGH-ON-MENDIP—a parish in the liberty of Mells and Leigh, and locally in the hundred of Kilmersdon, 5½ miles W. from Frome; containing 149 inhabited houses, and as many families, 148 of whom are employed in agriculture. The church is a Gothic structure, dedicated to St. Giles, and consists of a nave, chancel, two side aisles and porch, with an embattled tower containing six bells, and is a chapel to the adjoining parish of Mells. Population, 1801, 534—1811, 562—1821, 666.

LILSTOCK—a parish in the hundred of Williton and Free-manners, 7 miles E. from Watchet, bounded on the north by Bridgewater-Bay; it contains 12 inhabited houses, and 13 families, the whole of whom are employed in agriculture. Adjoining to the hamlet of Honibere, at the south-east extremity of this parish, is *Fairfield*, the seat of Sir John Palmer Acland, Bart. The church is a small building, dedicated to St. Andrew, and is a rectory united with Stoke-Courcy, both forming one presentation. Population of Lilstock, including Honibere, 1801, no return—1811, 91—1821, 71.

LITTLETON-HIGH—a parish in the hundred of Chewton, 11 miles N. N. E. from Wells, and 10½ miles S. S. E. from Bristol; containing 172 inhabited houses, and 181 families, 16 of whom are employed in agriculture, 46 in trade, &c. and 119 not included in either class, the principal part of the population being employed in the coal-works, there being several mines in this and the adjoining parishes. The church is dedicated to the Holy Trinity, and consists of a nave, chancel, and south aisle, with a tower containing three bells. The living is a vicarage, in the deanery of Redcliff and Bedminster; Rev. H. H. Mogg, incumbent; instituted 1804. Population, 1801, 811—1811, 804—1821, 864.

LITTON—a parish in a detached part of the hundred of Wells-Forum, 7 miles N. N. E. from Wells, on the left of the turnpike-road from that city to Bristol; it contains 81 inhabited houses, and 96 families, 55 of whom are employed in agriculture. The church is dedicated to St. Mary, and consists of a nave, chancel, and south aisle, with a well-built tower, in which are five bells. The living is a rectory and a peculiar, in the deanery of Frome, belonging to the prebendary; Rev. David Williams, incumbent; instituted 1814. Population, 1801, 366—1811, 347—1821, 378.

LOCKING — a parish in the hundred of Winterstoke, 7 miles N.W. from Axbridge, containing 26 inhabited houses, and 35 families, 30 of whom are employed in agriculture. The church is dedicated to St. Augustin, and consists of a nave, with a tower containing four bells; the living is a vicarage, in the deanery of Axbridge; Rev. David Dowell, incumbent; instituted 1812. Population, 1801, 137—1811, 168—1821, 198.

LOXTON—a parish in the hundred of Winterstoke, 4 miles W. from Axbridge, containing 29 inhabited houses, and 30 families, 27 of whom are employed in agriculture. A small brook, rising in the parish of Winscomb, divides this parish from Compton-

Bishop, and falls into the river Ax. The church is dedicated to St. Andrew, and consists of a nave, with a tower on the south side containing three bells; the living is rectorial, in the deanery of Axbridge; Rev. D. S. Moncriefe, incumbent; instituted 1801. Population, 1801, 97—1811, 165—1821, 165.

LOPEN—a parish in the hundred of South-Petherton, 3½ miles N. from Crewkerne, containing 94 inhabited houses, and 98 families, 46 of whom are employed in agriculture, and 50 in trade and manufacture, principally that of dowlas. The church is a small building, dedicated to All-Saints; it consists of a nave, with a turret at the west end. The living is a curacy, in the deanery of Crewkerne; Rev. J. Templeman, incumbent. Population, 1801, no return—1811, 331—1821, 425.

LOVINGTON—a parish in the hundred of Catash, 3 miles S. W. from Castle-Cary, on the left of the turnpike-road to Ilchester, containing 30 inhabited houses, and 44 families, 40 of whom are employed in agriculture. The church is a small structure, dedicated to St. Thomas-à-Becket. The living is a perpetual curacy, in the gift of the Dean and Chapter of Wells; Rev. J. C. Palmer, incumbent; instituted 1810. Population, 1801, 174—1811, 195—1821, 206.

LUCKHAM-EAST—a parish in the hundred of Carhampton, 2½ miles S. E. from Porlock, and 4 miles W. S.W. from Minehead, containing 86 inhabited houses, and 106 families, 54 of whom are employed in agriculture. Several springs, rising on Dunkery-Hill and in the Forest of Exmoor, form a rivulet, which runs through this parish under two stone bridges, and falls into the sea. The church is dedicated to St. Mary, and is a handsome Gothic structure, consisting of a nave, chancel, and south aisle, with an embattled tower, 82 feet high, containing a clock and two bells. The living is a rectory, in the deanery of Dunstead; Rev. R. F. Gould, incumbent; instituted 1782. Population, 1801, 457—1811, 417—1821, 481.

LULLINGTON — a parish in the hundred of Frome, 3 miles N. from Frome, containing 37 inhabited houses, and 39 families, 25 of whom are employed in agriculture. This parish contains 790 acres of land, chiefly applied to pasture: the river Frome divides it on the east from Beckington. At the south-west extremity of the parish is *Orchardleigh*, the seat of Sir T. S. Champneys, Bart. The church of Lullington is a very ancient structure of Saxon architecture, dedicated to All-Saints, consisting of a nave and chancel, with a large tower in the centre. It is a rectory, in the deanery of Frome; Rev. F. Skurray, incumbent; instituted 1807. Population, 1801, 157—1811, 178 —1821, 224.

LUSTON—a small parish in the hundred of Stone, 3 miles W. from Yeovil, containing only 5 inhabited houses, and as many families, 4 of whom are employed in agriculture. It is a rectory; the Rev. Elias Taylor, incumbent; instituted 1802. Population, 1801, no return—1811, 26—1821, 21.

LUXBOROUGH—a parish in the hundred of Carhampton, 5 miles S. from Dunster; containing 76 inhabited houses, and 77 families. The church is dedicated to St. Mary, and consists of a nave and chancel, with a tower at the west end containing four bells. The living is a vicarage, annexed to Cutcombe. Population, 1801, 332—1811, 344—1821, 387.

LYDEARD St. LAURENCE—a parish in the hundred of Taunton and Taunton-Dean, 8 miles N. W. from Taunton; containing 128 inhabited houses, and 134 families, 118 of whom are employed in agriculture. This parish had its additional title from St. Laurence, the second Archbishop of Canterbury, and successor to St. Augustine, to whom the church is dedicated. Here are several streams that run through the parish, one of which flows from a medicinal spring that rises in the village, and has been efficacious in scrophulous disorders. The church stands on

rising ground at the south of the village, and consists of a nave,
chancel, and north aisle, with an embattled tower at the west
end 70 feet high, ornamented with eight pinnacles, and contains
a clock and five bells. The living is a rectory, in the deanery
of Taunton; Rev. C. Russell, incumbent. Population, 1801,
604—1811, 575—1821, 618.

LYDFORD-EAST—a parish in the hundred of Somerton, 4½
miles W. from Castle-Cary, and 7 miles N. N. E. from Ilchester;
containing 23 inhabited houses, and 30 families, 16 of whom are
employed in agriculture. The church is a small building, consisting of a nave, with an open turret at the west end in which
are two bells. The living is a rectory, in the deanery of Cary;
Rev. N. Ryall, incumbent; instituted 1784. Population, 1801,
143—1811, 139—1821, 137.

LYDFORD-WEST—a parish in the hundred of Catash, 5 miles
W. from Castle Cary, and 7 miles N. N. E. from Ilchester; containing 64 inhabited houses, and 89 families, 60 of whom are
employed in agriculture. This place obtained its name from its
situation, there having formerly been a broad ford over the river
Brew, which runs through the parish, and over which is a good
stone bridge near the church. In the reign of Henry the Third,
William Martin, then lord of the manor, obtained a charter for
a weekly market on Tuesday, likewise two annual fairs, the one
on Holy Thursday, and the other on the 12th August; the
market has been discontinued long since, but the fairs are still
held. The church consists of a nave, chancel, and north aisle,
with a small tower at the west end containing five bells. The
living is a rectory, in the deanery of Cary, and a peculiar belonging to the prebendary; Rev. W. H. Colston, D. D. incumbent;
instituted 1810. Population, 1801, 313—1811, 402—1821, 437.

LYMINGTON—a parish in the hundred of Stone, 1½ mile E. S. E.
from Ilchester, on the river Yeo, or Ivel, which divides this

parish from Yovelton; containing, with the tything of Draycott, 54 inhabited houses, and 57 families, 46 of whom are employed in agriculture. The church, which is dedicated to St. Mary, consists of a nave, chancel, and north aisle or chapel, with a tower at the west end containing four bells. The living is a rectory, in the deanery of Ilchester; Rev. E. C. Forward is both patron and incumbent; instituted 1810. Population, 1801, 242 —1811, 243—1821, 268.

LYMPSHAM—a parish in the hundred of Brent with Wrington, 8 miles W. from Axbridge; containing 95 inhabited houses, and 118 families, 77 of whom are employed in agriculture. The church is dedicated to St. Christopher, and consists of a nave and north aisle, with an embattled tower 100 feet in height containing five bells. The living is a rectory, in the deanery of Axbridge; Rev. J. W. Stephenson, incumbent; instituted 1809. Population, 1801, 334—1811, 408—1821, 496.

LYNG-EAST—a parish in the hundred of Andersfield, 8 miles E. N. E. from Taunton; containing 62 inhabited houses, and 69 families, 61 of whom are employed in agriculture. Between the hamlet of Boroughbridge, and the church of East-Lyng, is a spot of rising ground, whereon is Alfred's monument, and denominated the Isle of Athelney, from two Saxon words signifying the Isle of Nobles, rendered famous as being the retreat of the illustrious Alfred, who, after having bravely encountered his enemies for nine years, was at length reduced to the necessity of taking refuge in this place, which at that time was rendered inaccessible on account of the bogs and inundations of the lakes. After the subjugation of his enemies, he founded a monastery for Benedictine Monks, which he dedicated to the honour of St. Saviour and St. Peter, and endowed it with the Isle of Athelney, and other benefactions were afterwards added thereto by different kings and nobles. The church of East-Lyng, which was formerly appropriated to the Abbey, consists of a nave, chancel and porch, with a tower 60 feet high containing five bells. The living is a vicarage, in the deanery of Bridge-water; Rev. Aaron Foster, incumbent; instituted 1806. Population, 1801, 253—1811, 264—1821, 335.

MAPERTON—a parish in the hundred of Catash, 3½ miles W.S.W. from Wincanton; containing 23 inhabited houses, and 30 families, 25 of whom are employed in agriculture. The church, which stands on an eminence, is dedicated to St. Peter and St. Paul, and consists of a nave and chancel, with a tower containing three bells. The living is a rectory, in the deanery of Cary; Rev. T. S. Phelps, incumbent; instituted 1802. Population, 1801, 171—1811, 178—1821, 165.

MARK—a parish in the hundred of Bempston, 10 miles N.W. from Glastonbury; containing 198 inhabited houses, and 219 families, 60 of whom are returned as being employed in agriculture, 28 in trade, &c. and 131 not comprised in either class. It is a parish of large extent, bounded on the south by the river Brew. The church is a noble building, consisting of a nave, chancel, and two side aisles, with a well-built tower at the west end, containing a clock and six bells. The living is rectorial, and a peculiar belonging to the Dean of Wells; Rev. J. Jarman, incumbent. Population, 1801, 875—1811, no return—1821, 1150.

MARKSBURY—a parish in the hundred of Keynsham, 6½ miles W.S.W. from Bath; containing, with the tything of Houndstreet, 65 inhabited houses, and 69 families, 53 of whom are employed in agriculture. About 2 miles west of the village is *Houndstreet-Park*, the residence of General Popham; the mansion stands on the site of the old manor-house, which belonged to the abbots of Glastonbury. The church is dedicated to St. Peter, and consists of a nave, with a tower containing four bells. The living is a rectory, in the deanery of Redcliff and Bedminster; Rev.

R. W. White, incumbent; instituted 1816. Population, 1801, 283—1811, 306—1821, 354.

MARSTON-BIGOTT—a parish in the hundred of Frome, $2\frac{1}{4}$ miles S. S. W. from Frome, containing 86 inhabited houses, and as many families, 55 of whom are employed in agriculture : on the south-east of the turnpike-road is the elegant seat of the Earl of Cork and Orrery. Dr. Collinson relates the following anecdote respecting an ancestor of the present noble lord :—
" Upon the death of King Charles the First, Roger Earl of Orrery quitted the service of the parliament in Ireland, and re- tired to his seat at Marston, which his father had purchased of Sir John Hippisley : the parish church was very near the mansion, and Lord Orrery never failed to go thither on Sundays ; but having one day sat there some time, and being disappointed of the then qualified minister, his lordship was preparing to go home, when his steward told him a person in the church offered to preach : his lordship (though he looked on the proposal only as a piece of enthusiasm) gave·permission, and was never more surprized or delighted than with the sermon, which was filled with learning, sense, and piety. His lordship would not suffer the preacher to escape unknown, but invited him to dinner, and inquiring of him his name, life, and fortune, received this answer—' My lord, my name is Asberry ; I am a clergyman of the church of England, and a loyal subject to the King : I have lived three years in a poor cottage under your garden-wall, within a few paces of your lordship's house ; my son lives with me, and we dig and read by turns ; I have a little money, and some few books, and I submit cheerfully to the will of Provi- dence.' This worthy and learned man (for such Lord Orrery always called him) lived some years longer at Marston, under an allowance of £30 per annum, which his lordship obtained for him, without an obligation of taking the covenant, and died there deservedly lamented." A neat cottage, consisting of one room only, was fitted up in the pleasure-grounds belonging to this seat, by the late Earl, in commemoration of the above

circumstance. The church of Marston-Bigott is a small modern structure, dedicated to St. Leonard, and is a rectory, in the deanery of Frome; Rev. R. J. Meade, incumbent; instituted 1821; patron the Earl of Cork and Orrery. Population, 1801, 366—1811, 301—1821, 471.

MARSTON-MAGNA—a parish in the hundred of Horethorne, 6 miles N. E. from Yeovil; containing 53 inhabited houses, and 62 families, 32 of whom are employed in agriculture. The church is dedicated to St. Mary, and consists of a nave, chancel, and north aisle, with an embattled tower at the west end, containing a clock and four bells. The living is a vicarage, in the deanery of Marston; Rev. J. Williams, incumbent; instituted 1785. Population, 1801, 303—1811, 303—1821, 324.

MARTOCK — a market-town and parish of considerable extent, and a hundred of itself: it is situated 4 miles S. W. from Ilchester, and 7 from Somerton, Yeovil, and Ilminster, and contains 376 inhabited houses, and 544 families, 260 of whom are employed in agriculture, 232 in trade, manufacture, or handicraft, and 52 not comprised in either class. The principal street is nearly a mile and a half in length, and in the centre of the town stands the market-house; but the market is now inconsiderable, having so many market-towns in its vicinity. The church is an elegant Gothic structure, 150 feet long, and 62 feet wide, consisting of a nave, chancel, north and south aisles, and porch, with a noble embattled tower at the west end, containing a clock and five bells. The interior of this church is well fitted up, and has an elegant altar-piece in stucco plaister, and a handsome organ. The living is a vicarage, in the deanery of Ilchester, and has been augmented with Queen Anne's bounty; Rev. Henry Bennett, incumbent; instituted 1798; patron, the Treasurer of Wells. At Load, a hamlet in this parish, is a chapel annexed to this church. Population of Martock, 1801, 2102—1811, 2356—1821, 2560.

MERE—a parish in the hundred of Glaston-Twelve-Hides, 4 miles N.W. from Glastonbury, containing 185 inhabited houses, and 213 families, 188 of whom are employed in agriculture. This parish was formerly a large moor, overflown by the sea, comprising upwards of 6000 acres of land; but the inclosures which have been made at different periods have rendered it valuable, and it is now well cultivated. At Godney, about 3 miles E. N. E. from the village, the Abbots of Glastonbury (who had a manor-house here), erected a chapel, and dedicated it to the Holy Trinity, on the site of which, in the year 1737, another was erected, having this inscription at the west end — "This chapel (sacred to the Holy Trinity) was restored to its ancient use, by Peter Davis, Esq. Recorder of Wells, in the year 1737." The church of Mere is a large Gothic structure, dedicated to St. Mary, and consists of a nave, chancel, and side aisles, with an embattled tower at the west end, containing a clock and six bells. The living is a vicarage, in the jurisdiction of Glaston; Rev. R. M. Austin, incumbent; instituted 1819. Population, 1801, 753—1811, 972—1821, 1151.

MELLS and LEIGH—a liberty on the E. side of the county, near Frome, locally situated in the hundred of Kilmersdon, of which it anciently formed a part; it comprises the two parishes of Mells and Leigh-on-Mendip; containing 380 inhabited houses, 409 families, 903 males, and 910 females. Total population, 1813.

MELLS — a parish in the above liberty, 3½ miles W. from Frome, containing 231 inhabited houses, and 260 families, 50 of whom are employed in agriculture, 126 in trade, manufacture, or handicraft, and 84 not comprised in either class. A considerable proportion of the population is employed in the coal and iron works. Here are two fairs annually; one on the Monday after Trinity week, and the other on Michaelmas-day. *Mells-Park*, delightfully situated at a short distance W. S.W. of the village, is the seat of T. S. Horner, Esq. The church is a handsome structure, consisting of a nave, chancel, and two side aisles, with a tower at the west end, containing a clock and six bells. The living is a rectory, in the deanery of Frome; Rev. John Bishop, D. D. incumbent; instituted 1783. Population, 1801, 1113—1811, 1061—1821, 1147.

MERRIOT—a parish in the hundred of Crewkerne, 2 miles N. from Crewkerne, containing 223 inhabited houses, and 235 families, 188 of whom are employed in agriculture. The church is dedicated to All-Saints, and consists of a nave and side aisles, with a tower at the west end, containing a clock and five bells. The living is a vicarage, in the deanery of Crewkerne, and in the gift of the Dean and Chapter of Bristol; Rev. Thomas Price, incumbent; instituted 1775. Population, 1801, 1017 — 1811, 1058—1821, 1212.

ST. MICHAEL— a parish in the hundred of North-Petherton, 5 miles S. from Bridgewater, containing 8 inhabited houses, and 10 families, the whole of whom are employed in agriculture. This small parish is entirely insulated in the parish of North-Petherton. The church is a small Gothic structure, with a low tower. It is a vicarage, in the deanery of Bridgewater; Rev. J. A. Templer, incumbent; instituted 1821. Population, 1801, no return—1811, 48—1821, 50.

MIDDLEZOY — a parish in the hundred of Whitley, 6 miles E. S. E. from Bridgewater, containing 106 inhabited houses, and 110 families, 99 of whom are employed in agriculture. The church, which stands on an eminence, at the north-west end of the village, is dedicated to the Holy Cross, and consists of a nave, chancel, south aisle, and a chapel on the north side; at the west end is a tower 70 feet high, containing a clock and six bells. The living is a vicarage, in the patronage of the Bishop of the diocese; Rev. W. B. Buller, incumbent; instituted 1821. Population, 1801, 494—1811, 536—1821, 605.

MIDSOMER-NORTON—a parish in the hundred of Chewton, 8½ miles S.S.W. from Bath, containing 418 inhabited houses, and 476 families, 130 of whom are employed in agriculture, 90 in trade, manufacture, or handicraft, and 256 not comprised in either class. This parish is very extensive, and the lands are equally applied to pasture and arable: here are several coal-works, in which the greater part of the population is employed. It has a fair, on the 25th April, for cattle, pigs, and pedlery. The church is an ancient edifice, dedicated to St. John the Baptist, and consists of a nave and side aisles, with a modern tower at the west end, containing a clock and eight bells—three of which were presented to this church by Charles the Second, whose statue was placed in a niche on the south side. The living is a vicarage, in the deanery of Frome, and in the gift of Christ Church College, Oxford; Rev. J. T. Becher, incumbent; instituted 1802. Population, 1801, 1552—1811, 1717—1821, 2326.

MILBORNE-PORT—a borough town in the hundred of Horethorne, 12 miles from Ilchester, 8 from Wincanton, and 114 from London, containing 281 inhabited houses, and 283 families, 98 of whom are employed in agriculture, 159 in trade, manufacture, or handicraft, and 26 not included in either class. It is a borough by prescription, and sent two members to parliament in the reign of Edward the First, but ceased to enjoy that privilege from the thirty-fifth year of that monarch till the fourth of Charles the First, when it was restored to that franchise. The parish is divided into three tithings, called Milborne-Port, Milborne-Wick, and Kingsbury-Regis; the latter lies in many places, promiscuously intermixed with some parts of the borough, both in the town and at Milborne-Wick. The principal manufacture consists in dowlas, linsey, stockings, and shoes. Here are two fairs annually, viz. June 5, and October 28. A short distance to the south-east of the town, is *Venn-House*, the seat of Sir W. C. Medlicott, Bart. The church is dedicated to St. John the Baptist, and is an ancient structure, built in the form of a cross, with a large quadrangular tower, containing six bells. The living is a rectory, in the gift of Winchester College; the Bishop of Hereford, incumbent; instituted 1798. Population, 1801, 953—1811, 1000—1821, 1440.

MILTON-CLEVEDON—a parish in the hundred of Bruton, 2½ miles N. N. W. from Bruton, on the turnpike-road to Shepton-Mallet, containing 38 inhabited houses, and 42 families, 26 of whom are employed in agriculture. The church is a small building, dedicated to St. James, and consists of a nave, chancel, and south aisle, having a low tower at the west end, containing four bells. The living is a vicarage, in the deanery of Cary; Rev. T. Selwyn, incumbent; instituted 1811; patron the King. Population, 1801, no return——1811, 199—1821, 189.

MILTON-PUDDIMORE—a parish in the hundred of Whitley, 2 miles N. E. from Ilchester; containing 23 inhabited houses, and 35 families, 31 of whom are employed in agriculture. The church is dedicated to St. Peter, and consists of a nave, with a tower in which are three bells. It is a rectory, in the deanery of Ilchester; Rev. Thomas Pearson, incumbent; instituted 1776. Population, 1801, no return—1811, 158—1821, 178.

MILVERTON—a market-town and parish, which gives name to the hundred in which it stands, situated 8 miles W. from Taunton, 4 miles N. N. W. from Wellington, and 152 from London, and contains 38 inhabited houses, and 415 families, 220 of whom are employed in agriculture, 166 in trade, manufacture, or handicraft, and 29 not comprised in either class. This town was anciently a borough, and carried on an extensive manufactory of serges, druggets, and flannels, some of which continue to be made here. It is governed by a portreeve and inferior officers, annually appointed. The market is on Friday, and here are three annual fairs, viz. on Easter Tuesday, July 25, and October 10. About 2 miles S. W. of Milverton, is *Spring-*

Grove, the residence of John Cridland, Esq. The church is dedicated to St. Michael, and consists of a nave, chancel, side aisles, and a vestry-room, with a tower containing six bells. The living is a vicarage, and a peculiar in the deanery of Taunton; Rev. Richard Darch, incumbent; instituted 1819. Population, 1801, 1669—1811, 1637—1821, 1930.

MINEHEAD—a sea-port, borough, and market-town, in the hundred of Carhampton, 25 miles from Taunton and Bridgewater, and 162 from London; containing 258 inhabited houses, and 280 families, 106 of whom are employed in agriculture, 76 in trade, manufacture, or handicraft, and 98 not included in either class. Minehead was formerly a place of considerable importance, and in the early part of the last century there were upwards of forty vessels belonging to this town engaged in the Irish trade alone. Several were also employed in trading to the West Indies, and 4000 barrels of herrings were annually exported to the Mediterranean; this trade has been on the decline for many years, and but little now remains, except in the article of coals. This town was incorporated by Queen Elizabeth, and endowed with considerable privileges. It was formerly governed by a portreeve, but now by two constables, chosen at the court-leet of the lord of the manor. Minehead returns two members to parliament, who are elected by such of the parishioners of Minehead and Dunster as are housekeepers, and do not receive alms: the constables are the legal returning officers. The market is on Wednesday, and here is a fair on the Wednesday in Whitsunweek. The country around Minehead is extremely beautiful and picturesque, and the mildness of the climate is such, that vegetation is a month earlier here than in most parts of England, which, with the advantages of a fine shore, commodious machines, and reasonable lodging, has induced a number of persons to resort to this place for sea-bathing. The church is situated on a considerable eminence, and is 116 feet long, and 42 wide, consisting of a nave, chancel, north aisle and vestry-room, with an

embattled tower 90 feet high, containing a clock, chimes, and
five bells. The living is a vicarage, in the deanery of Dunster;
Rev. T. F. Luttrell, incumbent; instituted 1821. Population,
1801, 1168—1811, 1037—1821, 1239.

MISTERTON—a parish in the hundred of Crewkerne, 2 miles
S. E. from Crewkerne; containing 77 inhabited houses, and 83
families, 42 of whom are employed in agriculture. The church
is a small edifice, consisting of a nave, chancel, and south aisle,
and is dedicated to St. Leonard. It is a vicarage, annexed to
Crewkerne. Population, 1801, 368—1811, 347—1821, 362.

MONK-SILVER—a parish in the hundred of Williton and Freemanners, 4½ miles S. from Watchett; containing 49 inhabited
houses, and 60 families, 43 of whom are employed in agriculture. The church is a small building, dedicated to All Saints,
consisting of a nave, chancel, and south aisle, with a tower containing a clock and four bells. The living is a rectory, the
advowson of which belongs to the Dean and Canons of Windsor;
Rev. William Walker, incumbent; instituted 1803. Population,
1801, 260—1811, 233—1821, 306.

MONKTON-COMBE—a parish in the hundred of Bath-Forum,
2½ miles S. S. E. from Bath; containing 151 inhabited houses,
and 155 families, 7 only of whom are employed in agriculture.
A considerable proportion of the population is employed in
cutting stone from the quarries on Combe-Down, of which the
greater part of the new streets, &c. in Bath have been built.
The church is dedicated to St. Michael, and consists of a nave
and chancel, with an open stone turret, in which hang two bells.
The living is a vicarage, in the deanery of Bath, annexed to
South Stoke. Population, 1801, 369—1811, 525—1821, 855.

MONKTON-WEST—a parish in the hundred of Whitley, 4 miles
N. E. from Taunton; containing 150 inhabited houses, and 198

families, 103 of whom are employed in agriculture. The church
is dedicated to St. Augustine, and consists of a nave, chancel, and
two side aisles, with a tower containing a clock and five bells.
The living is rectorial, in the deanery of Taunton ; Rev. F. G.
Crossman, D. D. incumbent in his own right; instituted 1812.
Population, 1801, 794—1811, 903—1821, 1004.

Montacute—a parish in the hundred of Tintinhull, 4½ miles
W. from Yeovil; containing 195 inhabited houses, and 237
families, 92 of whom are employed in agriculture. A short
distance from the village is St. Michael's-hill, the base of which
contains nearly twenty acres ; the ascent is very steep, and the
top terminates in a flat area of half an acre, on which is built a
round tower 60 feet high, and crowned with an open balustrade,
on which a flag is occasionally displayed. The summit commands a fine view, extending over a circumference of 300 miles,
in which on a clear day eighty churches may be distinctly seen.
The hill is covered all round with a plantation of oaks, elms,
firs and sycamores. This manor formerly belonged to Robert
Earl of Morton, brother to William the Conqueror, who built a
castle here, and named it after his friend Drogo de Montagu,
who came over to England with him. His son and successor
erected a monastery, and endowed it with the borough and
market of Montacute, and several other manors. At the general
dissolution of monasteries, the site of the priory was granted to
Sir William Petre, who sold it to Mr. Robert Freke, from whom
it came by purchase into the family of its present possessor,
John Phelips, Esq. The church is dedicated to St. Katherine,
and consists of a nave, chancel, and side aisles, with an embattled tower containing a clock and five bells. The living is
vicarial, in the deanery of Ilchester ; Rev. William Langdon,
incumbent ; instituted 1790. Population, 1801, 827—1811,
857—1821, 973.

Moorlinch—an extensive parish in the hundred of Whitley,

7 miles E. from Bridgewater; containing 54 inhabited houses, and 59 families, 53 of whom are employed in agriculture. The church is dedicated to St. Mary, and consists of a nave, with an embattled tower, containing six bells. The living is a vicarage, in the jurisdiction of Glastonbury, with the chapels of Catcot, Chilton, Edington, Stawell, and Sutton-Mallet, annexed; Rev. R. J. Luscombe, incumbent; instituted 1818. Population, 1801, 234—1811, 239—1821, 251.

MUCHELNEY—a parish in the hundred of Pitney, 2 miles S. S. E. from Langport; containing 51 inhabited houses, and 63 families, 53 of whom are employed in agriculture. This parish has been denominated the Great Island, from its having been insulated by the stagnant waters, occasioned by the overflowing of the rivers Ivel and Parret. Here was formerly a monastery, said to have been founded by King Athelstan, for Benedictine monks. Its ruins have been converted into a barn; part of the ancient kitchen and stone staircases may still be seen. The church of Muchelney is dedicated to St. Peter and St. Paul, and consists of a nave, chancel, and side aisles, with a tower containing five bells. The living is a vicarage, in the deanery of Ilchester, and in the patronage of the Dean and Chapter of Bristol; Rev. J. H. Mules, incumbent. Population, 1801, 283—1811, 261—1821, 329.

MUDFORD—a parish in the hundred of Stone, 3 miles N. N. E. from Yeovil; containing 76 inhabited houses, and 77 families, 70 of whom are employed in agriculture. This parish received its name from there having formerly been a ford through the river Ivel, which passes near the village, having over it a bridge with two arches. The church is a large structure, dedicated to St. Mary, and consists of a nave, chancel, and north aisle, with a tower, containing a clock and five bells. The living is a vicarage, in the deanery of Marston, and in the presentation of the Dean and Chapter of Wells; Rev. John Bowen, incumbent; instituted 1796. Population, 1801, 352—1811, 315—1821, 375.

NAILSEA—a parish in the hundred of Portbury, 5½ miles N. from Wrington; containing 289 inhabited houses, and 335 families, 186 of whom are employed in agriculture, 127 in trade, manufacture, or handicraft, and 22 not comprised in either class : here are several coal-mines in this parish, and a crown-plate glass manufactory has been established upwards of thirty years. The living is a curacy, in the deanery of Redcliff and Bedminster, and is a chapel to Wraxall, but the inhabitants have the privilege of burial at their own church, which consists of a nave, chancel, and side aisle, with a tower containing five bells. Population, 1801, 1093—1811, 1313—1821, 1678.

NEMPNETT—a parish in the hundred of Hartcliff with Bedminster, 9½ miles S. S. W. from Bristol ; containing 44 inhabited houses, and 53 families, 49 of whom are employed in agriculture. Between the church of Nempnett and that of Butcombe, near Nempnett-farm, is a tumulus, or barrow, 60 yards in length, 20 in breadth, and 15 in height; it is a mass of stones, supported on each side by a wall of thin flakes ; the space between contains two rows of cells, or cavities; these cells are entered from north to south, and are divided from each other by large stones, placed on their edges, and covered by others still larger ; several skulls, and a quantity of human bones, were found at the time it was opened, but no coins or other reliques were discovered that could afford any clue as to the time when this ancient sepulchre was constructed. The church of Nempnett is a small structure, consisting of a nave, with a tower containing five bells ; it is a chapel to Compton-Martin. Population, 1801, 253—1811, 225—1821, 264.

NETHER-STOWEY—a small market-town and parish, in the hundred of Williton and Freemanners, 9 miles W. N. W.

from Bridgewater, and 149 from London ; containing 153 inhabited houses, and 155 families, 66 of whom are employed in agriculture, 72 in trade, manufacture, or handicraft, and 17 not included in either class. The town consists of three streets, and has a market on Tuesdays, likewise a fair for cattle on the 18th September. On a hill to the west of the town formerly stood a castle, and near to it was a church, dedicated to St. Michael, neither of which now remain. The church of Stowey stands nearly half a mile east from the town, and is dedicated to St. Mary; it is a substantial building, 70 feet long, and 18 feet wide, with a tower at the west end, containing six bells. The living is a vicarage, and a peculiar ; the advowson belongs to the Dean and Canons of Windsor ; Rev. John Keate, incumbent ; instituted 1820. Population, 1801, 586—1811, 620—1821, 773.

NETTLECOMBE—a parish in the hundred of Williton and Freemanners, 7 miles S. S. W. from Watchett ; containing 59 inhabited houses, and 66 families, 54 of whom are employed in agriculture. *Nettlecombe-House,* the seat of Sir John Trevelyan, Bart. is pleasantly situated in a vale near the church, surrounded with well-cultivated hills, having to the west a beautiful plantation of oaks. The church is a handsome structure, dedicated to St. Mary, consisting of a nave, chancel, and side ai-les, with an embattled tower, containing a clock and three bells. The living is a rectory, in the deanery of Dunster ; Rev. G. Trevelyan, incumbent ; instituted 1797. Population, 1801, 329—1811, 328,—1821, 372.

NEWTON ST. LOE—a parish in the hundred of Wellow, 3 miles W. from Bath ; containing 50 inhabited houses, and 84 families, 6 of whom are returned as being employed in agriculture, 6 in trade, manufacture, or handicraft, and 72 not comprised in either class ; of the latter number, a great proportion is engaged in working the coal-pits. *Newton-Park,* a short distance south-west of the village, is the seat of William Gore

Langton, Esq. The church is dedicated to the Holy Trinity, and consists of a nave, chancel, and south aisle, with a tower containing a clock and five bells. The living is a rectory, in the deanery of Bath; Rev. Peter Gunning, incumbent; instituted 1820. Population, 1801, 371—1811, 384—1821, 431.

NINEHEAD—a parish in the hundred of Taunton and Taunton-Dean, 2 miles N. from Wellington; containing 38 inhabited houses, and 57 families, 49 of whom are employed in agriculture. *Ninehead-Court,* the seat of W. A. Sanford, Esq. is pleasantly situated a short distance to the south of the turnpike-road; the river Tone runs through the park. The church is dedicated to All Saints, and consists of a nave, chancel, and side aisles, with an embattled tower, containing five bells. The living is a rectory, in the patronage of the Crown; Rev. J. Sanford, incumbent; instituted 1810. Population, 1801, 371—1811, 324—1821, 308.

NORTHOVER—a parish in the hundred of Tintinhull, divided from the town of Ilchester, on the north, by the river Ivel; it contains 21 inhabited houses, and as many families, 12 of whom are employed in agriculture. The church, which is dedicated to St. Andrew, consists of a nave, chancel, and a tower, in which are four bells. The living is a vicarage, in the deanery of Ilchester; Rev. Nathaniel Bartlett, incumbent; instituted 1780. Population, 1801, 56—1811, 73—1821, 121.

NORTON-FERRARS (*vulgo* NORTON-FERRIS) — the name of a hundred, bordering on the counties of Wilts and Dorset; it received its name from a hamlet, in the parish of Kilmington, called Norton-Ferrars, from its having been long possessed by the family of Ferrars, of Chartley, who were also lords of this hundred, and kept their court for it at Norton-Ferrars, where they had their mansion. It contains the following parishes; viz. BRATTON, CHARLTON-MUSGRAVE, CUCKLING-

TON, KILMINGTON, PEN-SELWOOD, SHEPTON-MONTAGUE, STOKE-TRISTER, and WINCANTON, containing 876 inhabited houses, 980 families, 2404 males, and 2543 females. Total population, 4947.

NORTON-FITZWARREN—a parish in the hundred of Taunton and Taunton-Dean, 2 miles W. N. W. from Taunton ; containing 67 inhabited houses, and 94 families, 57 of whom are employed in agriculture. The church is dedicated to All Saints, and consists of a nave, chancel, north aisle, and tower. The living is a rectory, in the deanery of Taunton ; Rev. Joseph Guerin, incumbent ; instituted 1797. Population, 1801, 371—1811, 422—1821, 475.

NORTON-MALREWARD—a parish in the hundred of Chew, 5½ miles S. from Bristol ; containing 19 inhabited houses, and 22 families, 16 of whom are employed in agriculture. The church consists of a nave, chancel, and porch, with a tower at the west end, containing two bells. The living is rectorial, in the deanery of Redcliff and Bedminster ; Rev. W. P. Wait, incumbent in his own right ; instituted 1819. Population, 1801, 114 —1811, 142—1821, 118.

NORTON-MIDSOMER—See MIDSOMER-NORTON.

NORTON-ST. PHILIPS—a small town in the liberty of Hinton and Norton, and locally in the hundred of Wellow, situated 7 miles S. from Bath, and containing 134 inhabited houses, and 150 families, 34 of whom are employed in agriculture, 84 in trade, manufacture, or handicraft, and 32 not comprised in either class. This town had formerly a weekly market, and four annual fairs ; two of the latter are still held, one on May 1st, and the other on August 29th. The church is dedicated to St. Philip and St. James, and is an ancient building, consisting of a nave, chancel, and side aisles, with a neat embattled tower at the west end 70 feet high, containing a clock and six bells. The living is a vicarage, in the deanery of Frome, and in the gift of the Bishop of the diocese; Rev. J. Cammeline, incumbent; instituted 1819. Population, 1801, 557—1811, 593—1821, 669.

NORTON under HAMDON—a parish in the hundred of Houndsborough Berwick and Coker, 6 miles W. from Yeovil; containing 67 inhabited houses, and 106 families, 43 of whom are employed in agriculture : to the north-east of this village is Hamdon-hill, one of the most extensive Roman encampments in this part of the kingdom, being nearly three miles in circuit; vestiges of several parts of the works still remain, and a number of Roman coins have been dug up : this hill is likewise remarkable for its free-stone quarries. Most of the churches for several miles round, in this and the adjoining county, have been built with this stone, which possesses the excellent quality of hardening by time. The church of Norton is dedicated to St. Mary, and consists of a nave, chancel, and side aisles, with a tower at the west end, containing a clock and five bells. The living is a rectory, in the deanery of Ilchester; Rev. William Tarish, incumbent; instituted 1806. Population, 1801, 334—1811, 417—1821, 482.

NUNNEY—a parish in the hundred of Frome, 3 miles S. W. from Frome; containing, with the hamlet of Trudox-hill (which is within this parish) 237 inhabited houses, and 246 families, 92 of whom are employed in agriculture. On the west side of this village stands the castle, which is a fine vestige of antiquity; it was built by Sir John Delamere about the thirteenth century; its form is a double square, with a round castellated tower at each corner, 63 feet high, and crowned with four lofty turrets, covered with ivy ; the whole is surrounded by an elliptical moat, which communicates with a river called Holwell, that runs through the parish. This castle was garrisoned for the King, in the civil war, but was taken by the parliament army September

8, 1645, and burnt, to prevent its future service to the royalists.
Here is a fair for cattle, &c. on November 11th.   The church of
Nunney is dedicated to St. Peter, and consists of a nave, chancel,
two side aisles, and a porch, with a handsome tower 63 feet
high, surmounted with four pinnacles, and containing a clock
and six bells.   The living is a rectory, in the deanery of Frome ;
Rev. Charles Richards, incumbent ; instituted 1817.   Population,
1801, 919—1811, 1124—1821, 1120.

OAKE—a parish in the hundred of Taunton and Taunton-
Dean, 2½ miles E. from Milverton, containing 27 inhabited
houses, and 32 families, 29 of whom are employed in agriculture.   This village derived its appellation from the number of
oaks with which this neighbourhood formerly abounded, its
ancient names being *Ac*, *Acha*, and *Ache*, all signifying an oak
tree.   The church is dedicated to St. Bartholomew, and consists
of a nave, chancel, and south aisle, with a tower containing four
bells.   The living is rectorial, in the deanery of Taunton ;   Rev.
T. F. Foord Bowes, incumbent ; instituted 1803.   Population,
1801, 172—1811, 182—1821, 189.

OARE—a parish in the hundred of Carhampton, 6 miles W.
from Porlock, at the north-west extremity of the county, on
the borders of Devonshire ; containing 11 inhabited houses, and
12 families, 11 of whom are employed in agriculture.   The
village is situated in a vale, through which runs a stream,
formed by several springs that rise in the hills on the south and
east sides of the parish, and pursuing its course under Moles-
mead-bridge, falls into the sea to the west of Foreland-Point.
The church is a small structure, consisting of a nave and tower,
with one bell.   The living is a rectory, in the deanery of Dunster ;   Rev. John Blackmore, incumbent ;   instituted 1809.
Population, 1801, no return—1811, 57—1821, 66.

ODCOMBE—a parish in the hundred of Houndsborough Berwick and Coker, 3 miles W. from Yeovil ; containing 76 in-

habited houses, and 106 families. The church consists of a nave and chancel, with a tower in the centre, and is dedicated to St. Peter and St. Paul. The living is a rectory, in the deanery of Ilchester, and in the patronage of the Dean and Canons of Christ Church, Oxford; Rev. P. A. French, incumbent; instituted 1803. Population, 1801, 428—1811, 477—1821, 540.

OLD-CLEVE—*See* CLEVE-OLD.

ORCHARDLEIGH—a small parish in the hundred of Frome, 2½ miles N. from Frome; containing 9 inhabited houses, and as many families, 6 of whom are employed in agriculture. *Orchard-leigh-Park*, the seat of Sir T. S. Champneys, Bart. comprises nearly the whole of the parish. The church is a small structure, consisting of a nave only. The living is a rectory, in the deanery of Frome; Rev. Joseph Algar, incumbent; instituted 1818. Population, 1801, 32—1811, 32—1821, 27.

ORCHARD-PORTMAN—a parish in the hundred of Taunton and Taunton Dean, 3 miles S.S.E. from Taunton; containing 15 inhabited houses, and 21 families, 14 of whom are employed in agriculture. This parish received its adjunctive name from the ancient family of Portman, to distinguish it from the manor of Orchard-Wyndham, near Watchet. The church is dedicated to St. Michael, and consists of a nave, chancel, south aisle, and an embattled tower containing four bells. The living is a rectory, in the deanery of Taunton; Rev. Henry Bowen, incumbent; instituted 1806. Population, 1801, 131—1811, 100—1821, 100.

OTTERFORD—a parish in the hundred of Taunton and Taunton-Dean, 7 miles S. from Taunton; containing 55 inhabited houses, and 64 families, 54 of whom are employed in agriculture. This parish is bounded on the south and west by the county of Devon, on the north is Blagdon-Hill, from which there is an extensive prospect over the whole of Taunton-Dean, and commands a fine view of the Welch mountains. The church is dedicated to St. Leonard, and consists of a nave and chancel, with a tower, in which are four bells. The living is a curacy, in the deanery of Taunton; Rev. John Gale, incumbent; instituted 1810. Population, 1801, 259—1811, 286—1821, 366.

OTTERHAMPTON—a parish in the hundred of Cannington, 6 miles N. W. from Bridgewater; containing 33 inhabited houses, and 41 families, 35 of whom are employed in agriculture. The church consists of a nave, with a tower at the west end containing four bells. It is a rectory, in the deanery of Bridgewater; Rev. J. Jeffrey, incumbent; instituted 1804. Population, 1801, 239—1811, 209—1821, 221.

OTHERY—a parish in the hundred of Whitley, 7 miles E. S. E. from Bridgewater; containing 95 inhabited houses, and 104 families, 88 of whom are employed in agriculture: The church, which stands upon an eminence, is dedicated to the Holy Cross, and consists of a nave, chancel, and two side aisles, with a tower 70 feet high, containing a clock and six bells. The living is a vicarage, in the patronage of the Bishop of the diocese; Rev. G. G. Beadon, incumbent; instituted 1821. Population, 1801, 384—1811, 433—1821, 509.

OVER-STOWEY—a parish in the hundred of Cannington, 1 mile S. S. W. from Nether-Stowey, containing 71 inhabited houses, and 132 families, 129 of whom are employed in agriculture. A silk manufacture has lately been established in this parish. The church consists of a nave, chancel, and north aisle, with a tower at the west end containing five bells. The living is a vicarage, in the deanery of Bridgewater; Rev. W. B. Buller, incumbent; instituted 1820. Population, 1801, 468—1811, 461—1821, 587.

PAULTON—a parish in the hundred of Chewton, 10 miles S. W.

from Bath, and 10 N. E. from Wells; containing 272 inhabited houses, and 297 families, 28 of whom are returned as being employed in agriculture, 54 in trade, manufacture, or handicraft, and 215 not comprised in either class. Most of the latter number are employed in working the coal-mines, which are numerous in this parish. The church was rebuilt in 1753, of stone, from the quarries at Doulting, and consists of a nave and chancel, with a tower containing a clock and five bells. The living is a curacy, annexed to Chewton-Mendip, Population, 1801, 1019 —1811, 1160—1821, 1380.

PAWLET—a parish in the hundred of North-Petherton, 5 miles N. from Bridgewater; containing 69 inhabited houses, and 98 families, 83 of whom are employed in agriculture. The church is dedicated to St. John the Baptist, and consists of a nave, chancel, and cross aisle, with a tower containing a clock and five bells. The living, which is a vicarage, and denominates a deanery, is in the gift of the Crown; Rev. Edward Crosse, incumbent; instituted 1789. Population, 1801, 429—1811, 433 —1821, 529.

PENDOMER—a parish in the hundred of Houndsborough Berwick and Coker, 5 miles S. S. W. from Yeovil; containing 15 inhabited houses, and as many families, the whole of whom are employed in agriculture. The church stands on an eminence, and is a small Gothic building, consisting of a nave and chancel, with a turret, in which are two bells. The living is a rectory, in the deanery of Ilchester; Rev. H. Helyar, incumbent; instituted 1810. Population, 1801, 95—1811, 78—1821, 70.

PENNARD-EAST—a parish in the hundred of Whitestone, 4½ miles S. from Shepton-Mallet; containing 131 inhabited houses, and 153 families, 38 of whom are employed in agriculture. The church is dedicated to All-Saints, and consists of a nave, chancel, and side aisles, with a tower at the west end containing a clock and five bells. The living is a vicarage, in the deanery of Cary, and in the gift of the Bishop of the diocese; Rev. Henry Gould, incumbent; instituted 1790. Population, 1801, 644—1811, 629—1821, 755.

PENNARD-WEST—a parish in the hundred of Glaston-Twelve-Hides, 3½ miles E. from Glastonbury, and 5 S. W. from Shepton-Mallet; containing 123 inhabited houses, and 157 families, 45 of whom are employed in agriculture. The church is a large Gothic structure, dedicated to St. Nicholas, and consists of a nave, chancel, and side aisles, with a large tower at the west end containing five bells. The living is a curacy, annexed to St. John's church, Glastonbury. Population, 1801, 727—1811, 831—1821, 890.

PENSFORD—a hamlet and chapelry in the parish of Publow, and in the hundred of Keynsham, 6 miles S. S. E. from Bristol; containing 71 inhabited houses, and 76 families, 49 of whom are employed in agriculture. Here was formerly a very considerable market on Tuesdays, and a large manufacture of woollen cloth, now declined. The church is a neat modern edifice, dedicated to St. Thomas-à-Becket, and is a chapel to Stanton-Drew. Here are two annual fairs, one on the 6th May, and the other November 8th. Population, 1801, 306—1811, 296—1821, 319.

PEN-SELWOOD—a parish in the hundred of Norton-Ferrars, 4 miles N. E. from Wincanton; containing 53 inhabited houses, and 68 families, 41 of whom are employed in agriculture. The church is dedicated to St. Michael, and consists of a nave, chancel and porch, with a square embattled tower 50 feet high, containing three bells. The living is vicarial, in the deanery of Cary; Rev. Charles Digby, incumbent; instituted 1806. Population, 1801, 265—1811, 299—1821, 332.

PARRET-NORTH—a parish in the hundred of Houndsborough

Berwick and Coker, 4 miles E. from Crewkerne, on the borders of Dorsetshire, seated on the river Parret, from which it derives its name; it contains 71 inhabited houses, and 86 families, 47 of whom are employed in agriculture. Near the church is a handsome stone mansion, the residence of William Hoskins, Esq. The church is built in the form of a cross, with a tower in the centre, containing a clock and three bells. The living is a rectory, in the deanery of Ilchester; Rev. Henry Hoskins, incumbent; instituted 1814. Population, 1801, 426—1811, 364—1821, 387.

PETHERTON-NORTH—the name of a hundred in the western part of the county, lying around Bridgewater, and comprises the following parishes, viz. BAWDRIP, BRIDGEWATER, (Borough), CHEDZOY, CHILTON-TRINITY, DURSTON, PAWLET, PETHERTON-NORTH, St. MICHAEL, THURLOXON and WEMBDON, containing 934 inhabited houses, 1036 families, 2595 males, and 2650 females. Total population, 5245.

PETHERTON-NORTH—a parish in the above hundred, 3 miles S. from Bridgewater; containing 581 inhabited houses, and 603 families, 405 of whom are employed in agriculture. This parish is very extensive, and derives its name from the river Parret, which partly bounds it on the east in its course to Bridgewater. Here was formerly a large market on Saturdays, and an annual fair, the latter of which is still held on the 1st of May. The church is a large handsome structure, dedicated to St. Mary, and consists of a nave, chancel, and side aisles, with an elegant castellated tower of Gothic architecture. The living is a vicarage, in the deanery of Bridgewater; Rev. William George, incumbent; instituted 1801. Population, 1801, 2346—1811, 2615 —1821, 3091.

PETHERTON-SOUTH—the name of a hundred in the southern part of the county, divided into three parts; the first contains five parishes around the town from which it receives its name ; the second part is separated from the former by a narrow tract of the hundred of Tintinhull ; and the third part contains one parish on the borders of Devonshire : the whole comprises the following parishes, viz. BARRINGTON, CHAFFCOMBE, CHILLINGTON, CRICKET ST. THOMAS, CUDWORTH, DOWLISH-WAKE, KNOWLE ST. GILES, LOPEN, PETHERTON-SOUTH, SEAVINGTON ST. MARY, SEAVINGTON ST. MICHAEL, DINNINGTON, SHEPTON-BEAUCHAMP, and WHITE-STANTON, containing 1039 inhabited houses, 1207 families, 2784 males, and 2941 females. Total population, 5725.

PETHERTON-SOUTH—an ancient market-town and parish in the hundred to which it gives name, 7 miles S.W. from Ilchester, 7 N. from Langport, and 137 from London ; containing 401 inhabited houses, and 436 families, 246 of whom are employed in agriculture, 107 in trade, manufacture, or handicraft, and 83 not comprised in either class. The river Parret, from which the town takes its name, bounds it on the east side, over which, on the Roman Fosse-road, there is a stone bridge of three arches ; this bridge was formerly of wood, which had become ruinous, and two children having been drowned in the river near it, the parents of those children rebuilt it of stone, and caused their infant effigies to be placed thereon, to commemorate the circumstance. In a field near this bridge, a pot of Roman coins was dug up in the year 1720, containing about six pecks. The town principally consists of three streets, which meet in a triangular form. It had formerly a very considerable market on Thursdays, now nearly declined, on account of the larger market-towns in its vicinity. A fair on July 5, for cattle, sheep, pedlery, and toys, is still held here. The church stands in the centre of the town, and is a large structure, dedicated to St. Peter and St. Paul. It is built in the form of a cross, with a large octangular tower, containing a clock, chimes, and six bells, surmounted with a spire, covered with lead. Behind the altar is a vestry-room, having two doors, formerly used for auricular confession. The living is a vicarage, in the gift of the Dean and Chapter of Bristol; Rev. F. Simpson, incumbent; instituted 1813. Population, 1801, 1674—1811, 1867—1821, 2090.

PILTON—a parish in the hundred of Whitestone, 2 miles S. S. W. from Shepton-Mallet; containing 209 inhabited houses, and 227 families, 152 of whom are employed in agriculture. About a mile N. W. from the village is *Westholm-House,* the residence of Thomas Henry Ernst, Esq. The church is a spacious building, consisting of a nave, chancel, and north aisle, with a tower at the west end 60 feet high, containing a clock and six bells. In the year 1782 the turret, and one of the pinnacles on the tower were damaged by lightning; three men were in the belfry at the time, one of whom was instantly struck dead, and the other two were rendered for some time insensible. The living is a vicarage, and a peculiar belonging to the precenter of Wells; Rev. W. H. Barnard, incumbent; instituted 1821. Population, 1801, 780—1811, 1158—1821, 1100.

PITCOMBE—a small parish in the hundred of Bruton, 1½ mile S. from Bruton, containing, with the tything of Hadspen, 65 inhabited houses, and 83 families, 68 of whom are employed in agriculture. *Pitcombe-House,* situated a short distance from the church, is the residence of Capt. N. Jekyl; and about a mile and a half to the south-west is *Hadspen-House,* the seat of Henry Hobhouse, Esq. The church of Pitcombe is a neat edifice, dedicated to St. Leonard, and consists of a nave, with a tower at the west end containing three bells. The living is a curacy, in the deanery of Cary; Rev. John Dampier, incumbent; instituted 1819. Population, 1801, 326—1811, 310—1821, 431.

PITMINSTER—a parish in the hundred of Taunton and Taunton-Dean, 4 miles S. from Taunton, containing, with the tythings of Blagdon, Duddlestone, Fulford, Leigh, Poundesford, and Trendle,

262 inhabited houses, and 280 families, 220 of whom are employed in agriculture. *Barton-Grange,* the seat of Frederick Grey Cooper, Esq. is situated a short distance north-east of the village, adjoining to the parish of Corfe. The church of Pitminster is a handsome Gothic structure, dedicated to St. Andrew and St. Mary, and consists of a nave, chancel, and side aisles, with an octangular tower surmounted by a neat spire. The living is a vicarage, in the deanery of Taunton; Rev. M. Dickson, incumbent; instituted 1789. Population, 1801, 1070—1811, 1206—1821, 1416.

PITNEY—the name of a hundred in the southern part of the county, including the town of Langport, and the parishes of Pitney and Muchelney, and contains 247 inhabited houses, 318 families, 833 males, and 801 females. Total population, 1634.

Pitney—a parish in the hundred to which it gives name, pleasantly situated a short distance north from the centre of the turnpike-road leading from Langport to Somerton : it contains 64 inhabited houses, and 70 families, 66 of whom are employed in agriculture. The church is dedicated to St. John the Baptist, and consists of a nave, chancel, and south aisle, with a tower containing four bells. The living is a rectory, and a peculiar in the deanery of Ilchester; Rev. Charles Wightwick, incumbent; instituted 1819. Population, 1801, 243—1811, 279—1821, 301.

Pointington—a parish in the hundred of Horethorne, 2 miles W. N. W. from Milborne-Port, on the confines of Devonshire, containing 36 inhabited houses, and 37 families, 31 of whom are employed in agriculture. The village is surrounded with hills, and is watered by a stream formed from seven springs that rise about 1½ mile to the north, on Horethorne-Down. The church is dedicated to All-Saints, and consists of a nave, chancel, and south aisle. It is a rectory, in the deanery of Marston; Rev. T. Woodforde, incumbent; instituted 1810. Population, 1801, 157—1811, 172—1821, 162.

PORLOCK—a small sea-port town and parish in the hundred of Carhampton, 5½ miles W. from Minehead; containing 138 inhabited houses, and 151 families, 78 of whom are employed in agriculture, 49 in trade, manufacture, or handicraft, and 24 not included in either class. The situation is very romantic, being nearly surrounded on all sides, except the sea, by steep and lofty hills, intersected by deep vales and hollow glens. A weekly market was formerly held here by royal licence; there are now only three in the year, which may be more properly called fairs, viz. on the Thursday before the 12th May, Thursday before the 9th October, and the Thursday before the 12th November. The quay is situated at the western corner of the bay, which forms a concave of nearly three miles. The chief trade consists in importing coal and lime from the opposite coast. The church is dedicated to St. Dubritius, and consists of a nave, chancel, south aisle, vestry-room, and porch, with a low tower at the west end. The living is a rectory, in the deanery of Dunster; Rev. John Pitman, incumbent; instituted 1811; patron, the King. Population, 1801, 600—1811, 633—1821, 769.

PORTBURY—the name of a hundred at the northern extremity of the county, near Bristol, comprising the parishes of ABBOTS-LEIGH, CLAPTON, CLEVELAND, FLAX-BOURTON, EASTON ST. GEORGES, NAILSEA, PORTBURY, PORTISHEAD, TICKENHAM, WALTON in GORDANO, WESTON-NORTH, or WESTON in GORDANO, and WRAXALL, containing 1339 inhabited houses, 1536 families, 3807 males, and 3773 females. Total population, 7580.

PORTBURY—a parish in the above hundred, 7 miles W. N. W. from Bristol; containing 105 inhabited houses, and 127 families, 84 of whom are employed in agriculture. This place was formerly a town of considerable importance, having had a weekly market and an annual fair, a charter for which was procured by Robert Fitz-Harding, afterwards Earl Berkley, which title he received in consideration of the services he rendered to the

Empress Maud, and her son Henry, in opposition to King Stephen. A fair continues to be held here on Whit Monday, for cattle, sheep, &c. The church is a large structure, dedicated to St. Mary, and consists of a nave, chancel, north and south aisles, and chapel, with a large tower at the west end containing five bells. The living is a vicarage, in the deanery of Redcliff and Bedminster; Rev. C. Newsam, incumbent; instituted 1806. Population, 1801, 509—1811, 552—1821, 594.

PORTISHEAD—a parish in the hundred of Portbury, 10 miles W. N. W. from Bristol; containing 86 inhabited houses, and 112 families, 97 of whom are employed in agriculture. The church is a good building, remarkable for its lofty and elegant tower. The living is a rectory, in the deanery of Redcliff and Bedminster, and in the gift of the Corporation of Bristol; Rev. J. Shipton, D. D. incumbent; instituted 1791. Population, 1801, 387—1811, 369—1821, 506.

PRESTON—a parish in the hundred of Stone, 1½ mile W. from Yeovil; containing 53 inhabited houses, and 63 families, 39 of whom are employed in agriculture. The church consists of a nave, chancel, and side aisles, with a tower at the west end containing four bells. It is a vicarage, in the deanery of Marston, united with Yeovil; Rev. John Hammond, incumbent; instituted 1820. Population, 1801, 260—1811, 284—1821, 317.

PRIDDY—a parish in the hundred of Wells-Forum, 5 miles N. N. W. from Wells; containing 28 inhabited houses, and 32 families, the whole of whom are employed in agriculture. A large fair for cattle, horses, &c. is held here on the 21st of August. The church is dedicated to St. Lawrence, and consists of a nave, chancel, and side aisles, with a tower containing three bells. The living is a curacy, united to Westbury. Population, 1801, 119—1811, 109—1821, 141.

PRIORS ASH, or ASH PRIORS—a parish in the hundred of West Kingsbury, 6 miles N.W. from Taunton; containing 42 inhabited houses, and 46 families, 39 of whom are employed in agriculture. This parish was designated Priors Ash, from having formerly belonged to the Priors of Taunton, who had a court here. The church is a small structure, consisting of a nave, chancel, and north aisle, with a tower in which are three bells. The living is a curacy, in the deanery of Taunton; Rev. Nicholas Spencer, incumbent; instituted 1821. Population, 1801, 155 —1811, 150—1821, 201.

PRISTON—a parish in the hundred of Keynsham, 5 miles S.W. from Bath; containing 56 inhabited houses, and 61 families, 18 of whom are employed in agriculture. The church is dedicated to St. Luke, and consists of a nave, with a tower containing five bells. The living is a rectory, in the deanery of Redcliff and Bedminster; Rev. John Hammond, incumbent; instituted 1820. Population, 1801, 314—1811, 318—1821, 286.

PUBLOW—a parish united with Pensford, in the hundred of Keynsham, 6 miles S.S.E. from Bristol; containing 167 inhabited houses, and 175 families, 63 of whom are employed in agriculture. The church is dedicated to All Saints, and consists of a nave, chancel, and two side aisles, with a tower at the west end in which are six bells. The living is an impropriate curacy, in the deanery of Redcliff and Bedminster; Rev. A. Dawberry, incumbent. Population, 1801, 786—1811, 820—1821, 836.

PUCKINGTON—a parish in the hundred of Abdick and Bulstone, 3 miles N. N. E. from Ilminster; containing 31 inhabited houses, and 39 families, 30 of whom are employed in agriculture. The church is dedicated to St. Andrew, and consists of a nave, chancel, and small aisle, with a tower 60 feet high, containing five bells. The living is a rectory, in the deanery of Crewkerne, in the gift of the Bishop of the diocese by lapse;

Rev. E. B. Troyte, D. D. incumbent; instituted 1787. Population, 1801, 171—1811, 151—1821, 220.

PUDDIMORE-MILTON—*See* MILTON-PUDDIMORE.

PURITON—a parish in the hundred of Huntspill and Puriton, 4 miles N. N. E. from Bridgewater; containing 66 inhabited houses, and 76 families, 61 of whom are employed in agriculture. The church is a Gothic edifice, consisting of a nave and chancel, with a large tower, in which are six bells. The living is a vicarage, united with Woolavington. Population, 1801, 332—1811, 332—1821, 350.

PUXTON—a parish in the hundred of Winterstoke, 5 miles N. N. W. from Axbridge; containing 27 inhabited houses, and 30 families, the whole of whom are employed in agriculture. The church consists of a nave and chancel, with a tower containing two bells. Previous to the year 1772 the church was a chapel of ease to Banwell; it is now a perpetual curacy, and a peculiar, in the deanery of Axbridge, and in the gift of the Dean and Chapter of Bristol; Rev. R. Davis, incumbent; instituted 1804. Population, 1801, no return—1811, 122—1821, 137.

PYLLE—a parish in the hundred of Whitestone, 4 miles S. from Shepton-Mallet; containing 28 inhabited houses, and 36 families, 32 of whom are employed in agriculture. The church is dedicated to St. Thomas-à-Becket, and consists of a nave, chancel, and north aisle, or chapel, with a tower at the west end containing five bells. The living is a rectory, in the deanery of Cary; Rev. William Langdon, incumbent; instituted 1765. Population, 1801, 150—1811, 182—1821, 176.

QUANTOCKSHEAD-EAST—a parish in the hundred of Williton and Freemanners, 4 miles E. from Watchet; containing 52 inhabited houses, and 53 families, 29 of whom are employed in agri-

culture. The church is dedicated to St. Mary, and consists of a
nave, chancel, and a small chapel on the north side, with a tower
at the west end containing four bells. The living is rectorial, in
the deanery of Bridgewater ; Rev. A. F. Luttrell, incumbent ; instituted 1818. Population, 1801, 262—1811, 261—1821, 276.

QUANTOCKSHEAD-WEST, or ST. AUDRIES—a parish adjoining
the above, and in the same hundred, 3 miles E. from Watchet ;
containing 42 inhabited houses, and 45 families, 34 of whom
are employed in agriculture. A short distance N. W. from the
church is St. Audries-House, the residence of Miss Balch. The
church consists of a nave, chancel, and south aisle, with a tower
at the west end, in which are two bells. The living is a rectory,
in the deanery of Dunster ; Rev. Charles Alford, incumbent ;
instituted 1814. Population, 1801, 192—1811, 187—1821, 225.

QUEEN-CAMEL—a parish in the hundred of Catash, 4½ miles
E. from Ilchester; containing 144 inhabited houses, and
as many families, 77 of whom are employed in agriculture.
This is an extensive parish, situated on the river Camel, and
had its additional name from having been formerly vested in the
Queens of the realm : about two centuries since it was a town
of some note, having had a charter for two weekly markets, and
four annual fairs ; two of the latter are still held, one on Trinity
Tuesday, and the other on the 25th October. Within a short
distance from the river rises a spring, the water of which has
been used with success in scrophulous cases ; it is very cold,
and offensive to the smell, which is much like that of burnt gun-
powder mixed with water. The church consists of a nave,
chancel, north and south aisles, and porch, with a tower 20 feet
high, containing a clock and six bells. The living is a vicarage,
in the deanery of Marston ; Rev. T. H. Pearson, incumbent ;
instituted 1785. Population, 1801, 584—1811, 656—1821, 712.

QUEEN-CHARLTON—a parish in the hundred of Keynsham,

2 miles S. W. from Keynsham, and 4½ S. E. from Bristol; containing 25 inhabited houses, and 33 families, 29 of whom are employed in agriculture. This parish contains about 1200 acres, chiefly applied to pasture. In the year 1573 Queen Elizabeth passed through the village, and granted a charter for an annual fair, to be held on the 20th of July, which is still continued. The church is a small structure, dedicated to St. Margaret, and consists of a nave, chancel, and two side aisles, with a tower at the west end containing a clock and four bells. The living is a rectory, in the deanery of Redcliff and Bedminster; Rev. T. R. Ireland, incumbent; instituted 1798. Population, 1801, no return—1811, 149—1821, 147.

RADDINGTON—a parish in the hundred of Williton and Free-manners, 4½ miles W. S. W. from Wiveliscombe; containing 13 inhabited houses, and 17 families, 15 of whom are employed in agriculture. The church is dedicated to St. Michael, and consists of a nave and chancel, with a tower containing four bells. The living is a rectory, in the deanery of Dunster; Rev. William Darch, incumbent; instituted 1807. Population, 1801, no return—1811, 101—1821, 101.

RADSTOCK—a parish in the hundred of Kilmersdon, 7 miles S. S. W. from Bath, on the turnpike-road from that city to Wells; it contains 164 inhabited houses, and 169 families, 29 of whom are returned as being employed in agriculture, 34 in trade, manufacture, or handicraft, and 106 not comprised in either class; the latter number are nearly all employed in the coal-works, which are numerous in this parish. The church is a small structure, dedicated to St. Nicholas. The living is rectorial, in the deanery of Frome; Rev. Richard Boodle, incumbent; instituted 1814. Population, 1801, no return—1811, 567—1821, 902.

REDLYNCH—a tything in the parish and hundred of Bruton,

1½ mile S. E. from Bruton; containing 21 inhabited houses, and 24 families, 22 of whom are employed in agriculture. It is the seat of the Earl of Ilchester, who receives the title of Baron from this place. The chapel is a modern edifice, and over the entrance are the Ilchester arms; the Rev. J. Goldesborough, junior, is the present incumbent. Population, 1801, no separate return—1811, no separate return—1821, 93.

RIMPTON—a parish in a distinct portion of the hundred of Taunton and Taunton-Dean, 5½ miles W. N. W. from Milborne-Port; containing 30 inhabited houses, and 42 families, 35 of whom are employed in agriculture. This parish was attached to the hundred of Taunton and Taunton-Dean, in consequence of its having belonged in ancient times to the bishopric of Winchester, and the tenants were bound to do their suit at the bishop's court in Taunton; the manor is still vested in the bishopric of Winton. The church is a small Gothic structure, dedicated to St. Mary, and consists of a nave, chancel, and south aisle, with an embattled tower at the west end containing three bells. The living is a rectory, in the deanery of Marston, and in the presentation of the Bishop of Winchester; Rev. R. A. Burney, incumbent; instituted 1802. Population, 1801, 195—1811, 201—1821, 219.

ROAD—a parish in the hundred of Frome, 5 miles N. N. E. from Frome; containing 232 inhabited houses, and 257 families, 42 of whom are employed in agriculture, 213 in trade, manufacture, or handicraft, and 2 not comprised in either class. Road was formerly a large market-town, the charter for which was obtained by Laurence de St. Maur, from Edward the First: it has no market at present, but is a very considerable village, and the population has increased nearly one-fourth within the last ten years, in consequence of the improved state of the very handsome houses in the neighbourhood. The river Frome woollen manufacture, the proprietors of which have built some runs through the parish, turning several mills in its course : a fair is held here on the Monday after August 29th. The church is situated nearly half a mile from the village; it is dedicated to St. Lawrence, and consists of a nave, chancel, and side aisles, with a tower at the west end containing six bells. The living is a rectory, in the deanery of Frome, and is consolidated with Woolvington; Rev. Charles Glossop, incumbent; instituted 1812. Population, 1801, 927—1811, 957—1821, 1217.

Rodden—a parish in the hundred of Frome, 2 miles E. from Frome; containing 34 inhabited houses, and 50 families, 30 of whom are employed in agriculture. The land, which comprises about 1000 acres, is principally applied to meadow and pasture; a number of streams run through the parish, one of which, called Rodden Trout-Stream, turns several mills in its course to the river Frome. The chapel was built at the expense of the inhabitants, about the year 1640, by the rector of Boynton, in Wilts, pursuant to an order obtained from the Archbishop of Canterbury, to which the said rector annexed the chancel. The presentation is in the rector of Boynton for the time being ; Rev. J. M. Rogers, incumbent. Population, 1801, 200—1811, no return—1821, 272.

Rodney-Stoke—a parish in the hundred of Winterstoke, 5 miles N. W. from Wells ; containing 56 inhabited houses, and 60 families, 32 of whom are employed in agriculture. This place was anciently written Stoke, and received the additional title of Rodney, from a family of that name who were its former possessors, and from whom descended Sir George Bridges Rodney, who was created a baronet, January 21, 1754, and Baron Rodney, of Rodney Stoke, June 19, 1782, for the eminent services he rendered to his country as a naval commander during the American war. The church of Rodney-Stoke is dedicated to St. Leonard, and consists of a nave, chancel, and south aisle or chapel. The living is a rectory, in the deanery of Axbridge ;

Rev. T. A. Salmon, incumbent; instituted 1794; patron, the Bishop of Bath and Wells. Population, 1801, 186—1811, 257 —1821, 272.

Rowbarrow—a parish in the hundred of Winterstoke, 4 miles N. N. E. from Axbridge; containing 46 inhabited houses, and as many families, 4 only of whom are employed in agriculture. The greater part of the population are miners, considerable quantities of lapis-calaminaris being found here: the fumes arising from the burning of the calamine is very destructive to vegetation. The church is a neat structure, dedicated to St. Michael, with a tower at the west end containing six bells. The living is a rectory, in the deanery of Axbridge, and in the gift of the Bishop of Bristol; Rev. John Price, incumbent; instituted 1795. Population, 1801, 249—1811, 263—1821, 334.

Ruishton—a parish in the hundred of Taunton and Taunton-Dean, 2 miles E. from Taunton; containing 58 inhabited houses, and 66 families, 51 of whom are employed in agriculture. About a mile and a half S. S. E. from the village is *Henlade-House*, the residence of C. P. Anderdon, Esq. The church is an ancient structure, dedicated to St. George, and consists of a nave, chancel, and south aisle, with a tower at the west end containing a clock and three bells. It was formerly a chapel to St. Mary Magdalen, Taunton, but is now a curacy; Rev. Richard Winsloe, incumbent. Population, 1801, 518—1811, 267—1821, 329.

Runnington—a parish in the hundred of Milverton, 2 miles N. W. from Wellington, from which it is divided by the river Tone: it contains 12 inhabited houses, and 22 families, 7 of whom are employed in agriculture. The greater part of the population is employed in spinning, &c. for the manufacture at Wellington. The church is a small building, with a tower at the west end, in which are two bells. The living is rectorial, in the deanery of Taunton, and in the gift of the Crown; Rev.

Edward Webber, incumbent; instituted 1809. Population, 1801, 82—1811, 94—1821, 90.

SALTFORD—a parish in the hundred of Keynsham, 5 miles W. N. W. from Bath ; containing 60 inhabited houses, and 66 families, 60 of whom are employed in agriculture. The church is a small structure, dedicated to St. Mary. The living is rectorial, in the deanery of Redcliff and Bedminster ; Rev. John Wightman, incumbent ; instituted 1818. Population, 1801, 223—1811, 249—1821, 327.

SAMPFORD-ARUNDEL—a parish in the hundred of Milverton, 2½ miles S. W. from Wellington ; containing 72 inhabited houses, and 78 families, 56 of whom are employed in agriculture. A short distance to the east of the village is *Easter-Land*, the residence of Capt. Bellett. The church is dedicated to the Holy Cross, and consists of a nave and chancel, with a tower containing four bells. The living is a vicarage, in the deanery of Taunton ; Rev. George Bellett, incumbent ; instituted 1821. Population, 1801, 319—1811, 303—1821, 376.

SAMPFORD-BRETT—a parish in the hundred of Williton and Freemanners, 3 miles S. E. from Watchet ; containing 29 inhabited houses, and 40 families, 28 of whom are employed in agriculture. The church is dedicated to St. George, and consists of a nave, chancel, and north aisle, with an embattled tower on the south side containing a clock and five bells. The living is a rectory, in the deanery of Dunster ; Rev. Thomas Tanner, incumbent ; instituted 1821. Population, 1801, 180—1811, 185 —1821, 194.

SANDFORD-ORCAS—a parish in the hundred of Horethorne, 4 miles W. N. W. from Milborne-Port ; containing 64 inhabited houses, and 71 families, 62 of whom are employed in agriculture. The church is dedicated to St. Nicholas, and consists of a nave, chancel, and south aisle, with a tower containing five bells. The living is a rectory, in the deanery of Marston; Rev. T. Belamey, incumbent; instituted 1816. Population, 1801, 269—1811, 290—1821, 332.

SEABOROUGH—a parish in the hundred of Crewkerne, 2½ miles S.S.W. from Crewkerne, on the borders of Dorsetshire; containing 18 inhabited houses, and as many families, 27 of whom are employed in agriculture. The church consists of a nave, chancel, and north aisle. The living is a rectory, in the deanery of Crewkerne; Rev. William Butler, incumbent; instituted 1806. Population, 1801, 82—1811, 100—1821, 92.

SEAVINGTON ST. MARY — a parish in the hundred of South Petherton, 3 miles east from Ilminster; containing 44 inhabited houses, and 65 families, 58 of whom are employed in agriculture. About half a mile north is Scavington-Abbots, so designated from having formerly belonged to the abbey of Athelney: one of the abbots built a chapel here, which continued till the dissolution of the monasteries. The church of Seavington St. Mary consists of a nave and chancel, with an embattled tower containing three bells. The living is a curacy, in the deanery of Crewkerne, united with Seavington St. Michael. Population, 1801, no separate return—1811, no separate return—1821, 212.

SEAVINGTON ST. MICHAEL—a parish in the hundred of South Petherton, 3½ miles east from Ilminster; containing 22 inhabited houses, and 42 families, 32 of whom are employed in agriculture. The church is dedicated to St. Michael, which gave the additional name to the parish. It consists of a nave and chancel, having a wooden turret containing three bells. The living is a rectory, in the deanery of Crewkerne; Rev. Thomas Evans, incumbent; instituted 1809. Population, 1801, no return—1811, 222—1821, 212.

SELWORTHY—a parish in the hundred of Carhampton, 3 miles
W. from Minehead ; containing 83 inhabited houses, and 100
families, 69 of whom are employed in agriculture. About a
mile from the village, on the left of the turnpike-road to Porlock, is *Holnicote*, the seat of the Hon. Mathew Fortesque.
The church is pleasantly situated on rising ground, and consists
of a nave, chancel, and side aisles, with an embattled tower
containing a clock and six bells. The living is a rectory, in the
deanery of Dunster ; Rev. J. Stephenson, incumbent; instituted
1802. Population, 1801, 418—1811, 458—1821, 483.

SHAPWICK—a parish in the hundred of Whitley, 8½ miles E. from
Bridgewater, and 7 W. from Glastonbury; containing 76 inhabited
houses, and as many families. This parish is very extensive, and
is situated to the north of the Poldon-hills. In the year 1777 an
act of parliament was obtained for dividing and enclosing
Shapwick-moor, which contained nearly 1020 acres. A short
distance north of the village is *Shapwick-House*, the residence
of the Rev. Elias Taylor. The church is dedicated to the
Virgin Mary, and consists of a nave and chancel, with a tower
in the centre which contains five bells. The living is a vicarage,
in the jurisdiction of Glastonbury ; Rev. G. H. Templar, incumbent in his own right ; instituted 1810. Population, 1801,
399—1811, 418—1821, 414.

SHEPTON-BEAUCHAMP—a parish in the hundred of South-
Petherton, 4 miles E. N. E. from Ilminster, and 2 miles S. from
South-Petherton ; containing 105 inhabited houses, and 115
families, 71 of whom are employed in agriculture. The church
is a handsome structure, consisting of a nave, chancel, and two
side aisles, with a noble embattled tower at the west end 70
feet high, containing a clock, chimes, and six bells ; on the
west side is the statue of St. Patrick, with his crosier. The
living is a rectory, in the deanery of Crewkerne ; Rev. Joseph
Domett, incumbent ; instituted 1789. Population, 1801, 439
—1811, 559—1821, 567.

SHEPTON-MALLET—a market-town and parish in the hundred of Whitestone, situated 6 miles E. from Wells, 10 W. S. W. from Frome, and 18 S. S. W. from Bath, on the turnpike-road from that city to Ilchester, and a short distance to the east of the old Roman Foss. It received its adjunctive name from the Mallets, its ancient lords, who had been for many generations in possession of this manor, and made it the head of their barony. The town consists of about twenty narrow streets and lanes, and has for many years carried on an extensive manufacture of various kinds of woollen cloths and knit stockings. It is a very populous parish, containing 1060 inhabited houses, and 1075 families, 217 of whom are employed in agriculture, 744 in trade, manufacture, or handicraft, and 114 not comprised in either class. Here is a good market on Fridays, well supplied with all kinds of provisions ; the market-cross is a very curious structure, consisting of five arches, supported by pentagonal columns ; in the centre is a large hexagonal pillar, standing on two rows of steps, and supporting a flat roof, over which rises a lofty pyramidal spire adorned with Gothic niches, and crowned with an oblong entablature, on which is the figure of our Saviour on the cross between the two malefactors. It was erected by Walter and Agnes de Buckland, in the year 1500, as appears from a brass plate affixed to the central pillar : lands of considerable value have been appropriated to the reparation of this structure. The church is a handsome edifice, built in the form of a cross, and consists of a nave, chancel, north and south aisles, north and south transept, and a sepultural chapel on each side of the chancel, with a well-built tower at the west end containing a clock and eight bells, and on the west side are the statues of the Virgin Mary, St. Peter, and St. Paul. The living is rectorial, in the deanery of Cary; Rev. W. F. Blomberg, incumbent; instituted 1787. Here are also several places of worship belonging to various denominations of protestant dissenters, a free grammar-school, and two alms-houses, one for four men and the other for four women. Population, 1801, 5104—1811, 4638—1821, 5021.

SHEPTON-MONTAGUE, or MONTACUTE—a parish in the hundred of Norton-Ferrars, 2½ miles S. from Bruton ; containing 60 inhabited houses, and 79 families, 71 of whom are employed in agriculture. This place received its additional name from Droge de Montacute, of Montague, a township in Normandy, who came over to England with Earl Morton, brother to William the Conqueror, and held this manor with Montacute, near Yeovil. The church is dedicated to St. Peter, and consists of a nave and chancel, with a tower on the south side containing three bells. The living is a curacy, in the deanery of Cary ; Rev. J. Goldesborough, incumbent; instituted 1803. Population, 1801, 365—1811, 371—1821, 367.

SHIPHAM—a parish in the hundred of Winterstoke, 3 miles N. N. E. from Axbridge ; containing 128 inhabited houses, and 140 families, 11 of whom are employed in agriculture, 25 in trade, &c. and 104 not comprised in either class ; of this latter number 80 families are employed in the lead mines and calamine works, which are very numerous in this parish. Dr. Collinson describes the calamine stone as a kind of fossilly bituminous earth, principally used in converting copper into brass. It lies in a strata nearly perpendicular, and mostly in a direction from east to west : when the ore is first raised it has the appearance of brownish yellow gravel, and is often intermixed with eyes, or small veins of lead ; when dug it is washed or budded (as the miners call it) in running water, which carries off the earthy parts, leaving the calamine, lead, and sparry concretions at the bottom ; they then put it into a sieve, and shake it in the water, by which means the lead sinks lowest, the sparry parts rise on the top, and the calamine remains in the middle : thus prepared, they bake it in an oven four or five times, the flames being so directed as to pass over it, by which means it is calcined : it is then picked and sifted, and sent in bags to Bristol, where it is ground as fine as flour, and mixed with powdered charcoal and water into a mass or paste : seven pounds of this calamine is put into a gallon melting pot, and on the top five pounds of copper; it is then let down into a wind furnace, and remains there about twelve hours, in which time the whole is converted into brass ; when melted, it is cast into plates, or lumps : forty-five pounds of calamine produces thirty when calcined, and sixty pounds of copper make with calamine one hundred pounds of brass. Here is an annual fair for cattle, sheep, &c. on the 17th of November. The church is dedicated to St. Leonard, and consists of a nave, chancel, and south aisle, with a tower at the west end surmounted by a small spire, and contains five bells. The living is a rectory in the deanery of Axbridge, and in the gift of the Dean and Chapter of Wells ; Rev. William Jones, incumbent ; instituted 1791. Population, 1801, 493—1811, 539—1821, 635.

SKILGATE—a parish in the hundred of Williton and Free-manners, 5 miles E. from Dulverton, and bounded on the south by the county of Devon ; containing 41 inhabited houses, and as many families, 30 of whom are employed in agriculture. About a mile west of the village is *Leigh-House*, the residence of H. H. Henley, Esq. The church is a small structure, 64 feet long and 13 feet wide, with a tower containing three bells. The living is rectorial, in the deanery of Dunster; the Rev. Richard Bere, junior, incumbent in his own right. Population, 1801, 226—1811, 201—1821, 226.

SOMERTON—the name of a hundred in the southern part of the county, containing the town which designates it, and the following parishes ; viz. ALLER, CAMEL-WEST, CHARLTON-ADAM, CHARLTON-MACKERELL, KINGSDON, LONG-SUTTON, LYD-FORD-EAST, and YEOVILTON; containing 829 inhabited houses, 1040 families, 2419 males, and 2452 females. Total population, 4871.

SOMERTON — an ancient market-town, from which the county received its name, having derived its own from the pleasantness of the surrounding country, being beautifully varied, with well-cultivated hills and rich luxuriant vallies. It lies in latitude 51° 3′ 17″ 3. N. and longitude 2° 43′ 5″ 1. W. being 17 miles W. from Taunton, 17 from Bridgewater, 13 from Wells, and 126 from London. That part called the Borough consists principally of five streets, and with Somerton-Early and the hamlet of Hurcot, contains 301 inhabited houses, and 379 families, 239 of whom are employed in agriculture, 104 in trade, manufacture, or handicraft, and 36 not included in either class. This town was frequently the residence of the West Saxon kings, who built a castle here, and which was many years afterwards used as a state prison. John, King of France, who was made prisoner by Edward the Black Prince, was confined here after his removal from Hereford. The hall in which the Justices hold their meetings is in the centre of the town, and near the church is an excellent free-school; here is also a well-endowed almshouse for eight poor women. The town is governed by a bailiff and constables, annually chosen, and has a market on Tuesdays well attended, also several fairs, viz. on Palm-Tuesday, and the third, sixth, and ninth Tuesdays following, likewise September 30th and November 8th. The inhabitants had formerly a right of common on an extensive moor north-west of the town, which is now enclosed, and portions allotted to the parishes adjoining it. The church is an ancient building, dedicated to St. Michael, and consists of a nave, chancel, two side aisles, vestry-room and porch, with an octagonal embattled tower on the south side containing six bells. The living is a vicarage, in the deanery of Ilchester; Rev. Henry Davis, incumbent; instituted 1810. Population, 1801, 1145— 1811, 1478—1821, 1643.

SPARKFORD—a parish in the hundred of Catash, 6 miles E. N. E. from Ilchester; containing 37 inhabited houses, and 52 families, 40 of whom are employed in agriculture. The church consists of a nave and chancel, with a strong quadrangular embattled tower containing three bells. The living is rectorial, in the deanery of Cary; Rev. E. S. Newman, incumbent; instituted 1798. Population, 1801, 239—1811, 228—1821, 273.

SPAXTON—a parish in the hundred of Cannington, 5 miles W. from Bridgewater; containing 144 inhabited houses, and 183 families, 116 of whom are employed in agriculture. The church is a handsome structure, dedicated to St. Margaret, and consists of a nave, chancel, and south aisle, with an embattled tower at the west end containing a clock and five bells. The living is a rectory, in the deanery of Bridgewater; Rev. William Gordon, incumbent in his own right; instituted 1816. Population, 1801, 662—1811, 737—1821, 816.

STANTON-DREW—a parish in the hundred of Keynsham, 8 miles S. from Bristol; containing 135 inhabited houses, and 141 families, 101 of whom are employed in agriculture. To the north-east of the church is a remarkable Druidical circle, consisting of a number of huge massive stones, some of them weighing from ten to fifteen tons each. The church is dedicated to St. Mary, and consists of a nave, chancel, two side aisles, and a chapel on the north side, with a tower, the belfry under which forms the principal entrance into the church. The living is a vicarage, in the deanery of Redcliff and Bedminster, and in the patronage of the Archdeacon of Bath; Rev. James Phillot, incumbent; instituted 1815. Population, 1801, 660—1811, 682—1821, 622. The decrease in the population of this parish has been occasioned by the removal of a manufactory since the return in 1811.

STANTON-PRIOR—a parish in the hundred of Keynsham, 5½ miles W. S. W. from Bath; containing 26 inhabited houses, and as many families, 23 of whom are employed in agriculture. At the north-west extremity of this parish is a large knoll, called

Stantonbury-hill, supposed to have been a Roman encampment, as many of their coins have been dug up in the valley that surrounds it. Previous to the conquest this village belonged to the Saxon kings, and was given to the Priors of Bath, and from them it received the name by which it is now distinguished. The church is a small building, dedicated to St. Lawrence, and consists of a nave and chancel, with an embattled tower at the west end. The living is a rectory, in the deanery of Redcliff and Bedminster; Rev. James Phillot, incumbent; instituted 1815. Population, 1801, 130—1811, 144—1821, 158.

STAPLE-FITZPAIN—a parish in the hundred of Abdick and Bulstone, 5 miles S. S. E. from Taunton; containing 61 inhabited houses, and 70 families, 68 of whom are employed in agriculture. The church, which is dedicated to St. Peter, is a handsome Gothic structure, consisting of a nave, chancel, and porch, with an elegant tower 70 feet high, crowned with eight handsome pinnacles, and containing five bells. The living is a rectory, in the deanery of Crewkerne; Rev. Henry Bowen, incumbent; instituted 1811. Population, 1801, 279—1811, 310—1821, 385.

STAPLEGROVE — a parish in the hundred of Taunton and Taunton-Dean, 1½ mile N. W. from Taunton; containing 55 inhabited houses, and 78 families, 48 of whom are employed in agriculture. The church consists of a nave, chancel, and two side aisles, with a tower containing five bells. The living is a rectory, in the deanery of Taunton ; Rev. H. W. Rawlins, incumbent in his own right ; instituted 1810. Population, 1801, 319—1811, 350—1821, 403.

STAWELL—a hamlet and chapelry in the parish of Moorlinch and hundred of Whitley, 5½ miles E. N. E. from Bridgewater; containing 28 inhabited houses, and 41 families, the whole of whom are employed in agriculture. The church is a small building, and is a curacy annexed to Moorlinch. Population, 1801, 144—1811, 168—1821, 200.

STAWLEY—a parish in the hundred of Milverton, 4 miles S. S. W. from Wiveliscombe; containing 27 inhabited houses, and 32 families, 22 of whom are employed in agriculture. The church is a small Gothic edifice, dedicated to St. Michael, consisting of a nave and chancel, with a tower containing three bells. The living is a rectory, in the deanery of Taunton; Rev. R. T. Cornac, incumbent; instituted 1819. Population, 1801, 148—1811, 170—1821, 195.

STOCKLAND-BRISTOL—a parish in the hundred of Cannington, 6¼ miles N. N. W. from Bridgewater; containing 30 inhabited houses, and 43 families, 29 of whom are employed in agriculture. This parish is called Stockland-Bristol from the manor thereof having been given in trust to the Chamber of Bristol, by Henry the Eighth, at the dissolution of religious houses, for the free-school in that city, erected on the site of Gaunt's hospital, the master and brethren of which were formerly in possession of this estate. The church consists of a nave and south aisle, with an embattled tower, containing a clock and four bells. The living is a vicarage, in the patronage of the Mayor and Corporation of Bristol; Rev. N. Ruddock, incumbent; instituted 1814. Population, 1801, 144—1811, 173—1821, 199.

STOCKLINCH-MAGDALEN—a very small parish in the hundred of Abdick and Bulstone, 3 miles N. E. from Ilminster; containing 14 inhabited houses, and 17 families, the whole of whom are employed in agriculture. The church is a small building, 50 feet long and 14 wide. The living is a rectory, in the deanery of Crewkerne; Rev. James Upton, incumbent; instituted 1803. Population, 1801, 89—1811, 85—1821, 79.

STOCKLINCH-OTTERSEY—another small parish adjoining the

above, and in the same hundred, $3\frac{1}{2}$ miles N. E. from Ilminster; containing 17 inhabited houses, and 26 families; the whole of whom are employed in agriculture. The church is a small Gothic edifice, consisting of a nave, chancel, and south aisle, with a tower at the west end containing three bells. The living is a rectory, in the deanery of Crewkerne; Rev. C. S. Allen, incumbent; instituted 1821. Population, 1801, 119—1811, 130 —1821, 140.

STOGUMBER—a small market-town and parish in the hundred of Williton and Freemanners, 14 miles N. W. from Taunton, and 11 S. E. from Minehead; containing 202 inhabited houses, and 243 families, 158 of whom are employed in agriculture, 55 in trade, manufacture, or handicraft, and 30 not comprised in either class. The town principally consists of two streets of tolerable appearance. Here is a small market on Saturday, and a fair on the 6th of May. The parish is very extensive, comprising several hamlets : there were formerly chapels at Halsway and Hartrow; at the latter place the Rev. Thomas Sweet Escott has a pleasant residence. In this parish is an alms-house for six poor widows, endowed with a provision from the estate of Combe-Sydenham, on the opposite side of the turnpike-road, formerly the residence of an ancient family of that name. The church of Stogumber is a handsome structure, consisting of a nave, chancel, two side aisles, and two chapels, with an embattled tower containing a clock and five bells. The living is a vicarage, in the deanery of Dunster, and in the patronage of the Dean and Chapter of Wells; Rev. S. Trevelyan, incumbent; instituted 1820. Population, 1801, 1285—1811, 1214—1821, 1281.

STOKE-COURCEY—a parish in the hundred of Cannington, 2 miles N. from Nether-Stowey; containing 250 inhabited houses, and 260 families, 132 of whom are employed in agriculture. This town is styled in ancient records the Borough and Honour

of Stoke-Courcey; and in the 34th year of Edward the Third,
John Bakeler and Adam Mareys represented it in parliament,
but it returned no members afterwards. It was formerly privileged with a weekly market and two annual fairs ; the latter
are still held, one on the 14th of May and the other the 23d of
September. *Fairfield*, the seat of Sir John Palmer Acland,
Bart. is situated at the western extremity of this parish; the
boundary between the hundreds of Carhampton and Williton
and Freemanners runs through the park. The church of Stoke-
Courcey is an ancient edifice, with a tower in the centre supported by four arches. The living is a vicarage, in the deanery
of Bridgewater, and in the gift of Eton College ; Rev. Edward
Palmer, incumbent; instituted 1788. Population, 1801, no
return—1811, 1208—1821, 1362.

STOKE-UNDER-HAMDEN—a parish in the hundred of Tintinhull, 6 miles W. from Yeovil ; containing 220 inhabited houses,
and 240 families, 167 of whom are employed in agriculture.
The church consists of a nave, chancel, and south aisle, with a
tower on the north side of the nave containing a clock and five
bells. The living is a curacy, in the deanery of Ilchester ; Rev.
W. Langdon, incumbent. Population, 1801, 766—1811, 868—
1821, 1072. The manufactnre of gloves is mentioned in the
return as having caused an increase in the population of this
parish.

STOKE-LANE, or STOKE ST. MICHAEL—a parish in the hundred of Whitestone, 5 miles N. E. from Shepton-Mallet ; con-
containing 228 inhabited houses, and 229 families, 72 of whom
are employed in agriculture. A number of springs rising in
this and the adjoining parish of Doulting, form a small river,
which turns several mills in the hamlet of Stokebottom. The
church consists of a nave, chancel, and north aisle, with an
embattled tower at the west end containing a clock and one
bell. The living is a curacy, in the deanery of Cary, annexed to
Doulting. Population, 1801, no return—1811, 861—1821, 1000.

STOKE-NORTH—a parish in the hundred of Bath-Forum, 5 miles N. W. from Bath ; containing 24 inhabited houses, and as many families, 17 of whom are employed in agriculture. This parish is bounded on the north by Gloucestershire, and on the west by the river Avon. At Swineford, a hamlet nearly a mile west from the village, was formerly a chapel, now destroyed. The church is dedicated to St. Martin, and consists of a nave and chancel, with a tower at the west end. The living is a rectory, in the deanery of Bath, and in the gift of the Crown ; Rev. H. H. Hayes, incumbent ; instituted 1811. Population, 1801, 108—1811, 113—1821, 129.

STOKE-PERO—a parish in the hundred of Carhampton, 3 miles E. from Porlock ; containing 13 inhabited houses, and 17 families, 16 of whom are employed in agriculture. The church is a small building, with a tower at the west end. The living is a rectory, in the deanery of Dunster; Rev. W. H. Quick, incumbent; instituted 1818. Population, 1801, 63—1811, 61 —1821, 81.

STOKE-RODNEY—*See* RODNEY-STOKE.

STOKE ST. GREGORY—so called from the dedication of its church, is situated in the hundred of North-Curry, 5½ miles W. from Langport ; containing, with the hamlet of Stathe, 261 inhabited houses, and 280 families, 180 of whom are employed in agriculture. This parish is very extensive, and is almost surrounded by moors ; that of West-Sedgemoor, on the southeast, is now enclosed, and portions are allotted to this and the neighbouring parishes. The church is built in the form of a cross, and has an octagonal tower at the west end containing five bells. The living is a curacy, and a peculiar annexed to North-Curry. Population, 1801, 907—1811, 1031—1821, 1369.

STOKE ST. MARY—a parish in the hundred of Taunton and Taunton-Dean, 3 miles E. S. E. from Taunton ; containing 49 inhabited houses, and as many families, 46 of whom are employed in agriculture. The church is a small structure, with a tower at the west end, in which are three bells. The living is a curacy, united with Thurlbear. Population, 1801, no return— 1811, 210—1821, 248.

STOKE-SOUTH—a parish in the hundred of Bath-Forum, 2 miles S. from Bath, containing 50 inhabited houses, and 57 families, 30 of whom are employed in agriculture. About half a mile east from the church, on the turnpike-road from Bath, stands *Midford-Castle*, the residence of Charles Conolly, Esq. The church is a small structure, dedicated to St. James, and consists of a nave, chancel, and porch, with a tower at the west end crowned with pinnacles. The living is a vicarage, in the deanery of Bath; Rev. Charles Johnson, incumbent; instituted 1792. Population, 1801, 177—1811, 188—1821, 258.

STOKE-TRISTER—a parish in the hundred of Norton-Ferrars, 2 miles E. from Wincanton; containing, with the hamlet of Bayford, 57 inhabited houses, and 77 families, 52 of whom are employed in agriculture. The church consists of a nave and chancel, with a tower containing three bells. The living is a rectory, in the deanery of Cary; Rev. William Phelips, incumbent; instituted 1807. Population, 1801, 336—1811, 382— 1821, 377.

STONE—the name of a hundred in the southern part of the county, comprising the town of Yeovil, and the parishes of ASHINGTON, BRIMPTON, CHILTHORNE-DOMERE, LYMINGTON, LUSTON, MUDFORD, and PRESTON; containing 1023 inhabited houses, 1145 families, 2857 males, and 3219 females. Total population, 6076.

STON-EASTON— a parish in the hundred of Chewton, 8½ miles N. E. from Wells; containing 78 inhabited houses, and 82 families, 39 of whom are employed in agriculture. Here is an extensive park, the seat of Sir John Coxe Hippisley, Bart. The church is an ancient structure, consisting of a nave, chancel, and north aisle, with a tower containing five bells. The living is a curacy, annexed to Chewton-Mendip. Population, 1801, 389—1811, 394—1821, 419.

STOWELL—a parish in the hundred of Horethorne, 2½ miles N. from Milborne-Port ; containing 21 inhabited houses, and 25 families, 21 of whom are employed in agriculture. The church is dedicated to St. Mary, and consists of a nave and chancel, with a tower containing three bells. The living is a rectory, in the deanery of Marston ; Rev. James Hooper, incumbent ; instituted 1820. Population, 1801, 88—1811, 97—1821, 102.

STOWEY—a parish in the hundred of Chew, 9½ miles S. from Bristol ; containing 31 inhabited houses, and 45 families, 30 of whom are 'employed in agriculture. A short distance north from the village is *Sutton-Court*, the residence of Sir Henry Strachey, Bart. The church consists of a nave and chancel, with a tower containing five bells. The living is a vicarage, in the deanery of Redcliff and Bedminster, and in the patronage of the Bishop of the diocese ; Rev. Edward Whitby, incumbent ; instituted 1799. Population, 1801, 170—1811, 195—1822, 208.

STRATTON—a parish in the hundred of Kilmersdon, 6½ miles N. N. E. from Shepton-Mallet ; containing 74 inhabited houses, and as many families, 24 of whom are employed in agriculture. This place is generally called Stratton-on-the-Fosse, from its situation, the Roman Fosse passing through the village. About a mile north from the church is *Stratton-House*, the residence of Charles Gordon Gray, Esq. This manor belongs to the Dutchy of Cornwall, and is the property of the King, as Prince of Wales, who likewise presents to the living. The church is dedicated to St. Vigor, and consists of a nave, chancel, and north aisle, with a tower at the west end. The living is a rectory, in the deanery of Frome (now vacant.) Population, 1801, 267—1811, 269—1821, 317.

STREET—a parish in the hundred of Whitley, 1½ mile S. S.W. from Glastonbury; containing 103 inhabited houses, and 148 families, 98 of whom are employed in agriculture. The church consists of a nave and chancel, with a tower containing six bells. The living is a rectory, in the jurisdiction of Glastonbury; Rev. C. F. Fenwick, incumbent; instituted 1820. Population, 1801, 540—1811, 634—1821, 791.

STRINGSTON—a parish in the hundred of Cannington, 2 miles N. N.W. from Nether-Stowey; containing 26 inhabited houses, and 27 families, 24 of whom are employed in agriculture. In a detached portion of this parish, near the Quantock-hills, is a remarkable eminence, called Danes-Burrow, being an entrenchment about three quarters of a mile in circumference, and consisting of a double rampire, with a very deep fosse: the whole is covered with an oak coppice wood. The church consists of a nave, chancel, and south aisle, or chapel. The living is a rectory, in the deanery of Bridgewater, annexed to Kilve. Population, 1801, 120—1811, 130—1821, 131.

SUTTON-BINGHAM — a parish in the hundred of Houndsborough Berwick and Coker, 4 miles S. from Yeovil; containing only 7 inhabited houses, and 12 families, the whole of whom are employed in agriculture. A small rivulet, formed by a spring rising in this parish, divides it from Closworth, and turns a mill near the church, in its course to the river Ivel. The church is a Gothic edifice, consisting of a nave and chancel, with a turret at the west end containing two bells. The living is a rectory, in the deanery of Ilchester; Rev. H. W. Helyer, incumbent; instituted 1821. Population, 1801, 65—1811, 72—1821, 78.

SUTTON-LONG—a parish in the hundred of Somerton, $2\frac{1}{2}$ miles S. S. W. from Somerton; containing 138 inhabited houses, and 174 families, 140 of whom are employed in agriculture. This parish is denominated Long-Sutton, on account of its extent, and to distinguish it from others of the same name. Here are several hundred acres of moor land, in which this parish, with Martock and Somerton, have a right of common. The river Yeo bounds this parish on the south, and divides it from Martock. The church of Long-Sutton is dedicated to the Holy Trinity, and consists of a nave, chancel, north and south aisles, and two porches, with a tower 100 feet in height, and crowned with 12 Gothic pinnacles; it contains a clock and five bells. The living is a vicarage, and a peculiar, in the deanery of Ilchester, and in the patronage of the Dean and Chapter of Wells; Rev. William James, incumbent; instituted 1817. Population, 1801, 735—1811, 725—1821, 856.

SUTTON-MALLET—a parish in the hundred of Whitley, $5\frac{1}{4}$ miles E. from Bridgewater; containing 18 inhabited houses, and 30 families, 26 of whom are employed in agriculture. The church is a small structure, with a tower containing three bells, and is a curacy annexed to Moorlinch. Population, 1801, 151 —1811, 144—1821, 164.

SUTTON-MONTIS, or MONTACUTE—a parish in the hundred of Catash, 5 miles S. from Castle-Cary; containing 25 inhabited houses, and 32 families, 26 of whom are employed in agriculture. The church consists of a nave and chancel, with a tower containing three bells. The living is a rectory, in the deanery of Cary; Rev. T. O. Bartlett, incumbent; instituted 1820. Population, 1801, 147—1811, 158—1821, 165.

SWANSWICK—a parish in the hundred of Bath-Forum, 3 miles N. from Bath; containing 76 inhabited houses, and 91 families,

60 of whom are employed in agriculture. The church consists of a nave, chancel, and two aisles, with a tower at the west end containing five bells. The living is a rectory, in the deanery of Bath, and in the gift of Oriel College, Oxford; Rev. John Poole, incumbent; instituted 1811. Population, 1801, 182—. 1811, 230—1821, 381.

SWELL—a parish in the hundred of Abdick and Bulstone, 4 miles S. W. from Langport; containing 26 inhabited houses, and 28 families, 26 of whom are employed in agriculture. The church is an ancient structure, dedicated to St. Katharine, and consists of a nave and chancel, with a turret containing three bells. The living is a vicarage, in the deanery of Crewkerne, and in the gift of the Dean and Chapter of Bristol; Rev. Thomas Price, incumbent; instituted 1782. Population, 1801, 120— 1811, 122—1821, 133.

TAUNTON—a borough and market-town in the hundred of Taunton and Taunton-Dean, 11 miles W. S. W. from Bridge-water, 32 miles S. W. from Wells, 52 S. W. from Bath, and 144 from London. It comprises two parishes, ST. JAMES and ST. MARY MAGDALEN, and contains 1503 inhabited houses, and 1706 families, 183 of whom are employed in agriculture, 1287 in trade, manufacture, or handicraft, and 236 not comprised in either class. The town is situated in a fertile plain, on the banks of the river Tone, extending nearly a mile in length, and chiefly consists of four principal streets, which are spacious, well paved, and contain a considerable number of well-built houses, and several good inns : in the centre is a commodious and handsome market-house, with several apartments appro-priated to various uses ; on the first floor is an elegant assembly-room, 50 feet long and 30 feet wide ; on each side of the house is a large wing, or arcade, for the accommodation of the farmers and tradesmen ; and in front is a spacious area, enclosed with chain posts, in which are erected moveable shambles, placed in

rows, for the use of the butchers : in the middle is a noble paved
footway, leading to the market-house, 216 feet in length and
18 broad. The Lent assizes are held in this town, for the
convenience of which here is a very spacious assize-hall, which
has been elegantly fitted up at a considerable expense. Taunton
is a borough by prescription, and has returned members to
parliament ever since the reign of Edward the First; the right
of election is in the parishioners residing within the limits of
the borough, not having received alms within the last twelve
months ; the legal returning officers are the bailiffs elected at
the annual court-leet of the Bishop of Winchester, as was
decided by a committee of the house of commons on the 3d
May, 1803. The corporation consists of a mayor, a recorder, a
justice of the peace, two aldermen, ten capital and ten inferior
burgesses ; the justice is always the last mayor, who, with the
two aldermen, is annually elected out of the capital burgesses :
the officers are a town-clerk, two serjeants at mace, a bellman
and a beadle ; there are also acting under the mayor two constables and six tithing-men, who with two portreeves and two
bailiffs, are chosen by a jury at an annual court held by the
Bishop of Winchester, who is lord of the manor. The corporation have neither lands, houses, or joint stock ; the last charter,
granted to them by Charles the Second, in 1677, precluding
them from any such possessions ; neither have the officers of
the borough any power to arrest : the only prison in this town
is a bridewell for vagrants ; the debtors are sent to the county
gaol at Ilchester, and the criminals are committed to that at
Wilton. The woollen manufacture flourished here soon after its
introduction into England from Flanders, nearly five centuries
since, but this branch has been for many years on the decline,
and the silk trade now affords employment to a considerable
proportion of the population. Here is an excellent free-school
in this town, founded in the reign of Henry the Seventh, by
Richard Fox, Bishop of Winchester; which was liberally endowed,
about the year 1553, by William Walbee and William Pool, of

Colyford, Esquires, with lands and tenements situated in the county of Dorset. Here are likewise two well-endowed almshouses, each having a chapel, and suitable apartments, one for thirteen poor men, and the other for eight men and ten women. A short distance from the town stands a noble edifice, for the reception and benefit of the diseased poor : this hospital is a square building, 90 feet on each side, having semicircular entrances leading to a suit of rooms, and meeting in an open circular court in the centre of the building ; each floor is divided into apartments suitable to the object of the institution. Taunton was formerly the residence of the Bishops of Winchester, one of whom built a castle here, on the site of a former one, said to have been erected by Ina, king of the West Saxons, in the year 700, and destroyed by his Queen Ethelburga : this castle was alternately in the hands of the king and the parliament during the civil war ; but the latter being ultimately successful, an act passed for the sale of all the Bishop's lands, and the manor, together with the castle and all other appurtenances, were sold by trustees appointed by the parliament, on March 20, 1647 ; but on the restoration of Charles the Second the castle was dismantled, and the manor was recovered by the Bishop of Winchester, and is still vested in that bishopric.

Among the religious foundations for which this town was formerly distinguished, was a priory of Black Canons, founded by William Giffard, Bishop of Winchester ; it was situated on the north side of the town, and near to the house now called the Priory Farm : besides this priory, there were several chapels and chantries in Taunton, all which were dependant on the mother-church in the convent, dedicated to St. Peter and St. John. There are at present two churches: that of St. Mary Magdalen, standing nearly in the centre of the town, is the most remarkable ; it is a beautiful Gothic structure, having a most magnificent tower at the west end, in which are thirteen windows, adorned with a variety of curious ornaments, which throw over it an air of lightness and delicacy, without injuring the grandeur of its appearance ; the figures which occupied a number of highly ornamented canopies, are entirely defaced, and the cherubs, lions, sphinxes, &c. are materially injured ; it is crowned with four elegant pinnacles 32 feet high, making the height of the whole 163 feet. The living is a vicarage ; Rev. Henry Bower, incumbent ; instituted 1819. The church of St. James is an ancient edifice, erected in the thirteenth century, and is a curacy ; Rev. John Townsend, incumbent ; instituted 1819. Exclusive of the above churches in the establishment, here are several places of worship belonging to the Dissenters ; also a meeting-house for the Society of Friends, and a Roman Catholic chapel. Population, 1801, 5794—1811, 6997—1821, 8534.

TAUNTON AND TAUNTON-DEAN—the name of a hundred lying on the south-west side of the county, bordering on Devonshire, comprising the borough of Taunton, and the following parishes ; viz. ANGERSLEIGH, BAGBOROUGH-WEST, BISHOP'S-HULL, BRADFORD, CHEDDON-FITZPAINE, COMBE-FLOREY, CORFE, COTHELSTON, HEATHFIELD, HILL-FARRANCE, KINGSTON, LYDIARD ST. LAWRENCE, NORTON-FITZWARREN, NINEHEAD, OAKE, ORCHARD-PORTMAN, OTTERFORD, PITMINSTER, RIMPTON, RUISHTON, STAPLEGROVE, STOKE ST. MARY, TOLLAND, TRULL, WILTON, and WITHIELL-FLOREY, containing 1722 inhabited houses, 2054 families, 5128 males, and 5273 females.—Total population 10,401.

TELLESFORD—a parish in the hundred of Wellow, 8½ miles S. S. E. from Bath, and 2 E. from Norton St. Philips, bounded on the east by Wiltshire. It contains 29 inhabited houses, and 34 families, 16 of whom are employed in agriculture. About a third part of the village was destroyed April 9, 1785, by an accidental fire. The church is dedicated to All Saints, and consists of a nave, with a tower at the west end, in which are three bells. The living is a rectory, in the deanery of Frome ; Rev. C. W. Baker, incumbent ; instituted 1821. Population, 1801, 153—1811, 125—1821, 167.

TEMPLE-COMBE, otherwise ABBAS-COMBE—a parish in the hundred of Horethorne, 5 miles S. from Wincanton; containing 89 inhabited houses, and 95 families, 75 of whom are employed in agriculture. The church consists of a nave, chancel, and south aisle, with an embattled tower at the west end containing a clock and five bells The living is rectorial, in the deanery of Marston; Rev. Thomas Fox, incumbent; instituted 1820. Population, 1801, 425—1811, 345—1821, 458.

THORN-COFFIN—a parish in the hundred of Tintinhull, 2 miles W. N. W. from Yeovil; containing 21 inhabited houses, and 23 families, 14 of whom are employed in agriculture. This parish received its additional name from Robert Coffin, who possessed the estate in the reign of Edward the Second. The church is a small structure, with a turret in which are two bells. The living is a rectory, in the deanery of Ilchester; Rev. J. H. Mules, jun. incumbent in his own right; instituted 1812. Population, 1801, 86—1811, 94—1821, 97.

THORNE-FALCON—a parish in the hundred of North-Curry, 4 miles E. from Taunton; containing 40 inhabited houses, and 45 families, 31 of whom are employed in agriculture. The church consists of a nave and chancel, with a tower containing three bells. The living is a rectory, in the deanery of Taunton; Rev. P. A. French, incumbent; instituted 1821. Population, 1801, 157—1811, 187—1821, 221.

THORNE ST. MARGARET — a parish in the hundred of Milverton, 3 miles W. from Wellington; containing 24 inhabited houses, and the same number of families, 22 of whom are employed in agriculture. The church is dedicated to St. Margaret (which gives the additional name to the parish,) and consists of a nave and chancel, with a tower containing three bells. The living is a curacy, and a peculiar in the deanery of Taunton, belonging to the Archdeacon thereof; Rev. Mr.

Webber, incumbent; instituted 1806. Population, 1801, 143—1811, 155—1821, 145.

THURLBEAR—a parish in the hundred of North-Curry, 3 miles S. E. from Taunton; containing 30 inhabited houses, and 38 families, the whole of whom are employed in agriculture. The church consists of a nave, chancel, and porch, with an embattled tower at the west end containing four bells. The living is a perpetual curacy, in the deanery of Taunton, and was formerly a chapel to St. Mary Magdalen in that borough, but the tithes were settled upon it by Sir William Portman, Knight; Rev. Charles Russell, incumbent; instituted 1768. Population, 1801, 151—1811, 202—1821, 215.

THURLOXTON—a parish in the hundred of North-Petherton, 5 miles S. S. W. from Bridgewater; containing 29 inhabited houses, and 35 families, 27 of whom are employed in agriculture. The church consists of a nave and chancel, with a tower containing four bells. The living is a rectory, in the deanery of Bridgewater; Rev. Charles Russell, incumbent; instituted 1768. Population, 1801, 136—1811, 156—1821, 178.

TICKENHAM—a parish in the hundred of Portbury, 10 miles W. from Bristol; containing 73 inhabited houses, and 81 families, 71 of whom are employed in agriculture. About a mile north from the church is a Roman encampment, occupying about an acre of ground; it is fortified by a double rampart 12 feet in length, and is composed of loose limestone, the produce of the spot. The church is an ancient structure, consisting of a nave, chancel, and two side aisles, with a tower at the west end containing five bells. The living is a vicarage, united with Portbury, and form one presentation, in the gift of the Bishop of Bristol; Rev. C. Newsam, incumbent; instituted 1806. Population, 1801, 276—1811, 388—1821, 405.

SOMERSETSHIRE. 191

TIMBERSCOMBE—a parish in the hundred of Carhampton, 2½ miles S. W. from Dunster; containing 74 inhabited houses, and 81 families, 54 of whom are employed in agriculture. Two streams, rising under Dunkery-hill, unite in this parish, and form a rivulet, which turns two mills, and pursues its course under a stone bridge of one arch, by Dunster, to the channel. The church is a Gothic edifice, dedicated to St. Michael, and consists of a nave, chancel, south aisle and porch, with an embattled tower surmounted by a low spire, and contains a clock and four bells. The living is a vicarage, and a peculiar in the deanery of Dunster, belonging to the prebendary; Rev. W. S. Bradley, incumbent; instituted 1819. Population, 1801, 356—1811, 388—1821, 409.

TIMSBURY—a parish in the hundred of Chew, 7 miles S. W. from Bath; containing 198 inhabited houses, and 208 families, 22 of whom are employed in agriculture, 20 in trade, &c. and 166 not comprised in either class; of the latter number of families the greater part are employed in the coal-works, from which the city of Bath is chiefly supplied: the population of this parish has increased one-third within the last twenty years. The church consists of a nave, chancel, south aisle and porch, with a square embattled tower at the west end, containing six bells. The living is a rectory, in the deanery of Redcliff and Bedminster, and in the gift of Baliol College, Oxford; Rev. W. H. Barter, incumbent; instituted 1783. Population, 1801, 714—1811, 841—1821, 1090.

TINTINHULL—the name of a hundred in the southern part of the county, having the hundred of Somerton on the north, and that of Houndsborough Berwick and Coker on the south. It comprises the following parishes, viz.; KINGSTON, MONTACUTE, NORTHOVER, STOKE under HAMDON, THORN-COFFIN and TINTINHULL; containing 732 inhabited houses, 849 families, 1991 males, and 1928 females. Total population, 3919.

TINTINHULL.—a parish in the hundred to which it gives name, 2½ miles S. S. W. from Ilchester; containing 68 inhabited houses, and 84 families, 59 of whom are employed in agriculture. The church is dedicated to St. Margaret, and consists of a nave and chancel, between which on the north side is a tower containing a clock and five bells. The living is a perpetual curacy, in the deanery of Ilchester; Rev. John Valintine, incumbent; instituted 1816. In this parish is the tithing of Sock-Dennis, formerly a very populous place, but now consisting only of two inhabited houses, and two families. It is a rectory, and a sinecure, the church having been destroyed long since; the Rev. J. E. Wyndham, is both patron and incumbent; instituted 1819. Population of Tintinhull, including Sock-Dennis, 1801, 333—1811, 388—1821, 398.

TOLLAND—a parish in the hundred of Taunton and Taunton-Dean, 10 miles N. W. from Taunton, containing 16 inhabited houses, and 22 families, 17 of whom are employed in agriculture. The church is a small building, dedicated to St. John the Baptist, and consists of a nave, chancel, and north aisle, with an embattled tower, containing three bells. The living is a rectory in the deanery of Dunster, and in the gift of the crown; Rev. Edward Cross, incumbent; instituted 1780. Population, 1801, 105—1811, 117—1821, 113.

TREBOROUGH—a parish in the hundred of Carhampton, 7 miles S. W. from Watchet, containing 20 inhabited houses, and the same number of families, the whole of whom are employed in agriculture. The church is dedicated to St. Peter, and consists of a nave and chancel, with a tower on the south side, containing three bells. The living is a rectory, in the deanery of Dunster; Rev. George Trevelyan, incumbent; instituted 1797. Population, 1801, 132—1811, 111—1821, 113.

TRENT—a parish in the hundred of Horethorne, 3 miles N. E.

from Yeovil, containing 81 inhabited houses, and 93 families, 44 of whom are employed in agriculture. Here is a free school, founded by Mr. William Young, formerly a merchant in London, who was a native of this village, and who devised the sum of £1000 to trustees, for the purchase of lands, the produce of which he directed should be applied to the repairs of the school-house, and the maintenance of the master. The church is a Gothic structure, dedicated to St. Andrew, and consists of a nave, chancel, north aisle and porch, with a tower at the south-east corner, surmounted by a well-proportioned hexagonal spire, and contains a clock and five bells. The living is a rectory in the deanery of Marston, and in the gift of Christ Church College, Oxford; Rev. Thomas Putt, incumbent; instituted 1802. Population, 1801, 302—1811, 422—1821, 479.

TRULL—a parish in the hundred of Taunton and Taunton-Dean, 2 miles S. from Taunton; containing 70 inhabited houses, and 99 families, 63 of whom are employed in agriculture. The church is dedicated to All Saints, and consists of a nave, chancel, and two side aisles, with a tower containing five bells. The living is a perpetual curacy, annexed to Pitminster. Population, 1801, 407—1811, 499—1821, 528.

TWIVERTON—generally pronounced Twerton, a parish in the hundred of Wellow, 1½ mile W. from Bath; containing 289 inhabited houses, and the same number of families, 36 of whom are employed in agriculture, 142 in trade, manufacture, or handicraft, and 111 not comprised in either class. The river Avon runs through this parish from east to west, on which are a number of mills. The church is dedicated to St. Michael, and consists of a nave and chancel, with an embattled tower at the west end, containing six bells; the living is a vicarage, in the deanery of Bath; Rev. W. B. Whitehead, incumbent; instituted 1815. Population, 1801, 764—1811, 1111—1821, 1500.

UBLEY—a parish in the hundred of Chewton, 10 miles S.S.W.

from Bristol; containing 66 inhabited houses, and 70 families, 40 of whom are employed in agriculture. The church, which is dedicated to St. Bartholomew, consists of a nave, chancel, and two side aisles, with a tower at the west end, containing four bells, and surmounted by a spire. The living is a rectory, in the deanery of Redcliff and Bedminster, in the gift of the Crown; Rev. T. S. Wylde, incumbent; instituted 1805. Population, 1801, 316—1811, 342—1821, 393.

UPHILL.—a parish in the hundred of Winterstoke, 8 miles W.N.W. from Axbridge, at the conflux of the river Ax with the Bristol Channel; containing 39 inhabited houses, and 51 families, 31 of whom are employed in agriculture. The church stands on the summit of a high hill, south of the village, and consists of a nave and chancel, with a tower in the centre containing five bells. The living is a rectory, in the deanery of Axbridge; Rev. Thomas Deacle, incumbent; instituted 1795. Population, 1801, 144—1811, 209—1821, 270.

UPTON—a parish in the hundred of Williton and Freemanners, 7 miles W. from Wiveliscombe; containing 49 inhabited houses, and 60 families, 43 of whom are employed in agriculture. The church is situated on an eminence, and consists of a nave and chancel, with a tower in which are three bells. The living is a curacy, in the deanery of Dunster; Rev. John Boucher, incumbent; instituted 1800. Population, 1801, 232—1811, 200—1821, 297.

UPTON-NOBLE—a parish in the hundred of Bruton, 4 miles N.N.E. from Bruton; containing 62 inhabited houses, and 69 families, 53 of whom are employed in agriculture. The church is a small structure, consisting of a nave, chancel, south aisle and porch, over which is a tower containing two bells. The living is a rectory, in the deanery of Cary, united with Batcombe. Population, 1801, 223—1811, 219—1821, 285.

WALTON—a parish in the hundred of Whitley, 3½ miles S. W.
from Glastonbury; containing 98 inhabited houses, and 126
families, 107 of whom are employed in agriculture. The church
is dedicated to the Holy Trinity, and consists of a nave and
chancel, with a tower in the centre, containing five bells. The
living is a curacy, annexed to the adjoining parish of Street.
Population, 1801, 397—1811, no return—1821, 635.

WALTON-IN-GORDANO—a parish in the hundred of Portbury,
12 miles W. from Bristol; containing 42 inhabited houses, and
the same number of families, 30 of whom are employed in
agriculture. About half a mile south-west from the village, on
the summit of a hill, stands *Walton-Castle*, the property of
Earl Poulett : it is of an octangular form, embattled round, and
adorned at each angle with a small turret. The keep, or
citadel, which stands in the centre of the area, is also octangular,
and has a small turret on the south-east side; the entrance is
through an embattled gateway on the east. The roof and floors
of the castle have fallen in, and the whole structure exhibits
evident marks of decay. The ruins of the original parish-church
stand at the bottom of the hill, westward of the castle ; the
present one, which is situated in the village, is a plain unadorned
fabric, of modern construction, with a turret and one bell. The
living is a rectory, in the deanery of Redcliff and Bedminster ;
Rev. Drax Durbin, incumbent; instituted 1810. Population,
1801, 147—1811, 151—1821, 161.

WANSTRAW — a parish in the hundred of Frome, 6 miles
S. W. from Frome ; containing, with the hamlet of Weston, 64
inhabited houses, and 93 families, 60 of whom are employed in
agriculture. The church is dedicated to St. Mary, and consists
of a nave, chancel, and two side aisles, with a tower containing
five bells. The living is a rectory, in the deanery of Frome ;
Rev. Thomas Valentine, incumbent; instituted 1818. Population, 1801, 325—1811, 365—1821, 397.

WATCHET—*See* St. Decumans.

Wayford—a parish in the hundred of Crewkerne, 3 miles
S. W. from Crewkerne; containing 35 inhabited houses, and
38 families, 34 of whom are employed in agriculture. The
church is a small building, consisting of a nave, chancel, and
porch, with a wooden turret, in which are two bells. The
living is a rectory, in the deanery of Crewkerne; Rev. R. S. Cox,
incumbent; instituted 1819. Population, 1801, 162—1811,
185—1821, 224.

Weare-Upper—a parish in the hundred of Bempston, 3 miles
S. W. from Axbridge; containing 127 inhabited houses, and
174 families, 148 of whom are employed in agriculture. This
place is called Upper, or Over-Weare, to distinguish it from a
hamlet about a mile to the N. W. called Lower-Weare, situate
on the turnpike-road from Bristol to Bridgewater, and which
was formerly a place of considerable note, having in the 34th
and 35th of Edward the First sent members to parliament, and
had the privilege of a market on Wednesdays, and an annual
fair. The river Ax runs through it, under a stone bridge. The
church of Upper-Weare is dedicated to St. Gregory, and consists
of a nave and chancel 100 feet in length and 30 in breadth,
with an embattled tower containing five bells. The living is a
rectory, in the deanery of Axbridge, and in the patronage of the
Dean and Chapter of Bristol; Rev. Henry Beeke, D. D. incumbent; instituted 1819. Population, 1801, 433—1811, 608
—1821, 800.

Wedmore—a parish in the hundred of Bempston, 8½ miles
W. from Wells; containing 590 inhabited houses, and 593
families, 478 of whom are employed in agriculture. This parish
is very extensive, and comprises several hamlets : the borough
is governed by a portreeve, annually chosen; the lord of the
manor holds a court yearly, at which are appointed water-
bailiffs, constables, and other officers. The improved state of

cultivation in this parish has caused a very considerable increase in the population. The church is a large Gothic edifice, dedicated to St. Mary, and is built in the form of a cathedral; it consists of a nave, north and south aisles, transept, chancel, with a chapel on each side, and a small chapel annexed to the south aisle; and in the centre over the transept is a noble tower 100 feet in height, with a ballustrade round the top, and contains a clock and six bells. The living is a vicarage, and a peculiar belonging to the Dean of Wells; Rev. John Richards, incumbent; instituted 1811. Population, 1801, 2122—1811, 2480—1821, 3079.

WELLINGTON—a populous market-town and parish in the hundred of Kingsbury-West, 7 miles S. W. from Taunton, on the turnpike-road from that town to the city of Exeter; it consists of four streets, the principal of which is the High-street, and is upwards of half a mile in length : the whole parish contains 837 inhabited houses, and 842 families, 207 of whom are employed in agriculture, 524 in trade, manufacture, or handicraft, and 111 not comprised in either class. The chief manufacture consists of serges, druggets, and other articles in the woollen trade; it has likewise an extensive pottery : the market is held on Thursday, and is well supplied with all kinds of provisions. It has two fairs, one on the feast of the nativity of St. John the Baptist, and the other on the 10th of November : both the market and the fairs were procured from the crown by the Bishops of Wells, who formerly possessed this manor. In the town is a hospital for twelve infirm poor people (six men and six women,) and likewise two children; it was built and endowed in pursuance of the will of Sir John Popham, Knt. bearing date September 21, 1604. The church, which is dedicated to St. John the Baptist, is a handsome Gothic structure, 110 feet in length and 61 in breadth, and consists of a nave, chancel, north and south aisles, two small chapels, a vestry-room and porch : at the west end is an elegant embattled tower, crowned with twelve highly-ornamented Gothic pinnacles; it is 100 feet in length, and contains a clock and eight bells. The living is a vicarage, in the deanery of Taunton, and in the gift of the Bishop of the diocese by lapse; Rev. Robert Jarratt, incumbent; instituted 1791. Population, 1801, 4032—1811, 3874— 1821, 4170.

WELLOW—the name of a hundred in the north-east part of the county, comprising the parishes of CAMERTON, COMBE-HAY, CORSTON, DUNKERTON, ENGLISH-COMBE, FARLEY-HUN-GERFORD, FORSCOTE, HINTON-CHARTERHOUSE, NEWTON ST. LOE, NORTON ST. PHILIP, TELLESFORD, TWIVERTON, and WELLOW, containing 1212 inhabited houses, 1330 families, 3455 males, and 3343 females. Total population, 6789. The parishes of Hinton-Charterhouse and Norton St. Philips, though locally in the above hundred, form a distinct liberty, called Hinton and Norton liberty.

WELLOW—a parish in the above hundred, to which it gives name, 4½ miles S. from Bath; containing 163 inhabited houses, and 175 families, 125 of whom are employed in agriculture. The river Cam runs through this parish, in its way to the Avon, parallel with which a canal was formed from Midford to Radstock : it is now filled up, and made into a railway. In this parish several tessellated pavements and other Roman antiquities have been discovered at different periods. The church is a handsome edifice, dedicated to St. Julian, and was built by Sir Walter Hungerford about the year 1372; it consists of a nave, chancel, and two side aisles, with a tower at the west end containing a clock and eight bells. The living is a curacy, in the deanery of Frome ; Rev. Frederick Gardiner, incumbent; instituted 1801. Population, 1801, 770—1811, 728—1821, 817.

WELLS—a city in the hundred of Wells-Forum, 19 miles S. W. from Bath, and the same distance S. from Bristol. It comprises the parishes of ST. CUTHBERT'S-WITHIN, ST. CUTH-BERT'S-WITHOUT, and ST. ANDREWS, the latter is extra-parochial; the whole contains 1862 inhabited houses, and 1275 families,

502 of whom are employed in agriculture, 524 in trade, manufacture, or handicraft, and 249 not comprised in either class. Wells, conjointly with Bath, forms a bishopric, and returns two members to parliament. It received its name from a remarkable spring, called St. Andrew's Well, that rises near the Episcopal Palace, from which issues a very copious stream, which, after encircling the palace, transmits itself through the town, and pursuing its course to the river Brew, turns several mills in its way. The town consists of several streets, most of them wide and well-paved, and the houses in general are spacious and well-built. At the east end of the city, near the market-place, stands the City Conduit, supplied from St. Andrew's well ; it is a modern triangular structure, and stands on the site where a beautiful hexagonal building, erected by Bishop Beckington for the same purpose, formerly stood. The corporation consists of a mayor, recorder, seven aldermen, sixteen common-councilmen, a town-clerk, and inferior officers ; and the city is divided into four verderies, or wards, each superintended by two constables. The only manufacture is that of knit stockings and lace. Here is a good town-hall, in which the assizes are held, alternately with Bridgewater and Taunton, and a spacious market-house ; the markets are held Wednesdays and Saturdays, and fairs May 14, July 25, October 25, and November 30. Here are several alms-houses for the infirm poor, and an excellent charity-school for an equal number of boys and girls. Ina, king of the West Saxons, first established a collegiate church at Wells, and dedicated it to the honour of St. Andrew, in the year 704, which continued till the year 905, when it was erected into a bishop's see, and the province of Somerset was assigned to the incumbent as his diocese and seat of jurisdiction. The foundation of the present cathedral was laid by Bishop Wifeline, which having been improved and adorned by his successors, is considered one of the most splendid specimens of religious architecture in England : it is built in the form of a cross, having a noble tower, which rises at the intersection of the transepts with the body of the church, and two other towers, lower, and of smaller dimensions, on the north and south sides of the west end, which,

from the dissimilarity of architecture, appear to have been built at different periods : this west front is esteemed a master-piece of Gothic architecture; it is adorned with a variety of figures of exquisite carved workmanship, placed in ornamental niches or canopies, supported by elegant slender pillars of beautiful polished marble ; at the top are the images of the twelve Apostles, and below them the hierarchs, popes, princes and bishops : one whole line of this front is occupied in the display of a curious grotesque representation of the Resurrection, in which is expressed the various attitudes of the resuscitated bodies emerging from their earthly mansions : the larger statues which adorn the lower part of this front, are also interspersed with other scriptural representations, pourtrayed in groups in high relief, and on each side of the great buttresses are canopies occupied with figures as large as life, of kings, queens, abbots, popes, and cardinals.

The church of St. Cuthbert stands at the west end of the city, and is a handsome structure, consisting of a nave, chancel, north and south aisles, and five chapels, with a lofty well-built tower at the west end, containing six bells. The living is a vicarage, in the patronage of the Dean and Chapter of Wells ; Rev. Samuel Serrel, incumbent; instituted 1798. Population, 1801, 4829—1811, 4827—1821, 5888.

WELLS-FORUM—the name of a hundred in the centre of the county, lying principally to the north of the city from which it is named, comprising the following parishes ; viz. BINEGAR, CRANMORE-WEST, DINDER, EVERCREECH, LITTON, PRIDDY, WELLS City, (ST. ANDREW, ST. CUTHBERT-WITHIN, and ST. CUTHBERT-WITHOUT,) WESTBURY, and WOOKEY, containing 1920 inhabited houses, 2217 families, 4826 males, and 5304 females. Total population, 10,130.

WEMBDON—a parish in the hundred of North-Petherton, 1½ mile N. W. from Bridgewater ; containing 43 inhabited houses, and 60 families, 49 of whom are employed in agriculture. The church is a small structure, dedicated to St. George, and is a vicarage, in the deanery of Bridgewater; Rev. Henry Parsons, incumbent; instituted 1791. Population, 1801, 279—1811, 296—1821, 293.

WESTBURY—a parish in the hundred of Wells-Forum, 4½ miles N. W. from Wells; containing 118 inhabited houses, and 128 families, 102 of whom are employed in agriculture. The river Ax bounds this parish on the south-west, and divides it from Wedmore. The church is dedicated to St. Lawrence, and consists of a nave, chancel, south aisle and chapel, with a tower at the west end, containing a clock and four bells. The living is a vicarage, and a peculiar in the deanery of Axbridge, and in the patronage of the Bishop of the diocese; Rev. Noblet Ruddock, incumbent; instituted 1814. Population, 1801, 429 —1811, 493—1821, 622.

WESTON—a parish in the hundred of Bath-Forum, 1½ mile N. W. from Bath; containing 369 inhabited houses, and 432 families, 289 of whom are employed in agriculture. A small stream, the source of which is in Lansdown-hill, runs through the village, and passing under a stone arch on the upper turnpike-road to Bristol, empties itself into the river Avon, on which are a number of mills. The church is a neat Gothic structure, dedicated to All Saints, and consists of a nave and chancel, with an embattled tower at the west end, containing a clock and six bells. The living is a rectory, in the deanery of Bath, and in the gift of the Crown; Rev. Thomas Wilkins, incumbent; instituted 1808. Population, 1801, 1010—1811, 1291—1821, 1919.

WESTON-BAMPFYLDE—a parish in the hundred of Catash, 6½ miles E. N. E. from Ilchester, and 7 W. S. W. from Wincanton; containing 25 inhabited houses, and 29 families, 25 of whom are employed in agriculture. This place was formerly the property and residence of the ancient family of Bampfylde, from whom it derived its additional name. The church is a small building, consisting of a nave and chancel, with a tower con-

2 D

taining three bells. The living is a rectory, in the deanery of Cary; Rev. F. Goldesborough, D.D. incumbent; instituted 1769. Population, 1801, 140—1811, 142—1821, 119.

WESTON-NORTH, or WESTON-IN-GORDANO—a parish in the hundred of Portbury, 11½ miles W. from Bristol; containing 20 inhabited houses, and 21 families, 18 of whom are employed in agriculture. It obtained the name of Weston from its western situation from the hundred town of Portbury; and that of North-Weston, from its being situated north from the parish of Weston-super-Mare; and the latter appellation it received from an ancient family named Gordano, that were in possession of this and several other manors near it, at an early period. The church is a small ancient building, dedicated to St. Paul, and consists of a nave, chancel, and chapel, with a tower on the south side containing five bells. The living is a rectory, in the deanery of Redcliff and Bedminster; Rev. D. S. Moncrieffe, incumbent; instituted 1817. Population, 1801, 90—1811, 113—1821, 111.

WESTON-SUPER-MARE—a parish in the hundred of Winterstoke, 10 miles W.N.W. from Axbridge; containing 126 inhabited houses, and 147 families, 6 only of whom are employed in agriculture, 57 in trade, &c. and 84 not comprised in either class; the latter number chiefly consists of families residing here for the benefit of sea-bathing, this place having of late become a fashionable place of resort; the number of houses have increased three-fourths during the last few years. The church is a small building, dedicated to St. John the Baptist, and consists of a nave and chancel, with a tower containing three bells. The living is a rectory, in the deanery of Axbridge, and in the gift of the Bishop of the diocese; Rev. James Scott, incumbent; instituted 1819. Population, 1801, 138—1811, 163—1821, 738.

WESTON-ZOYLAND—a parish in the hundred of Whitley, 4 miles E.S.E. from Bridgewater; containing 137 inhabited houses, and 185 families, 84 of whom are employed in agriculture. This village was formerly surrounded by moors, now principally enclosed, and brought into cultivation : a large fair is held here for cattle on the 9th of September. The church, which is dedicated to St. Mary, is built in the form of a cross, consisting of a nave, chancel, north and south transepts, and north and south aisles, with a noble tower at the west end, highly ornamented and crowned with Gothic pinnacles ; it is 105 feet high, and contains a clock and five bells. The living is a vicarage, in the jurisdiction of Glastonbury ; Rev. Caleb Rocket, incumbent ; instituted 1815. Population, 1801, 677—1811, 724—1821, 807.

WHATLEY—a parish in the hundred of Frome, 3 miles W. from Frome ; containing 77 inhabited houses, and 79 families, 40 of whom are employed in agriculture. The church is dedicated to St. George, and consists of a nave, chancel, and south aisle, with a tower at the west end surmounted by a spire. The living is a rectory, in the deanery of Frome ; Rev. T. Williams, incumbent ; instituted 1812. Population, 1801, 304—1811, 347—1821, 354.

WHEATHILL—a parish in the hundred of Whitley, 4 miles W. S. W. from Castle-Cary, and 6 N. N. E. from Ilchester ; containing 5 inhabited houses, and 10 families, 8 of whom are employed in agriculture. The church is dedicated to St. John the Baptist, and consists of a nave and chancel, with a turret in which are two bells. The living is a rectory, in the deanery of Cary ; Rev. John Harbin, incumbent ; instituted 1793. Population, 1801, 45—1811, 39—1821, 47.

WHITCHURCH, otherwise FILTON—a parish in the hundred of Keynsham, 3 miles S. S. E. from Bristol ; containing 51 inhabited houses, and 69 families, 42 of whom are employed in agriculture. The church is dedicated to St. Nicholas, and consists of a nave, chancel, south aisle and two chapels, with a tower containing two bells. The living is a perpetual curacy, in the deanery of Redcliff and Bedminster; Rev. Israel Lewis, incumbent; instituted 1794. Population, 1801, 362—1811, 378—1821, 403.

WHITE-LACKINGTON—a parish in the hundred of Abdick and Bulstone, 1½ mile E. from Ilminster; containing 38 inhabited houses, and 47 families, 36 of whom are employed in agriculture. The church, which is dedicated to the Virgin Mary, consists of a nave, chancel, north and south aisles, and two small semi transepts, with an embattled tower at the west end containing a clock and four bells. The living is a vicarage; Rev. R. Ireland, incumbent; instituted 1803. Population, 1801, 190—1811, 249—1821, 242.

WHITLEY—the name of a hundred, extending along the whole length of the Polden-hills, and comprising the following parishes; viz. ASHCOTT, BLACKFORD, BUTLEIGH, CATCOTT, CHILTON, COMPTON-DUNDON, COSSINGTON, EDINGTON, GREINTON, HIGH-HAM, HOLFORD, HOLTON, MIDDLEZOY, MONKTON-WEST, MOORLINCH, OTHERY, PUDDIMORE-MILTON, SHAPWICK, STAWELL, STREET, SUTTON-MALLET, WALTON, WESTON-ZOYLAND, WHEATHILL, and WOOLLAVINGTON, containing 1962 inhabited houses, 2315 families, 5772 males, and 5636 females. Total population, 11,408.

WICK-CAMPFLOWER—a chapelry in the parish and hundred of Bruton, 2 miles N. E. from Castle-Cary; containing 13 inhabited houses, and 14 families, 13 of whom are employed in agriculture. The church is a small structure, being only 46 feet in length and 16 in breadth, with a turret in which hangs one bell. The living is a curacy, in the deanery of Cary; Rev. W. Cozens, incumbent; instituted 1819. Population, 1801, 68—1811, 79—1821, 82.

WICK ST. LAWRENCE—formerly a hamlet and chapelry to Congresbury, but now a parish in the hundred of Winterstoke,

9 miles N.N.W. from Axbridge; containing 48 inhabited houses, and 52 families, 41 of whom are employed in agriculture. This parish received its additional name from the dedication of its church, which consists of a nave and chancel, with a tower at the west end containing five bells. The living is a curacy, in the deanery of Axbridge, and in the gift of the Mayor and Corporation of Bristol; Rev. Henry Bevan, incumbent. Population, 1801, 221—1811, 235—1821, 267.

WILLITON and FREEMANNERS—the name of a hundred lying at the western extremity of the county. It derived its name from the hamlet of Williton, in the parish of St. Decuman's, and was afterwards called Williton and Fremanners from the hundred court being held in that portion of Williton which belonged to the prior of St. John of Jerusalem, and which was entitled to greater privileges and freedoms than the other parts of the manor. It comprises the following parishes, viz. BICKNOLLER, BROMPTON-RALPH, BROMPTON-KING'S, BRUSHFORD, CHIPSTABLE, CHATWORTHY, CROWCOMBE, DECUMANS, ST. (which includes the Town of WATCHET) DODINGTON, DULVERTON, ELWORTHY, EXMOOR, EXTON, HALSE, HAWKRIDGE, HUISH-CHAMPFLOWER, KILTON, KILVE, LILSTOCK, MONKSILVER, NETHERSTOWEY, NETTLECOMBE, OLD CLEVE, QUANTOCKSHEAD-EAST, QUANTOCKSHEAD-WEST, RADDINGTON, SAMPFORD-BRETT, SKILGATE, STOGUMBER, UPTON, WINSFORD and WITHYPOOL; containing 2422 inhabited houses, 2705 families, 7054 males, and 6972 females. Total population, 14,026.

WILTON—a parish in the hundred of Taunton and Taunton-Dean, half a mile S. from Taunton; containing 96 inhabited houses, and 101 families, 50 of whom are employed in agriculture, 38 in trade, manufacture, &c. and 13 not comprised in either class. This parish forms a very considerable suburb to Taunton, and was formerly a chapelry to St. Mary Magdalen in that borough. A county gaol was erected here in the year 1755. The church is a Gothic edifice, dedicated to St. George, and consists of a nave, chancel, and side aisles, with a tower at the west end containing five bells. The living is a curacy, in the deanery of Taunton; Rev. Thomas Strangways, incumbent; instituted 1790. Population, 1801, 331—1811, 473—1821, 579.

WINCANTON—a small market-town and parish in the hundred of Norton-Ferrars, 5 miles S. S. E. from Bruton, and 8 N. N. E. from Milborne-Port. It is pleasantly situated on the western declivity of a hill, and watered by the river Cale, from which it derived its name. The town consists of four streets, in which are a number of well-built houses; the whole parish contains 390 inhabited houses, and 408 families, 119 of whom are employed in agriculture, 242 in trade, manufacture, or handicraft, and 47 not comprised in either class. The principal manufacture of this town for many years has been that of dowlas and tick, which continue to employ a great proportion of the population. The market is on Wednesday, and here are two fairs annually, one on Easter Tuesday, and the other September 29. The church is dedicated to St. Peter and St. Paul, and consists of a nave, chancel, and two side aisles, and at the west end is a square tower containing a clock and five bells. The living is a curacy, in the deanery of Cary; Rev. John Radford, incumbent; instituted 1812. Population, 1801, 1773—1811, 1850—1821, 2143.

WINFORD—a parish in the hundred of Hartcliff and Bedminster, 6½ miles S. S. W. from Bristol; containing 127 inhabited houses, and 162 families, 130 of whom are employed in agriculture. The church is dedicated to St. Mary and St. Peter, and consists of a nave, chancel, side aisles, and porch, with a tower at the west end. The living is a rectory, in the deanery of Redcliff and Bedminster; Rev. J. W. W. Horlock, incumbent; instituted 1797. Population, 1801, 641—1811, 751—1821, 849.

WINSCOMBE—a parish in the hundred of Winterstoke, 2 miles N. N. W. from Axbridge; containing 255 inhabited houses, and

314 families, 231 of whom are employed in agriculture. The population of this parish has been considerably increased, in consequence of a common having been inclosed, on which a number of cottages have been built. The church is a handsome structure, dedicated to St. James, and consists of a nave, chancel, and side aisles, with an elegant tower at the west end crowned with pinnacles, and contains six bells. The living is a vicarage, in the deanery of Axbridge, and in the gift of the dean and chapter of Wells; Rev. Edward Foster, incumbent; instituted 1794. Population, 1801, 922—1811, 1113—1821, 1428.

WINSFORD—a parish in the hundred of Williton and Free-manners, 6 miles N. from Dulverton, on the river Ax; containing 88 inhabited houses, and 97 families, 66 of whom are employed in agriculture. The church consists of a nave, chancel, and north and south aisles, with an embattled tower containing five bells. The living is a vicarage, in the deanery of Dunston, and in the gift of Emanuel College, Cambridge; Rev. Thomas Slade, incumbent; instituted 1782. Population, 1801, 503—1811, 486—1821, 518.

WINSHAM—a parish in the hundred of Kingsbury-east, 4 miles E. S. E. from Chard; containing 156 inhabited houses, and 184 families, 94 of whom are employed in agriculture, 82 in trade and manufacture, and 8 not comprised in either class: a considerable manufacture of narrow cloths is carried on in this village. The church is a Gothic structure, consisting of a nave, chancel, and porch, with a tower in the centre, containing a clock and five bells. The living is a vicarage and a peculiar, in the deanery of Crewkerne, and in the patronage of the Dean of Wells; Rev. F. J. H. Festing, incumbent; instituted 1798. Population, 1801, 764—1811, 844—1821, 878.

WITHAM-FRIARY—a parish forming of itself an extra-episcopal liberty, locally situated in the hundred of Bath-Forum, 6 miles

S. S. W. from Frome, and containing, with the hamlet of Charter-house-on-Mendip (which belongs to this parish,) 107 inhabited houses, and 114 families, 108 of whom are employed in agriculture. Henry the Second founded a monastery here, in 1181, for Carthu-sian Monks, (being the first house of that order in England) and endowed it with the manor of Witham-Friary and other valuable possessions. The ruins of this monastery were pulled down in 1764, except a small part connected with the east end of the church, and a farm-house and other buildings have been erected on its site. The church (which formerly belonged to the monastery) is a small structure, consisting of a nave and chancel, the ceiling of which is supported by stone arches. The living is a curacy and a peculiar, in the deanery of Frome; Rev. N. Mitchell, incum-bent. Population, 1801, 485—1811, 531—1821, 589.

WINTERSTOKE—the name of a hundred lying near the Bristol Channel, comprising the following parishes, viz. AX-BRIDGE, BADGWORTH, BANWELL, BLAGDON, BLEADON, CHEDDER, CHRISTON, CHURCHILL, COMPTON-BISHOP, CONGRESBURY, HARP-TREE-EAST, HUTTON, KENN, KEWSTOKE, LOCKING, LOXTON, PUXTON, RODNEY-STOKE, ROWBOROUGH, SHIPHAM, UPHILL, WES-TON-SUPER-MARE, WICK ST. LAWRENCE, WINSCOMBE, WORLE, and YATTON, containing 2985 inhabited houses, 3488 families, 8547 males, and 8572 females. Total Population, 17,119.

WITHIEL-FLORY—a parish in a detached portion of the hun-dred of Taunton and Taunton-Dean, 8 miles N. E. from Dul-verton, and 10 miles S. W. from Watchet; containing 12 inha-bited houses, and as many families, the whole of whom are employed in agriculture. The church is a small structure, dedicated to St. Mary Magdalen, and consists of a nave and chancel, with a tower containing three bells. The living is a curacy, in the deanery of Dunster, annexed to Upton. Population, 1801, 83—1811, 86—1821, 86.

WITHYCOMBE—a parish in the hundred of Carhampton, 2½ miles S.E. from Dunster; containing 44 inhabited houses, and 61 families, 41 of whom are employed in agriculture. The church is a small building, dedicated to St. Nicholas, and consists of a nave and chancel, with an embattled tower on the south side. The living is a rectory, in the deanery of Dunster; Rev. A. C. Verelst, incumbent; instituted 1819. Population, 1801, 283—1811, 283—1821, 319.

WITHYPOOL—a parish in the hundred of Williton and Free-manners, 7 miles N.W. from Dulverton; containing 35 inhabited houses, and as many families, 29 of whom are employed in agriculture. The church consists of a nave, chancel, and north aisle, with an embattled tower containing four bells. The living is a curacy, in the deanery of Dunster, annexed to Hawkridge. Population, 1801, 144—1811, 146—1821, 224.

WIVELISCOMBE—a market-town and parish in the hundred of Kingsbury-West, situated on the river Tone, 11 miles W. from Taunton, and 7 miles N.W. from Wellington; containing 543 inhabited houses, and 656 families, 209 of whom are employed in agriculture, 323 in trade, manufacture, or handicraft, and 124 not comprised in either class. The town is governed by a bailiff and a portreeve, annually chosen at a court held for that purpose, when inferior officers are appointed. A considerable woollen manufacture has been carried on here for more than two centuries, which still continues to afford employment to the industrious poor. Here were formerly two markets, one on Wednesdays, and the other on Saturdays; it has now only one on the Tuesday. The fairs are held May 2, and September 25. The church consists of a nave, chancel, and north and south aisles, with a tower at the west end, surmounted by a spire, and contains a clock, chimes, and six bells. The living is a vicarage, in the presentation of the Bishop of the diocese; Rev. John

Sunderland, incumbent; instituted 1816. Population, 1801, 2571
—1811, 2550—1821, 2791.

WOOKEY—a parish in the hundred of Wells-Forum, 2 miles
W. from Wells ; containing 190 inhabited houses, and 223
families, 147 of whom are employed in agriculture. About a
mile and a half from the village is Wookey-Hole, the most
celebrated cavern in the West of England ; the entrance is very
narrow, but at the distance of about 15 feet it expands into a
large cavern, resembling the body of a church, the parts of
which are very craggy, and abound with pendant rocks ; the
water dropping from the roof forms large projections of petrified
figures and nodules of pellucid spar on the floor : the passage
continuing hence, leads by a descent to another vault somewhat
smaller, from which you pass through another long and low
passage to a third vault, nearly circular, about 40 yards in
diameter, with a roof of a cylindrical form ; on one side of this
area is a fine sandy bottom, and on the other a stream of water,
very clear and cold, about 10 feet wide and two or three deep ;
after passing through the rock, it descends 40 or 50 feet, to a
level with the ground, and forms the first source of the river
Ax. The church of Wookey is a neat structure, dedicated to
St. Matthew, and consists of a nave, chancel, and side aisles,
with a tower at the west end containing five bells. The living
is a vicarage, and a peculiar in the deanery of Wells, belonging
to the Sub-Dean of Wells ; Rev. J. S. Phillot, incumbent; instituted 1801. Population, 1801, 740—1811, 859—1821, 1040.

WOOLLEY—a small parish in the hundred of Bath-Forum, 2
miles N. from Bath ; containing 18 inhabited houses, and 23
families, 22 of whom are employed in agriculture. The church
is a modern structure, 50 feet long and 19 feet wide, with a
tower at the west end covered with a handsome cupola, and
containing one bell. The living is a rectory, consolidated with
Bathwick. Population, 1801, 80—1811, 93—1821, 101.

WOOLAVINGTON—a parish in the hundred of Whitley, 4 miles
N. E. from Bridgewater; containing 66 inhabited houses, and
83 families, 47 of whom are employed in agriculture. Here is
a fair for cattle, sheep, &c. on the 18th October. The church,
which is dedicated to St. Mary, consists of a nave, chancel, and
small sepulchral chapel, with a tower at the west end containing
a clock and five bells. The living is a vicarage, united with
Puriton. Population, 1801, 294—1811, 325—1821, 381.

WOOLVERTON—a parish in the hundred of Frome, 5 miles N.
from Frome; containing 30 inhabited houses, and as many
families, 13 of whom are employed in agriculture. The church
is a small structure, consisting of a nave and chancel, with a
tower at the west end containing three bells. The living is a
rectory, in the deanery of Frome, consolidated with Road
Population, 1801, 169—1811, 159—1821, 184.

WOOTON-NORTH—a chapelry in the hundred of Glaston-Twelve-
Hides, 4 miles W. S. W. from Shepton-Mallet; containing 43
inhabited houses, and 54 families, 45 of whom are employed in
agriculture. The church consists of a nave and chancel, with
an embattled tower at the west end containing three bells. The
living is a curacy, in the deanery of Cary, annexed to Pilton.
Population, 1801, 224—1811, 248—1821, 278.

WOOTON-COURTNEY—a parish in the hundred of Carhampton,
3½ miles W. from Dunster; containing 57 inhabited houses, and
81 families, 64 of whom are employed in agriculture. A fair for
cattle, sheep, &c. is held here on the 19th September annually.
The church, which stands on an eminence, is dedicated to All
Saints, and consists of a nave, chancel, and north aisle, with an
embattled tower at the west end containing a clock and five
bells. The living is a rectory, in the deanery of Dunster, and
in the gift of Eton College; Rev. C. L. Scott, incumbent; instituted 1800. Population, 1810, 345—1811, 372—1821, 411.

WORLE—a parish in the hundred of Winterstoke, 8 miles N. W. from Axbridge; containing 130 inhabited houses, and 140 families, 70 of whom are employed in agriculture. The population of this parish has considerably increased in consequence of the demand for poultry, and other articles, for the supply of the adjoining parish of Weston-super-Mare, which has lately become a fashionable watering-place. The church of Worle is a neat Gothic structure, dedicated to St. Martin, and consists of a nave, chancel, and north aisle, with a tower at the west end surmounted by a small spire, and contains a clock and six bells. The living is a vicarage, in the deanery of Axbridge; Rev. J. Price, incumbent. Population, 1801, 422—1811, 467— 1821, 673.

WRAXALL—a parish in the hundred of Portbury, 7 miles W. from Bristol; containing 116 inhabited houses, and 143 families, 121 of whom are employed in agriculture. Near the church is *Wraxall-Court*, the residence of J. H. Smith, Esq. and about a mile north from the village is *Charlton-House*, the residence of Thomas Kington, Esq.; G. P. Seymour, Esq. has likewise a seat in this parish. The church is a handsome structure, consisting of a nave, chancel, and side aisles, with a tower at the west end containing a clock and five bells. The living is a rectory, in the deanery of Redcliff and Bedminster; Rev. James Vaughan, incumbent; instituted 1801. Population, 1801, 540—1811, 731—1821, 769.

WRINGTON—a small market-town and parish in the hundred of Brent-with-Wrington, 11 miles S. W. from Bristol; containing 215 inhabited houses, and 263 families, 157 of whom are employed in agriculture, 67 in trade, &c. and 39 not included in either class. A considerable traffic is carried on here in the cultivation of teasles, which are sold to the cloth manufacturers, and are used for the dressing of woollen cloth. A charter for a market on Tuesdays was procured by Adam de Sodbury, Abbot of Glastonbury, in the reign of Edward the Second; it is now but little attended. The celebrated John Locke, author of an essay on the Human Understanding, was born here in 1632; the whole of his works were published in three volumes folio, 1714. The church is a noble edifice, 120 feet long, and 52 feet wide, consisting of a nave, chancel, side aisles, and a porch, with an elegant embattled tower 140 feet high, crowned with four turrets, and sixteen Gothic pinnacles. It contains a clock and six bells. The living is a rectory, in the deanery of Redcliff and Bedminster; Rev. William Leeves, incumbent; instituted 1779. Population, 1801, 786—1811, 1109—1821, 1349.

WRITHLINGTON—a parish in the hundred of Kilmersdon; 8½ miles N.W. from Frome; containing 38 inhabited houses, and 41 families, 13 of whom are employed in agriculture. The church is dedicated to St. Mary Magdalen, and consists of a nave, chancel, and one small aisle and porch, with a low tower at the west end containing two bells. The living is a rectory, belonging to the prebend thereof in Salisbury cathedral, and is united with Fordington. Population, 1801, 108—1811, 167 —1821 216.

YARLINGTON— a parish in the hundred of Bruton, 4 miles W. from Wincanton; containing 34 inhabited houses, and 57 families, 51 of whom are employed in agriculture. A short distance S.E. from the village is *Yarlington-Lodge*, the residence of Mrs. Rogers. The church consists of a nave and chancel, 70 feet long and 17 wide, with an embattled tower on the south side containing three bells. The living is a rectory, in the deanery of Cary, and in the gift of the Archbishop of York; Rev. R. Frankland, incumbent; instituted 1797. Population, 1801, 252—1811, 286—1821, 301.

YATTON—a parish in the hundred of Winterstoke, 3 miles N.W. from Wrington; containing 225 inhabited houses, and

281 families, 177 of whom are employed in agriculture. The church is a noble structure, built in the form of a cross, with a large tower in the centre, formerly surmounted by a spire, the base of which only remains; the tower contains a clock and six bells. The living is a vicarage, and a peculiar, belonging to the prebendary thereof; Rev. Thomas Wickham, incumbent; instituted 1809. Population, 1801, 1147—1811, 1215—1821, 1516.

YEOVIL—a large populous market-town and parish, situated on the great western-road from London to Exeter, in the hundred of Stone, 5 miles S.S.E. from Ilchester; containing 780 inhabited houses, and 853 families, 137 of whom are employed in agriculture, 680 in trade, manufacture, or handicraft, and 36 not comprised in either class. This town derives its name from the river Yeo, or Ivel, which rises near Sherbourn, from seven springs called the Sisters, and passes this town on the east, under a stone bridge of three arches, and forms the boundary of the county of Dorset. The town of Yeovil consists of upwards of twenty streets and lanes; some of the former are wide and well built; many of the houses are built of stone. The woollen trade formerly flourished here, but the principal manufacture at present is that of gloves, which employs a great proportion of the population. It is governed by a portreeve and eleven burgesses; the former is a magistrate for the time, being chosen annually from among the burgesses; besides these officers, there are also a mace-bearer, and two constables for the borough, and two for the parish. Here is a good alms-house, founded by John Wobourne, minor canon of St. Paul's, in 1476, and endowed with 128 acres of land, for the maintenance of one master, two wardens, and twelve poor people of both sexes. In the town are several places of worship for the Protestant Dissenters. The market is on Fridays, well supplied with all kinds of provisions. Fairs, June 28 and November 16. The church is a handsome Gothic structure, dedicated to St. John the Baptist, and consists of a nave, chancel, north and south aisles, and transept, with a large stone tower at the west end 90 feet high, containing a clock and six bells. The living is a vicarage, and a peculiar, in the deanery of Ilchester, united with Preston. Population, 1801, 2774—1811, 3118—1821, 4655.

YEOVILTON—a parish in the hundred of Somerton, 2 miles E. from Ilchester; containing with the hamlet of Bridghampton, 40 inhabited houses, and 54 families, 44 of whom are employed in agriculture. The river Yeo, from which this parish derives its name, bounds it on the south, and divides it from Lymington. The church, which is dedicated to St. Bartholomew, consists of a nave and chancel, with a tower at the west end containing five bells. The living is a rectory, in the deanery of Ilchester, and in the patronage of the Bishop of the diocese; Rev. R. T. Whalley, incumbent. Population, 1801, 200—1811, 236 —1821, 255.